QUALITATIVE MARKET RESEARCH

To Yehudi Gordon and Lesley Goodman with all our love.

QUALITATIVE MARKET RESEARCH

A Practitioner's and Buyer's Guide

WENDY GORDON
and
ROY LANGMAID

with illustrations by Christopher Mills

Gower

Aldershot · Brookfield USA · Hong Kong · Singapore · Sydney

Published by
Gower Publishing Company Limited
Gower House
Croft Road
Aldershot
Hants GU11 3HR
England

Gower Publishing Company
Old Post Road
Brookfield
Vermont 05036
USA

Reprinted 1989, 1990, 1993, 1995, 1997

British Library Cataloguing in Publication Data

Gordon, Wendy
    Qualitative market research.
    1. Marketing research
    I. Title II. Langmaid, Roy
    658.8'3 HF5415.2

Library of Congress Cataloging-in-Publication Data

Gordon, Wendy, 1943–
    Qualitative market research.
    Bibliography: p.
    Includes index.
    1. Marketing research.   I. Langmaid, Roy, 1946–
    II. Title.
    HF5415.2.G564   1988   658.8'3   87–30021

ISBN 0 566 05115 X

Printed in Great Britain at the University Press, Cambridge

Contents

	Preface: The Reason for the Book	vii
	Introduction	ix
1.	Problems and Methodology	1
2.	Planning and Designing Qualitative Studies	20
3.	Group Discussions: Philosophy, Mechanics and Process	33
4.	Group Dynamics	43
5.	Interviewing – Getting Better	51
6.	The Individual 'Depth' Interview	64
7.	Non-verbal Communication	77
8.	Projective and Enabling Techniques	89
9.	One-way Mirror	127
10.	The Interpretation of Qualitative Research	132
11.	Recruitment	156
12.	The Presentation of Qualitative Research	165
13.	Research with Children	188
14.	Research Stimulus Material	209
15.	Qualitative and Quantitative Hybrid Methodologies	235
	Bibliography	252
	Index	255

Preface: The Reason for the Book

The qualitative research profession in the UK has experienced unprecedented growth in both popularity and sterling value since the mid-1970s. A conservative estimate would put the current value of *qualitative* work at £40 million per annum.

It seems extraordinary that all of this should have taken place in the absence of any collected or even episodic documentation of the theory or nature of this type of work. Even mere descriptions of qualitative studies, except as case histories or company presentations, are uncommon.

Part of the reason for this is company security; qualitative projects are subject to all of the rules of confidentiality surrounding corporate strategic decision-making. But while the findings may be veiled in secrecy, the processes certainly are not. This is the first book that attempts to draw together the practical and theoretical understandings of two experienced, practised qualitative workers as they have evolved over the years and present them to the industry at large and to a wider audience should it be interested. Quite simply, we wrote this book because there isn't another.

Another strange anomaly is that while qualitative research is very much a practical process, there are no guidebooks or instruction manuals on how to do it. We've tried as far as we were able to balance out theoretical orientation with practical guidance so that whether you are a buyer, a user, a doer or a layman, you may hopefully gain some insight into the process, content and meaning of this type of endeavour.

Our theoretical approach is based upon our experience in trying to understand human motivation. In our time we've tried variously to bring to bear both description and content analysis as well as the rather abstract conceptualizing of social psychology in our pursuit of our task, but increasingly we have needed to resort to deeper, more psychoanalytically based ideas to explain the configuration of desires, needs and behaviour that we've witnessed as the underpinning of consumerism. A woman said recently, rather dolefully, in one of our groups:

'I sometimes feel that the only place left to go is the shops.'

At least if market research can help us it can make sure that the shops, when we get there, contain the things we want!

Roy Langmaid and Wendy Gordon
January 1988

Introduction

Although market research may be defined operationally as 'meaning what market research agencies do',[1] some readers would no doubt prefer a less circular definition. Modern market research is best described as a process whereby information about the behaviour and/or attitudes of consumers or end users of a product or service is collected by means of some form of interrogatory procedure. There are many variants of the essential question and answer techniques, from the 5 minute street interview to the sequential monitoring of deep seated attitudes over a long period of time, just as there are many different ways and means of analysing or displaying the data from such investigations.

Much of this endeavour, usually termed quantitative research, is based upon the interviewing of statistically representative samples of the relevant population. Often, if not always, this provides findings which may be considered to be representative of the whole population.

This book is *not* about that kind of market research, but describes the practices and principles of a younger sister discipline – qualitative research. This type of market research usually focuses upon small, carefully selected numbers of individuals and does not claim any statistical validity but through the experience and sensitivity of its practitioners and their techniques offers valuable insights into the behaviour and motivations of consumers in their day to day lives and their interactions with the aforementioned products and services.

Since qualitative research is usually concerned with exploring people's views and feelings in some depth, it usually involves a fairly extended interviewing procedure with the same informants either singly or in groups. This accounts for the two principal methodologies of qualitative research – the *depth interview* and the *group discussion*. Much of this book is focussed on an exploration of the principles, practices and outcomes of these two key data-collection techniques.

The results of such insight or hypothesis checking techniques may or may not be subsequently checked by quantitative methods. Quite often this is not felt to be necessary. This is because qualitative research findings are only one of a number of different sources of information about the relationship between a brand and the consumers. Data from continuous monitoring such as retail audits or advertising tracking, TGI (Target Group Index), Ad Hoc quantitative research such as usage and attitude studies, observational feedback from the salesforce or marketing teams, competitive activity and broader information from the general and specialist media, all provide a context against which the qualitative findings make sense. Often a qualitative study is like finding the last piece of a jigsaw puzzle — it makes the whole picture clear. It has a face-validity, not when evaluated in isolation, but when viewed against a completed backdrop.

Sometimes, instead of being the final jigsaw piece, qualitative research outlines a possible shape, providing the buyer/user with a feeling about what the final picture might be. In this case, all the other pieces of information may be gathered and used to re-define the outline and add colour so that the picture is clearly understood.

THE GROWTH OF QUALITATIVE RESEARCH

The 1970s was the decade which saw a growth explosion in the qualitative market research industry. At the start of the decade, qualitative research was a fairly rare phenomenon and with the exception of a very few well-known companies, specialist qualitative agencies were relatively rare.

This was not so by the end of the decade. With its emphasis on individual skills (moderating, interpreting, presenting) and its low capital investment, qualitative work proved irresistible to many research executives in large organizations. Breakaways were common, either of individuals or of small groups who went on to form small independent companies or to establish themselves as freelance researchers. Given this individualistic piecemeal structure and competitive environment, there was little intercommunication between practitioners. Other than learning from experience or exchanging views with colleagues, there was almost no opportunity to learn from other senior practitioners who had specialized and were developing new approaches to qualitative research.

The Market Research Society in recognition of this growth has continually striven to provide more training courses, specialist meetings and special conference sessions to meet the growing interest in qualitative research. In the early 1980s, the Association of Qualitative Research Practitioners (AQRP) was formed and now has more than 450 members, some 35 per cent of whom are freelancers, the remainder being employed in research agencies, advertising agencies, manufacturers or service companies. The AQRP is now starting to run its own courses and hopes to add a new source of specialized training about its members' chosen discipline.

All this could not have happened, nor still continue to happen, without clients' (buyers and end-users) belief in the usefulness of qualitative research. To explain it simply, qualitative research is liked, even if not always agreed with. It stimulates, challenges and provokes, but above all it is user-friendly, allowing access into the way in which the target market thinks and talks. To extend the use of 80s computer jargon, it is 'high touch' rather than 'high tech'. When a good practitioner is presenting the findings, the presence of the consumer is almost palpable. What is more important, this consumer who is present in the boardroom is recognizable – not a number or statistic, but someone recognizable, known or easy to relate to.

There is an apocryphal story of a company chairman who angrily retorted 'that dumb consumer is my wife' in response to a deprecating comment about the user of a particular brand which goes some way towards explaining the fascination with qualitative research. It helps to understand the people with whom one is in contact, spouses, children, rebellious teenagers, redundant acquaintances, the punk on the corner, the woman managing the laundrette, the 'yuppie' couple down the road and even oneself.

A further reason for the growth in qualitative research is that it is relatively quick and cheap (compared to quantitative studies), flexible and adaptable. The open-endedness of the basic methodologies makes them infinitely variable, and together with the portable technology of tape-recorders, slide projectors and video, it is now possible to convey versions of 'the idea' (whether product, service or advertisement) on film, tape or cardboard to the general public.

OTHER USERS OF QUALITATIVE RESEARCH

There are many other practitioners of qualitative research, some operating in areas completely outside the scope of companies serving the general public with goods or services.

Local government, social services and community projects all have used, and are beginning to use more frequently, qualitative research methodologies.

Social marketing is a new concept in developing countries and uses qualitative methodologies to understand how best to introduce health measures · (eg vaccinations) or preventive behaviour (eg breast feeding rather than formula feeding; contraception) to a particular target group in such a way to ensure that the measure is not rejected.

The area of industrial research has been slow to respond to qualitative methods, but it is generally felt that an assumption of rationality in response to deciding upon which computer system, plant or chemical ingredient to buy has held sway for far too long in this area. Obviously, personality and motivation play a key part in technical decisions too, and this is leading to major growth in the industrial qualitative research business.

Inside organizations too, there is an increased use of qualitative techniques. Management consultancy and personnel training have employed Quality Circles or Task Forces which have the outline structure and methodology of qualitative work.

THE PRINCIPLES AND PROCEDURES DESCRIBED IN THIS BOOK

We have tried to avoid technical jargon, but a general statement of our orientation to our subject may not come amiss.

One of us has a psychology degree, the other a social anthropology degree; both of us have experienced clinical psychology first hand, but neither of us are clinical psychologists or academics.

We hope this book will provide a framework for understanding modern qualitative research *practices* (rather than theory). It is intended to be as open an attempt as we can to explain what we do with the hope that training practitioners, research buyers and users and those from other disciplines will use the book to increase their understanding of this fascinating area of commercial activity.

There are many aspects of the book that might provoke criticism. We did not set out to write the definitive textbook of qualitative market research, but to present two different but complementary views of the role of this type of research and the processes involved. If we succeed in enabling others to interrogate their own way of practising qualitative research or stimulate users and buyers to be a little more adventurous in the techniques they employ in the future and more confident that this approach has its own rigor which, although different from that of quantitative research, is equally demanding and valid, we feel we will have succeeded.

It has been enormously challenging to commit to paper the accumulated knowledge of forty years of combined experience. Given the background of individualism inherent to this specialist area of research and given our very different reputations in the research marketplace, we have been continually surprised by the extent to which we agreed with one another's approach. We hope therefore that other practitioners will find much of what we've written a reflection of their own experiences with qualitative research, with sufficient points of difference to add to their own unique skills and expertise.

On a point of detail, we have used the words 'him' and 'her' interchangeably in the book where the sex of the people being described may be either male or female without influencing the sense of the point under discussion. Where sex is an important variable we have used the correct gender.

ACKNOWLEDGEMENTS (WENDY GORDON)

I would like to thank all my teachers. Those from whom I learned the essential skills – John Blacking (Professor of Anthropology) who gave me an incurable curiosity for finding out how other people live, and conduct their lives, Bill Schlackman who taught me the real meaning of qualitative insight and intuition and Rodney Blankenberg who taught me to love advertising. I have also learned much from sharing qualitative research projects with other practitioners, particularly my partner Colleen Ryan whose firm belief that qualitative research is above all a tool for actionable decision making has added much to my more social perspective. I would also like to acknowledge a handful of individuals who may not realise how much I have valued their support and encouragement over the years – Rod Meadows, Don Cowley, Jackie Dickens, Sev D'Souza and Judy Lannon. Next I owe my heartfelt thanks to Yehudi, Gabi, Nick and Tanya for their tolerance and understanding over the years. Finally a thank you to the thousands of people whom I have interviewed over the past 20 years and who have been prepared to open an area of their hearts to my inquisitive probing.

I would also like to thank Ro Arnold and Ricardo Windrich for helping prepare the manuscript.

ACKNOWLEDGEMENTS (ROY LANGMAID)

My greatest gratitude must go to my earliest mentor Val Smith who stuck with me while I struggled to develop my techniques, and to my first colleague and clinical psychology teacher Keir Gregory PhD. Jeff Fergus and Nigel Bogle were sources of constant support and encouragement in these early years.

I have borrowed ideas from many and varied sources and put them to use experimentally and when they have worked empirically I have described them in the text. More specifically, I am grateful to Claire Mansfield for her foundation work on the projective techniques chapter and to Rebecca Wynberg for helping to complete it. I would also like to thank Rosie Campbell for useful suggestions that I have incorporated in the section on research with children. Lesley Goodman and Lisa Fry offered useful advice here too.

I should like to thank David Dawkins and Ed Newton for their help in understanding the mathematics involved in correspondence analysis and Vicky Johns for her contribution on the subject of the one-way mirror. I also owe a debt of appreciation to Angela Foster for turning me on to the ideas underlying group processes and dynamics.

Finally my thanks too to Jill Allaway who worked so hard in helping to prepare the manuscript.

NOTE

1. P. Kleinman (1985), *Market Research-Head counting becomes big business*, Comedia Publishing Group.

1 Problems and Methodology

WHAT IS QUALITATIVE RESEARCH?

At the most simplistic level the answer is as follows:

> Qualitative research answers such questions as 'What', 'Why' or 'How' but it cannot answer the question 'How many?'.

Qualitative research can be defined in a number of ways. It is frequently defined by *methodology*, and in fact, for many buyers it is synonymous with the group discussion.

In general terms, qualitative research:

- involves small samples of consumers which are not necessarily representative of larger populations;
- employs a wide variety of techniques to collect data, not simply a structured question-and-answer format;
- relies on interpretation of the findings which is an integral part of the data collection and indeed begins well before the fieldwork commences at the briefing;
- allows access to the ways in which consumers express themselves.

Ten to 15 years ago, qualitative research was frequently criticized on the grounds of its small sample methodology. Compared to survey methods, it was considered to produce 'soft' data and therefore lacking in both reliability and validity. Furthermore, its antagonists were and indeed still are suspicious of the influence and involvement of the moderator and unwilling to rely on his interpretation, which was seen to be highly subjective rather than objective (that is, not scientific).

For these reasons, qualitative research was the poor relation of quantitative research and was used, on the whole, as a first-stage pilot study prior to quantification. Its poor image also resulted from large motivation studies which yielded information which the end user often found fascinating, but which was complex and difficult to translate into marketing action.

In the last ten years in the UK there has been a boom in qualitative research and it now enjoys a status which previously used to be the prerogative of quantitative research. The main reason for this has been its proven effectiveness in increasing *understanding* of a particular market, brand, pack or advertising campaign.

This then is the crux of the definition of qualitative research. *It is centrally concerned with understanding things rather than with measuring them.*

The pursuit of understanding is a complex 'searching' type of procedure which cannot be rigid. Thus, qualitative projects are characterized by:

- a flexible interview structure;
- an evolutionary interview structure (which changes in response to growing understanding and hypotheses);
- a data base that is not entirely accessible to those who have only listened to the tapes or read the transcripts, since it includes
  - the verbal interchange between respondents and moderator (questions and answers);
  - the spontaneous verbal emissions of all those present whether in response to research stimuli or not;
  - the verbal omissions and silences of those present;
  - non-verbal communication – 'body language';
  - data from specialized generating techniques such as projective or enabling techniques (see Chapter 8).

Unlike quantitative research where the questionnaires form the data base (and can therefore be analyzed and interpreted by those who did not conduct the interviews but who are trained to understand figures and statistics), the tape recordings of interviews or groups in qualitative research are *not* a complete and objective data record. Often what is strongly expressed verbally by respondents on the tape recording of the discussion or interview, may have been discounted by non-verbal cues such as looking away or breaking eye contact. The transcript may read as if the product or advertising being discussed was condemned by respondents, yet it may have been only one or two dominant and articulate people who expressed their views frequently. Hence it is essential that the person(s) who conducted the qualitative interviews or groups interpret the database.

It should be pointed out that the pattern of results obtained in any survey (both qualitative and quantitative) may be open to several interpretations. There is never 'a right way' or 'the only way' of interpreting the findings. This will be discussed in a later chapter on 'Interpretation' (see Chapter 10).

QUALITATIVE AND QUANTITATIVE – FRIENDS NOT ENEMIES

Happily, the days of endless and sterile debates about the superiority of quantitative research over qualitative and vice versa are now over. Both have their strengths and weaknesses and most buyers and practitioners of research will discuss the two in terms of 'horses for courses'. In fact many hybrid methodologies have now been developed (see Chapter 15).

The strengths of qualitative and quantitative research, generally speaking, are summarized below:

Qualitative
- Open-ended, dynamic, flexible.
- Depth of understanding.
- Taps consumer creativity.
- Database – broader and deeper.
- Penetrates rationalized or superficial responses.
- Richer source of ideas for marketing and creative teams.

Quantitative
- Statistical and numerical measurement.
- Sub-group sampling or comparisons.
- Survey can be repeated in the future and results compared.
- Taps *individual* responses.
- Less dependent on research executive skills or orientation.

Thus, qualitative research is best used for problems where the results will increase *understanding*, *expand* knowledge, *clarify* the real issues, *generate* hypotheses, *identify a range* of behaviour, *explore* and *explain* consumer motivations, attitudes and behaviour, *identify* distinct behavioural groups, *provide input* to a future stage of research or development.

It is not feasible to describe all the problems qualitative research is employed to solve, but the most frequent problem areas will be discussed in this chapter. These are:

Basic exploratory studies
New product development
Creative development
Diagnostic studies
Tactical research projects

PROBLEM AREAS BEST SUITED TO QUALITATIVE RESEARCH

Basic market exploratory studies

Qualitative research is frequently conducted to examine consumer attitudes and behaviour in relation to a product category or service, usually (but not always) with the specific aim of understanding consumer relationships to a brand.

Basic qualitative studies are most frequently conducted in the following cases:

- When detailed information is required about the nature and elements of a market in order to look for opportunities for *new product development.*
- When consumer *markets change* and/or develop and up-to-date information is required to understand changing attitudes and behaviour. For example

a trend towards 'health consciousness' has emerged in most Western countries. This has affected the ways in which consumers think and act in relation to food products.

- When *new markets* require descriptive information in order to aid marketing or advertising development programmes. For example, technology markets, such as cellular telephones or computers, are relatively new and therefore lack information.

- When manufacturers, for reasons related to acquisition or new product development, require information on a market which is new to them.

These types of study are required to yield information of different types.

To define consumer perceptions of the market or product field

It is extremely important for manufacturers to know how their markets sub-divide into sectors and how these sectors are differentiated from one another.

Often manufacturing companies segment a market according to historical developments in the company, or according to production, distribution or marketing criteria. In some cases it may be a widely held belief that a product category competes with another, whereas consumer research indicates a completely different situation.

For example, the distinction between 'confectionery countlines' and 'biscuit countlines' (for example Mars versus Penguin) matters little to consumers who are in the process of making purchase decisions about what to pack in lunch-boxes, whereas the distinction between the two is critically important to a manufacturing company.

Levi's believed competitors were Wrangler and Lee, but in fact in a recent study in the USA we discovered that a major jeans manufacturer whose sales were slowing down among certain age groups was only monitoring the perceived image and attributes of his brand against other jeans. Out on the streets casual sports gear from companies like Nike and Reebok were drawing sales from his brand, unknown to him. For teenagers, for example, it was a very real choice between a new pair of denims and a pair of track shoes from Nike or a windcheater from Reebok — not just between one brand of jeans and another.

A qualitative study helps to understand the competitive relationships between different types of product and/or brand in any product category — from the consumer's point of view rather than the manufacturer's.

To define consumer segmentations in relation to a product category or brand

There have been many fashions in research since the 1960s in classifying types of consumers, not simply by demographic criteria but by more complex attitudinal or behavioural descriptors. Two, which continue to crop up in research documentation, are psychographics and life-style segmentations.

The first aims to increase understanding of consumer relationships to a product category or brand by describing psychological typologies which cut across demographic characteristics, such as age, social class or region. It draws on psychological (especially psychoanalytical) concepts, for example the purchase of high-performance cars may be much more closely related to aggression and the need to display than to any scientifically based notions of technical efficiency or engineering precision.

The second aims to increase understanding by describing typologies of consumers in sociological or social anthropological terms (again cutting across pure demographic descriptors). For example, purchase of a muesli-type cereal may be far more firmly based in a person's view of herself as modern and health-conscious rather than on any liking for fruit and nuts.

Many different theoretical starting points are used today to describe typologies (Transactional Analysis, Neuro Linguistic Programming (NLP),[1] etc.) but these are integrated into the qualitative approach. They are no longer heralded as great advances in research techniques which can be applied to the solution of every problem.

To understand the dimensions which differentiate between brands

There are two main ways in which consumers differentiate between brands – *rational criteria* and *emotional beliefs*.

Again in the 1960s, a great amount of research was conducted in the belief that if a unique set of discriminating criteria could be isolated for the brand, and these differences could be communicated to the larger market, then the brand would succeed by virtue of these differences. An example of the application of this idea was the use of Kelly's Repertory Grid in marketing research in Great Britain (Frost & Braine 1967). The technique was used to wring out as many differences (between brands), as humanly possible expressed in the language of the consumer to the exhaustion of both respondent and the interviewer. This led to marketing/advertising strategies based on what were called USP's (unique selling propositions).

Rational beliefs about brands are important, and today the role of qualitative research is to describe the rational criteria consumers use to differentiate between brands, not as an end in itself, but to understand their function in creating attitudes towards the brand and in motivating purchase. Qualitative research also provides insight into the consumer vocabulary which underpins rational beliefs. For example, what does 'crunchy' really mean? Does it mean the same thing when applied to a muesli as it does to a chocolate bar? Is there another word which means the same as 'crunchy' but is more precise and suffers less from overuse in advertising?

In many product fields today, the physical differences between competitive products are minimal, but the emotional differences are vast. For example, in the product fields of cars, toiletries, soap powders, alcoholic drinks, the brand images are crucial to differentiation. Brands can symbolize a lifestyle with which consumers may identify or aspire towards, or they may exude a 'personality' through the packaging or advertising; for example, 'warmth, homeliness and friendliness' or 'power and masculinity'.

These attributes of a brand are not superficially available to researchers because they function at an emotional level and are *felt* and *experienced* rather than *thought* or *spoken*. Here qualitative research comes into its own since a number of projective techniques which are now available enable the researcher to elicit these *feelings* and understand the cluster of added values which make up a brand (see Chapter 8).

To understand the purchase decision-making process and/or usage patterns

Qualitative research is extremely helpful in describing complex and detailed behaviour. For example, the purchase of a wallpaper design and paint colour for a room is the end of a very long, complicated sequence of decisions involving an individual or couple over a period of time. Qualitative research unravels the process from the initial decision to redecorate the room, through the reconnaissance visits to various stores, to the final purchase. Observation too may be important, for example watching people leafing through wallpaper pattern books and questioning them afterwards about their observed behaviour.

Qualitative research helps to understand the role of a product in daily life (when is it used, by whom, how often, where, why). Usage diaries kept by a respondent for a week prior to interview are surprisingly helpful in exploring behaviour patterns in an area which has a high level of manufacturer interest but low consumer involvement, e.g. the use of salt, pepper, herbs and seasonings.

Hypothesis-generation

Basic market studies are often conducted with the aim of generating hypotheses about the product field or brand. By understanding the aspirations, attitudes, needs and behaviour of consumers with regard to a general product area or a brand, qualitative research is able to indicate *which attitudinal* areas, *which consumer needs* and *which types of consumer* offer most potential for further development, whether this development lies in the area of new products, packaging, product reformulation, advertising or promotional activity.

Basic qualitative research helps the advertising and marketing teams to focus their energies in areas that are likely to be more fruitful. It can perform the role of a screening process, closing avenues that may have seemed obvious, and opening others.

New product development

Qualitative research has no rival when it comes to New Product Development.

There are various stages of new product development (NPD) which draw on qualitative research:

- understanding a market and the brands within it in order to find out where 'gaps' may lie for a new product;
- obtaining reactions to a large number of NPD product concepts or ideas to determine which directions seem worthy of further effort and development;
- understanding the strengths and weaknesses of a new product in order to guide product improvement;
- development of a total NPD proposition, i.e. product, packaging, positioning and advertising.

Creative development research

This is the one area of qualitative research which separates qualitative sheep from qualitative goats and which has been responsible for giving qualitative research an extremely poor reputation, especially in advertising agencies.

Creative development research is commissioned at three different stages in the advertising development process. Each one is subject to pressures of different kinds. It is essential, if conducting creative development research, to understand the relationship between the various functions within an agency (planner, account and creative)[2] and also the relationship between the agency and the client.

The three stages are:

- Strategy definition: *what* should the advertising be saying to consumers?
- Executional guidance: once the strategy is decided, *how* should the strategy be conveyed to consumers; that is, which creative idea(s) best succeed in meeting the strategy's objectives?
- Pre-testing the chosen execution to check the communication against the advertising objectives.

Strategy definition

The majority of users of qualitative research would agree that one of its most important roles in relation to advertising is its contribution to strategy development.

The basic types of study already discussed, particularly the relationship of the consumer both to the product category in general and to the brand in particular, will provide the groundwork for hypothesizing how to position the brand and what brand values will optimize its competitive position.

Qualitative research, at this stage of advertising development, acts as a bridge between the 'creatives' and the consumer. It helps the creative team to understand the consumers' relationship with the brand, and by the very nature of the data (anecdotal, consumer slang or technical terminology) it allows the copywriters and art directors to produce advertising relevant to the consumer rather than that based on how the creative team believes 'the average punter' feels, thinks and acts.

It must be remembered that those who work in advertising agencies or manufacturing companies are very far removed in terms of attitudes, behaviour and lifestyle from the majority of the population. An upmarket professional usually has no idea of the value structure of a downmarket unskilled labourer or his wife and children.

Executional guidance

It is in this area of advertising development research that the qualitative researcher should be most wary. It is here that the politics of an agency or agency-client relationship are most manifest, and here where research results are most open to differing interpretations based on the different goal-orientations of the end-users.

Essentially, the aim of qualitative research is to help nurture creative ideas or executions that promise to be the most memorable, distinctive and relevant (whilst at the same time meeting the strategy objectives) and conversely, helping to reject those which lack the qualities described above.

Such research, in order to be actionable, needs sensitivity and experience, both in terms of interpreting the reactions of consumers to the creative material *and* in communicating the understanding gained to the advertising agency and the client.

On no account should the qualitative research be positioned as a check on the creative team — winners and losers are not the name of the game — instead the research should increase understanding which can subsequently be used to aid judgement about how to develop better finished advertising.

Pre-testing

Pre-testing an almost finished television commercial or press/poster advertise-ment is also potentially hazardous, since by this point in the advertising develop-ment process both agency and client have become committed to the idea or its execution. Alternatively, the agency might be committed and the client unconvinced, or vice versa. In both instances, the debrief will be highly charged.

Pre-testing is essentially about communication — what is the advertisement 'getting across' to consumers and how does this match up to the advertising objectives already defined by client and agency?

The first thing to do is to make sure the advertising objectives are listed, and that the qualitative researcher has a copy.

Secondly, take care that in the sample design and methodology there is an opportunity to evaluate communication at an *individual* level. Once a commercial has been exposed in a group discussion and talked about, there is no way that individual communication effectiveness can be assessed.

Thirdly, be realistic. There is no earthly point in telling client or agency that consumers dislike the actor's clothes/manner/hairstyle, when this *did not* interfere with communication. The crucial consideration at this stage is whether or not there were any comprehension or executional problems that interfered with communication. If not, the executional negatives are best discussed in terms of 'points for future advertising development'. Additionally, practitioners need to ensure that if the strategy is found to be incorrect then no-one is left in doubt, and furthermore that the agency or client is warned that strategy will be discussed at the debrief so that they are prepared. Otherwise this type of last-minute bombshell is likely to result in the crucification of the qualitative researcher!

Diagnostic studies

These are often similar to broad market studies since the primary objective is to understand the consumer relationship to a particular aspect of the brand, for example the advertising, the packaging, the formulation.

Often such research is conducted in order to ascertain the degree of 'wear-out' of an advertising campaign or to determine to what extent the brand image has changed since the start of a campaign. Or because of a new competitor in the market or changing packaging conventions, a manufacturer may feel the need to evaluate a brand's packaging in order to determine whether it is still operating at an optimum level.

Sometimes qualitative research is commissioned to understand a competitor's activity (for example a new product, a new advertising campaign or promotional strategy). Usually such competitive 'snooping' is combined with the objective of updating current information on the brand.

Tactical qualitative studies

These are extremely numerous and in the UK are responsible for many of the '4 groups — 2 North, 2 South, 2 ABC1, 2 C2D' research designs of the 1980s. Such research is commissioned for a multitude of different reasons, all of which require a verbal debrief within two weeks of the date of commission! Examples are given below:

- Pack design alternatives — a winner is required from a range of 2–5.
- Press advertising — alternative headlines or copy lines.
- Casting — which model best represents the values of the brand?
- Advertising development — which execution (a) or (b)? — 'Neither' is not an answer!

- Product formulations – which of 2–3 recipes/formulations is most acceptable?
- Positioning alternatives – which one seems most motivating, relevant and worth development?
- Pack dispensing options – which one do consumers find most acceptable?
- Executional changes – do consumers notice the changed voice-over, pack design, logo position etc.?

The list is endless, and young qualitative researchers are likely to be 'broken in' on such projects. Indeed, they are fun to work on, since the results are immediately helpful to the end-user, aid decision-making and are relatively tension-free. The role of qualitative research in tactical studies is often 'judge' or 'arbitrator', and no one pretends otherwise.

CHOICE OF METHODOLOGY

What follows is an ABC guide to choice of qualitative approach. It is intended to outline the advantages and disadvantages of the most frequently used qualitative methodologies with indications of the type of problem to which each is most suited. It is not intended to cover the details of each type, which are discussed in Chapters 3, 4, 5 and 6.

Basically there are only two qualitative methodologies:

the group interview (discussion)
the individual interview (depth)

All other qualitative methodologies are a derivation or combination of these two approaches.

The group discussion

The group discussion methodological approach, particularly the dynamics operating within it, is covered elsewhere (Chapter 4). The basic concept is that seven to nine people, who are specially recruited according to a predetermined set of criteria, exchange experiences, attitudes and beliefs about a particular product category (or brand, pack, advertisement, promotion) under the guidance of a trained moderator, who

- directs the flow of the discussion over areas that are important to the moderator and/or client;
- recognizes important points and encourages the group to explore these and elaborate upon them;
- observes all the non-verbal communication between respondents, between

respondents and the moderator or between respondents and the subject matter;

- creates an atmosphere that allows respondents to relax and lower some of their defences;
- synthesizes the understanding gained with the problems and objectives defined by the client;
- tests out hypotheses generated by the information gained so far.

The advantages of group discussions are:

- the group environment with 'everyone in the same boat' is less intimidating than the individual depth interview (Gordon & Robson 1982);
- one person's experiences or feelings 'spark off' another's. It is a good vehicle for creativity;
- the process highlights the differences between consumers thus making it possible to understand a range of attitudes and behaviour in a relatively short time;
- groups can be observed, which is particularly useful for members of the creative/marketing development team who can experience consumer vocabulary, attitudes and reactions first hand;
- spontaneity of response is encouraged in a group setting;
- the social and cultural influences on attitudes and behaviour are highlighted.

The disadvantages of the group discussion are:

- group processes may inhibit the frank exchange of attitudes and beliefs and encourage unrealistic recounting of behaviour;
- the group may react negatively to the moderator, subject matter or the environment, and freeze;
- a strong personality (or perceived expert) may overawe the other members who either withdraw or simply agree;
- minority viewpoints may be lost by group members' feeling insecure at voicing opinions that appear to be different from the majority;
- loss of sense of perspective. The moderator, the group members and/or the observers can lose perspective by 'hot-housing' the problem under discussion or in evaluating possible resolutions or developmental directions.

Group discussions *alone* are not the most appropriate research technique in the following instances:

- intimate subject matter (contraception, sanitary protection products) or personal financial situations (e.g. banking, wealth management, insurance);
- when social norms strongly predominate, pressurizing conformity (such as teaching children road safety, bottle feeding);
- when a detailed life history is important or when a detailed understanding is required of a process (for example buying a car; deciding to go on holiday);
- when personal tastes are very varied and the group becomes too hetero-

geneous to obtain useful information (tastes in music, fashion, interior decor);
- where an understanding of a more complex psycho-sociological issue is involved (e.g. attitudes to women's roles; attachment to work; the meaning of motherhood etc.);
- when difficulties are encountered in recruiting the target sample, for example specialist doctors, AB men who travel abroad on business at least three times a month, farmers, pre-selected names from lists, minority brand users;
- where the product category involves different degrees of knowledge and understanding, such as DIY. Here the group discussion design needs to take this factor into account.

Variations on group discussions which can overcome some of the difficulties described above are:

> Mini-groups (4–6 respondents)
> Extended discussions (lasting 4 + hours)
> Reconvened groups (two sessions separated by a time gap)
> Sensitivity panels
> Synectic or brainstorming groups.

Mini-group discussions

Smaller group discussions consisting of 4–6 respondents instead of the conventional 8–9 are useful when:

- focussed information is required (for example, reactions to two press advertisements; or reactions to a graphic change on a pack);
- the subject matter is intimate or personal;
- longitudinal information on the individuals is required (such as understanding the dynamics of holiday choice, interior decoration, buying a car);
- interviewing adolescents or children for whom a large group of peers (either friends or strangers) encourages a greater level of posturing and 'showing-off'.

The main advantage of mini-group discussions is that the group environment is less threatening and rapport may develop more easily. Whilst it offers all the advantages of standard group discussions in terms of dynamics it also suffers from the same disadvantages, but it does enable the moderator to keep track of individual backgrounds, so relating these to reactions obtained or attitudes and beliefs expressed.

Extended discussions

These are group discussions lasting 3–4 hours (with a meal/coffee break) and are more than simply long groups. Extended discussions are characterized by:

- the use of enabling techniques which help respondents to 'form' into a cohesive group thus facilitating the potential to 'perform' subsequently (see Chapter 4);
- the use of the more time-consuming projective techniques such as role playing, psycho drawing and 'Words and Pictures' (see Chapter 8);
- the setting of tasks for respondents, either on their own, in pairs, in two teams or as a whole group so that experiential access to attitudes and feelings can take place.

The use of an extended discussion approach is indicated when we are required to:

- explore in depth more complex psychological issues associated with the product field or brand;
- provide new insight for over-researched brands;
- understand a commodity product (bread, eggs, bacon) when standard studies have not produced fresh information;
- use a great many research stimuli such as competitive products, competitive and current advertising, new advertising concepts, new pack designs;
- understand and describe the dynamics of a large and fragmented product sector, eg jams and marmalades;
- explore a very personal subject, eg AIDS, divorce, death.

The primary advantage of an extended group is the depth and breadth of data obtained. Enabling techniques at the start of the group facilitate the development of trust both between members and between members and the moderator, thus increasing rapport. The group atmosphere encourages respondents to express more heartfelt beliefs and attitudes, thus lowering some of the defensive posturing found in most standard group discussions.

Reconvened group discussions

These are two discussions, with the same group of respondents, separated by a time period. This approach offers some of the advantages of extended discussions since by the second session respondents have developed rapport and are likely to be less defensive. It is particularly useful for problems such as:

- NPD where the first session covers background attitudes and behaviour to the product category. The new product is then briefly discussed and respondents take it home for trial. The second session involves a discussion of the product (post trial) and the exploration of positioning concepts;
- setting up experimental experiences between discussions, e.g. asking credit card holders not to use their cards for a week or asking women not to clean the toilet for a week.

Sensitivity panels

Sensitivity panels were first invented by William Schlackman[3]. A group of respondents is selected according to usage or demographic characteristics and co-operation is obtained to attend weekly or fortnightly sessions for a set period. These respondents are then *trained* in the wide range of enabling techniques derived from psychoanalytical theory and encounter group practice such as free association, analogy generation, stream of awareness and gestalt dialogue, so that when given a research task the group requires almost no preparation. Rapport, trust and intimacy are well established so the group 'works' on the problem without the need for extensive warm-up procedures. Schlackman and other users of this technique claim that the reduction in defences together with a greater awareness of group processes, results in better quality qualitative data, that is, a more 'honest' expression of feelings and heightened creativity.

Sensitivity panels are most appropriate for complex research problems, particularly when conventional research approaches have been tried in the past and have proved of limited value. The kind of research problem summarized by the feeling 'where on earth do we go next', is probably a good candidate for this methodology. Its applicability lies in the areas of exploration, invention and diagnosis *not* evaluation.

Obviously, sensitivity panels are expensive to set up and maintain. They also outlive their usefulness after six or so sessions, by which time respondents are more concerned about exchanging feelings about life than they are about baked beans!

Methodologies such as this have an important role to play when combined with other methods.

'Brainstorming' and/or synectics

Synectics or brainstorming techniques were all the rage in the 1970s. Again, like most technical developments in research, their subsequent decline in popularity is due to the fact that the usefulness of such techniques was often overclaimed. Disillusionment often leads to total rejection.

Synectics and brainstorming are usually used interchangeably to describe techniques, skills and approaches used to encourage a set of people to solve problems by thinking in an innovative, open-minded and lateral-thinking manner.

In market research, a brainstorming group is one that is convened to solve a particular problem such as the generation of new product ideas. Such groups can also be used to generate hypotheses concerning strategic development for a brand, service or organization.

Brainstorming groups take a variety of different forms because different 'facilitators' support different procedures. Usually the participants include consumers pre-selected according to demographic and usage criteria as well as criteria such as 'creativity' or 'extroversion'. An example of this is to ask someone to think of as many uses for a brick as possible within a timed period or to join all the nine dots below with 4 straight lines (without lifting the pen)

```
0    0    0
0    0    0
0    0    0
```

Specialists such as pack designers, R & D personnel, marketing people or representatives from different functions within an advertising agency (creative, planning, account management) are often involved, either with consumers or in separate sessions.

The facilitator is especially trained in techniques to aid creativity such as the lateral thinking exercises described above, thinking by analogy, fantasy solutions, word associations and imagery. All of these are designed to help the group to suspend rational judgement and to free themselves of socially acceptable (or corporately acceptable) solutions to the problem being discussed.

Brainstorming is a very disciplined approach, and in order to produce successful results it needs to be carefully designed and executed by trained professionals.

The individual interview

The individual interview is both underrated and frequently misunderstood by buyers of qualitative research. A depth interview, as it is often named, can vary between half an hour or two hours, the two extremes obviously being quite different in terms of the relationship between interviewer and respondent and the depth/breadth of information obtained. A full discussion of the individual interview is given in Chapter 6.

For the purposes of this section, a depth interview is defined as:

- lasting approximately one hour;
- tape-recorded (no notes taken);
- orientated to penetrating below the superficial question-and-answer format of structured or semi-structured questionnaires;
- rapport building in order to facilitate the expression of heartfelt responses.

The strengths of the depth interview lie in many of the areas where the group interview technique is weak. They are as follows:

- longitudinal information can be gathered on one respondent at a time (for example purchase processes; decision-making sequences);
- both majority and minority opinion can be tapped irrespective of the dominance of personalities or problems of group processes;
- a sense of perspective is possible, particularly when a larger number of depths are being conducted (20 +) or when they are used to supplement group discussion data;

- very intimate and personal material can be discussed;
- peer group pressure is not operational;
- interviewing expertise can overcome the tendency to express socially acceptable norms of attitude and behaviour;
- recruitment difficulties can be overcome;
- the sample can be segmented and spread to cover more cells than is usually possible or practical in a group interview research design.

The main disadvantages of the depth interview are:

- that it is very time-consuming both in terms of conducting the interview and analysing the tapes;
- that it is costly (for the above reason);
- that there is a tendency for people to start thinking in terms of 'how many' rather than in 'how', 'why' or 'what'.

There are a number of variations of the individual interviews, namely:

> Mini-depth interviews
> Semi-structured interviews
> Pair interviewing
> Observation
> Accompanied shopping

Mini-depths

These are focussed individual interviews, which are less wide-ranging in the areas covered than are normal depth interviews. These interviews are conducted by fully qualified group moderators, who use a very flexible interview guide rather than a questionnaire.

Mini-depth interviews are very useful for problems requiring an evaluation of *communication* whether it be pack, promotion or advertising. A half-hour is sufficient to show a respondent one or two animatics (or near-finished TV commercials, press advertisements or pack designs) and to ask a series of questions to determine whether or not there are comprehension difficulties and to establish exactly what is being communicated about the brand. To attempt to pre-test the effectiveness of communication in groups is misleading, since intensive 'hot-housing' or the influence of an articulate minority can mask the relevant data.

Mini-depths are also very useful in parallel with a quantitative approach such as a halltest. A small qualitative sample conducted at the same time as the structured questionnaires or conducted with respondents who have already participated in the hall test helps to add qualitative flesh to the quantitative bones, thus yielding a richer end result.

Semi-structured interviews

This type of interview involves fully trained interviewers using a questionnaire which is essentially open-ended. They are trained in probing techniques but are required to ask the questions exactly as they are written and in the same order. They are not allowed to make up questions themselves, except to clarify a respondent's reply.

There are cost benefits to this method, but also limitations in the depth of data.

One of the hybrid methodologies referred to earlier is a combination of depths and semi-structured interviews. A qualitative executive conducts the first 10–20 individual depth interviews, and from this data designs an open-ended questionnaire which is then administered to a larger sample, by trained senior interviewers. The total number of interviews are then analysed by the qualitative executive responsible for the first set. The end result combines qualitative depth with extended sample coverage.

Paired interviews

Paired 'depths' are exactly what they seem — a depth interview with two respondents. These respondents can either be acquaintances, a married couple or strangers, depending on the subject matter and survey objectives.

Paired depths are very useful for interviewing children or adolescents where the two-to-one situation offers security (for the respondents) and the opportunity for the interviewer to explore differences in attitude and behaviour.

They are also useful when trying to understand a process of decision that involves two individuals, for example a young couple buying a new home; a married couple deciding on a holiday; two friends deciding on where to eat out.

Triangular interviews

These interviews are also what they seem — an interview with three respondents. However, the criteria by which each participant is recruited holds the key to understanding the usefulness of such a methodology. Each of the three participants is chosen to represent *a different viewpoint* on the subject matter for discussion. For example, in a survey to understand car-owner attitudes to Japanese cars, we recruited a current owner, a non-owner who was positively interested in buying a Japanese car 'next time', and a rejector of Japanese cars.

The interview is conducted in such a way as to encourage *the expression of differences in attitudinal perspective.* For this reason, such interviews are some-times termed conflict interviews but we believe this description is a little misleading since the dynamic that occurs is more like shifting alliances than overt argument, although the latter does occur!

To carry on the example above, as the interview progresses the moderator encourages the owner to persuade the other two about the virtues of Japanese cars, whilst a little later the rejector is encouraged to express the prejudices held against cars from Japan.

Other types of triangular combination are:

- a heavy user; a light user; a non-user.
- a new user; an established user; a lapsed user.
- a loyal user of brand X; a loyal user of brand Y; an own label user.

The combinations are unlimited, but usually revolve round the usership of the brand, rather than demographic or lifestage criteria which are kept constant so as not to introduce too many variables into the triangle.

Observation

Observation techniques have been part of the market research armoury for many years, to the extent that one well known American company, Mass Observation, included the term in its name.

However, in modern market research practice, observation methods are under-utilized and the majority of buyers are unaware of their potential. This is due to two factors. The first is that it is thought of as a time-consuming quantitative technique applicable only to large-scale studies such as observing football crowds at home and away matches, or observing how a new motorway affects surrounding traffic. The second is that in the present-day environment of qualitative research it is not thought to increase understanding, since those observed cannot be questioned about the reasons for their behaviour. Both are incorrect assumptions. Observation techniques can be applied to small samples and can also be applied qualitatively.

There are two types of observation: passive and active. Passive or *simple observation* entails the observer watching a particular activity. He simply notes down exactly what an individual does – the sequence of actions, the time taken over each and so on. The observer has no way of knowing what the actions *mean*. An obvious use of this type of observation is watching a baby/toddler play with a new toy, or watching a woman prepare a new recipe for the first time.

Active or *participant observation* entails the observer watching (first) and then asking questions (usually later). Thus for example a woman may be observed at the meat counter of a supermarket, and notes taken of her actions. Subsequently she will be asked what she had been thinking about when she picked up a roast and then replaced it. Participant observation addresses itself to the 'why' underlying behaviour, not only the 'what' or 'how'.

Accompanied shopping

This is a form of observation. The interviewer (with the respondent's agreement) accompanies her on a shopping expedition. The respondent may or may not have been given a sum of money to spend beforehand. The interviewer observes the selection process carefully, asking questions at appropriate times. An example of this was a study which aimed to understand how consumers select men's shirts. Both men and women were given a sum of money, sufficient for a good quality shirt, and were observed and questioned during the selection procedure.

The advantages of such a technique are:

- access to *real* behaviour (rather than recalled behaviour);
- an opportunity to evaluate the influence of point-of-sale material, displays, service;
- an opportunity to explore actions which the respondent may subsequently forget or perhaps is unaware of in the first place.

The disadvantages are that:

- it is time-consuming and therefore costly;
- the interviewer's presence may bias behaviour;

Accompanied shopping is rarely used as the only methodological approach. It is usually combined with other methods such as group discussions or depth interviews.

Conclusions on methodology

The main point to remember is to be flexible and open. Increasingly, sample designs are submitted which mix two or three methodological approaches (including quantitative) very successfully. Each method has strengths and weaknesses and therefore a sensible combination often results in a sounder data base than any one method alone.

NOTES

1. R. Bandler and J. Grinder (1979), *Frogs into Princes*, Real People Press.
2. C. Ryan and W. Gordon (1980), 'The Interface between Creative, Account and Research Groups in Advertising Agencies'. Article presented at Market Research Society Conference.
3. W. Schlackman (1984), 'A Discussion of the Use of Sensitivity Panels in Market Research', Market Research Society Annual Conference Proceedings.

2 Planning and Designing Qualitative Studies

INTRODUCTION

One of the problems of contemporary qualitative research both in UK and in America, and to a lesser extent in Europe, is that qualitative research is synonymous with the group discussion or 'focus' group. The syndrome of 'a few groups' has spread like a rampant disease that undermines the qualitative product itself, the degree to which qualitative insights and understanding are used to solve particular corporate or brand problems, and the professionalism of qualitative practitioners.

Planning and designing a qualitative research study involves more than the automatic commissioning of 'a few groups'. The problem itself requires evaluation and clarification followed by a consideration of the choices of methodology available today, and the size of the sample.

This chapter examines the crucial importance of the briefing – that is, the telephone or face-to-face meeting at which the client outlines the problem. It then discusses the alternatives available in terms of methodology and the criteria by which a sample is defined.

THE RESEARCH OBJECTIVES AND THE BRIEFING

The overt and the covert belief

It seems that all qualitative researchers practising in the 1980s accept the importance of understanding the covert responses of consumers and the dangers of accepting too much at face-value or merely reporting what we heard without thinking about it. Integral to our role is a firm belief that we get below the level of superficial responses, and for this reason anyone who is anyone in qualitative research claims to dig deeper than anyone else. Thus, the use of clay, psycho-drawings, sensitivity groups, transactional analysis, role playing and other projective techniques is cited as evidence of the ability to tap deeper levels of consumer response.

The assumption underlying all of this is that qualitative researchers understand what it is that clients want to understand about the consumer! It is in making this assumption that many qualitative researchers err. Insufficient thought and energy is given to ensuring that the brief from the client is clearly understood.

The reasons for this error make sense if one considers that clients are like consumers, and communicate in two different ways. There is the overt brief and the covert one, and it is our firm belief that it is as important to understand the covert as the overt brief and to make sure that the two do not contradict one another.

The reason that the covert brief exists in the first place relates directly to the political environment in which the client exists. This was made quite clear in a research study conducted in 1980 by Ryan and Gordon. This paper discusses in great detail the differing roles of independent researchers, creative teams, account handlers and planners within agencies, and describes their interaction at a particular point of time — the research debrief. The paper stated that a great deal of aggression, tension and anxiety exists at this time, as well as a number of other feelings such as boredom, irritation and lack of concentration.

The point to be made is that these emotional responses do not suddenly materialize at the debrief. They are there right from the outset of the project and are often exacerbated at the debrief unless the researcher has clearly understood the source of possible tension and spent some effort in considering whether or not she can reduce it in any way at all. Thus, we would like to suggest that qualitative researchers *must* be aware of the possibility of these tensions and can help to minimize them by understanding the *covert brief*. The two examples shown below illustrate the covert brief.

Example 1

Client/Agency *Overt*	Hello, Wendy — I have some research I'd like you to do. It is very important and as you know it is a complex brand. We have had the account for five years and our yearly review is in three weeks' time. There are no problems with the account — they're not contemplating a move. We've agreed on a strategy and have given the brief to three different creative teams. I think they've come up with some interesting ideas.
Covert	We're in danger of losing the account. We *have* to come up with the goods in three weeks' time. We're so anxious, we've briefed three different teams in the hope that one of them comes up with something. There is a lot of tension . . . . HELP!

Agency/Client	The three teams are having a great deal of fun...
Overt	you know, friendly rivalry, ha, ha! I need some sensitive research to point us in the right direction. By the way, our MD will be at the debrief, but don't worry, he's very nice.
Covert	The three teams are fighting. The atmosphere is terrible. I'm terrified I'll have to carry the can if the researcher doesn't perform well.... HELP ME! By the way, the MD scares me to death!

Example 2

Manufacturer/Client	Hello, Roy, we'd like you to do some more work
Overt	for us on stage II of the pack re-design work you did last month. The design company have finally agreed to take the research findings to heart and have submitted some new ideas.
Covert	Since you bombed out all their first designs there's been a lot of hassle and they were unwilling for you to research their designs again but we've won.

Manufacturer/Client	We also want to ask your opinion about the way
Overt	in which the designs should be presented to consumers. They have firm ideas but we want to know what you think.
Covert	We think they may be trying to bias the results by presenting the designs in a particular way. Will you act as objective advisor and protect us if necessary?

Manufacturer/Client	The new designs have moved on a little bit but
Overt	although I have strong views on how they will work, or not work as the case may be, we need guidance first.
Covert	I do not like the new designs and we need evidence fast.

How can one understand the covert brief?

The most important step is to ask questions subtly at the very initial stages of discussion of the research project. After all, if an individual thinks himself any good as a qualitative researcher, the subtle use of questions should not be difficult!

Secondly, the qualitative researcher should encourage informal conversations before the main briefing meetings, or even afterwards, particularly if the brief seemed to raise certain issues which signal a more complex underlying problem. The moral of the story is: when in doubt, try to clarify it.

Thirdly, it is important to reassure clients that it will not bias the qualitative researcher to know that there are differences of opinion. If the client and qualitative researcher have any relationship at all, the trust and rapport between them should be sufficient to counteract any feelings that such discussions will bias the results. Information, but not pressure, is what is needed by qualitative researchers.

Finally, it is essential to obtain the broadest picture possible and to understand for example how the strategy was arrived at; why a change of direction is taking place; what research information already exists; when the deadlines are; and so on. In other words, to establish quite clearly in one's own mind the historical who, when, how and why of the brand to date.

From a client point of view, of course, it is important to recognize that the qualitative researcher can only be expected to do a truly helpful job if she has been allowed to understand the problems fully. Many clients believe the myth that researchers must be unbiassed and objective in order to be effective researchers. It is simply an erroneous belief. The research process, whether quantitative or qualitative, is a subjective one. Rather like a river running over stones which direct and guide the pace and direction, information gathered in the course of qualitative interviewing run over the experience and theoretical viewpoint of the researcher. As we explain at length (see Chapter 10) data does not exist as an independent unity – it is an integral part of the researcher designing, conducting or interpreting the survey.

SAMPLE DESIGN

Preparatory stages

Having identified and clarified all the objectives for the study (both overt and covert) the next question is 'how do you go about it?'

Sample and methodology need to be considered separately as well as together. For example, if the sample consists of young teenagers it is less effective to interview them individually because of their likely defensiveness in relation to perceived authority figures, even though that may seem the best methodology in relation to the survey objectives.

The target sample

Assuming that the target market for the brand/advertising has been defined, it is necessary to consider the sample in terms of actual people. Some questions are itemized below:

Who do I want to talk to? Are these consumers identifiable by age, sex, or class demographics or are they types of people representing a particular attitude or lifestyle? If the latter is true, how can these individuals be identified in such a way that a recruiter or several recruiters can select them accurately? Will physical appearance suffice or is an attitude questionnaire necessary?

Are they people or statistics? Beware of consumer segments that have previously been identified using factor analysis or some other sophisticated statistical clustering exercise on quantitative data. The types of people will undoubtedly exist but they will not necessarily be easy to identify by using the same statements or scales as were used in the statistical analysis. We are talking about people, not correlations! The Acorn (A Classification of Residential Neighbourhoods) area classification system is a good example. Not everyone recruited in Acorn area J for example, will display the characteristics of this area, which are based on distributions which are higher or lower than the average.

Are you looking for the only individual in the world? Be careful not to 'overdefine' your sample, so that an interviewer is being asked to find a truly unique individual who meets the requirements. *Think* about the implications of the sample design – it may not be as straightforward as it looks at first glance.

An example of an overdefined sample is shown below:

A group discussion of housewives:

C1C2.
25–45 years.
Each to have one child under 5 and one child 6–10 years.
All must own a freezer.
Half to go to a specialist freezer shop at least once a month.
3 of the group to go to Bejams.
1 or 2 to go to other freezer shops.
Half must have the use of a car.
All must serve chips at least once a week.
Half to have tried oven chips and will buy again – some to have bought brands and some to have bought own label.
1 or 2 to have tried oven chips and rejected.
.... and so on!

Apparently an easy quota – a high penetration product with no particularly difficult requirements, but the combined effect of such a quota creates an almost impossible task for the recruiter.

Are these people prepared to be interviewed? Before specifying the methodology and sample size think about the target market. Perhaps they are unlikely to respond to market research requests. For example: men earning £30,000 a year; company directors of large multinationals; senior government officials, and so on. These people can, with time and patience (and consequently a higher cost per interview) be reached individually, but realistic timing and sample size needs to be set.

Do I want experienced or 'virgin' respondents? In the UK, recruiters work for a large number of market research companies with differing points of view about the advantages or disadvantages of interviewing people who have participated in market research before. Those in favour of experienced respondents claim that these people are more relaxed about the market research interviewing process and therefore are less inhibited in sharing their views. Gordon and Robson (1982) indicated that experienced respondents found the second and subsequent participation far less anxiety-provoking than the first and claimed to be more 'honest' in their responses. The opposing camp believe that after one or more exposures to qualitative market research, consumers become professional critics rather than unsophisticated participants.

The authors believe it is a matter of choice. For certain projects, experienced respondents are an advantage because they have undergone an informal training process in articulating their views about mundane products. In this respect such groups bear a superficial resemblance to 'sensitivity panels'. At other times and for other projects, completely inexperienced respondents may provide less contaminated information.

The sample size

Sample design is invariably a compromise between the ideal and budgetary and/or time constraints. So how are decisions made about what to cut out? How can maximum value from the sample be ensured? Start by trying to construct a cellular framework with the major variables along the top and sides. A simple example is shown below:

All married housewives C1C2[1]	Brand X users	Brand Y users	A four-cell approach yielding multiples of 4 (individual interviews or groups)
18–34 years	×	×	
35–50 years	×	×	

Note:
[1]See note 1 at end of chapter for clarification

Not all samples are as easy to construct. Take for example a survey conducted on behalf of a major bank, the objective of which is to understand current attitudes and behaviour regarding home-ownership with particular emphasis

Table 2.1:   Recent (last 12 months) experience of home purchase

Life stage	1st-time buyers		2nd or subsequent buyers	
Single	BC1* (mixed sex) Area 1		BC1 (mixed sex) Area 2	
Married or living together pre children	BC1 (female) Area 1	C2D (male) Area 2	BC1 (male) Area 3	C2D (male) Area 1
Married with children under 5 years	BC1 (male) Area 1	C2D (female) Area 1	BC1 (male) Area 3	C2D (male) Area 2
Married with children 5–16 years	BC1 (male) Area 2	C2D (female) Area 3	BC1 (male) Area 2	C2D (male) Area 1
Empty-nesters (children leaving/ left home)	BC1 (male) Area 3	C2D (male) Area 2	BC1 (female) Area 3	C2D (male) Area 1
Retiring in next 5 years	BC1 (male) Area 1	C2D (male) Area 3	BC1 (male) Area 2	C2D (female) Area 3

Notes:
*See note 1 at the end of the chapter

on financial services required. Commonsense indicates that there are likely to be a large number of variables which are influential such as life-stage, sex, marital status, socio-economic group, geographic location and whether or not the individual is a novice or experienced home purchaser.

   Table 2.1 shows a possible sample solution. It attempts to take account of as many variables as possible but even with this 22-cell solution, some compromises have to be made. The sample is purposely weighted towards men (past single lifestage) since women are less likely to be involved directly in the final financial decisions. However women cannot be ignored since they have enormous influence on their husbands in this type of decision. Thus the sample taps their views across the life stages but does not focus on them.

The decision on area is also simple. In an arbitrary manner, the cells are divided between three geographic areas so that a spread of geographic opinion is obtained thus lessening the likelihood of regional bias. The sample represents downmarket and upmarket consumers equally, since both are extremely important. They are separated because attitudes to home-ownership differ according to social class.

Having isolated a cell structure, the next task is to consider it as a totality. If the cells represent group discussions, is it really necessary to conduct 22, as in Table 2.1? Will there still be learning after the first eight are completed? Is the clients' budget being wasted? Answers to these questions might make re-evaluation of the cell structure necessary, perhaps resulting in a compression of the left-hand column to 4 key life-stages and a decision to design the total sample to represent social class differences, but *not* within each cell. If the cells represent individual interviews, it is generally the case that *more* cells are possible with only a few depth interviews in each.

Taking the house purchase example, it is highly likely that a compression of cells will be necessary, resulting in a 10- cell design, as shown in Table 2.2. This size sample is sensible both in terms of client budget *and* a practitioner's ability to cope with the vast amount of qualitative data which will be generated.

One of the points worth consideration in attempting to design commonsense samples is the issue of spread versus representation in order to determine real differences. For example should older and younger people be included in the sample to ensure a good spread of age and to avoid the possibilities of age bias, or are they both necessary in order to identify particular attitudes and behaviour of each age group? If the intention is to examine specific differences between younger and older consumers, it may not be necessary to cover the whole age range but rather to polarize the age difference. For example:

Younger cell 20–30 years
Older cell 40–50 years

Geographic distribution is always a thorny problem. If the intention is, as is often the case in the UK, to avoid biassing the findings towards London and the South East, then interviewing can be spread in an almost arbitrary manner between the North, the Midlands and the Greater London area. If, on the other hand, consumers in Scotland display different purchase patterns from those in the South East, these two areas need to be explored with sufficient coverage to understand the differences.

Thus, to summarize, the key to good sample design is to write down *all* the important variables. If the list is long, try to prioritize these. Then design an ideal sample. Finally apply commonsense criteria and collapse cells or spread variables within a cell in order to reach a compromised but none the less effective design. In our experience, enormous qualitative studies are not cost-

Table 2.2:   Recent (last 12 months) experience of home purchase

Life stage	1st-time buyers	2nd or subsequent buyers	Notes
Single/unmarried couples without children	BC1*	*C2D	mixed male/female. first-time buyers are most interesting to client
Married couples with children under 16	BC1* C2D	BC1 *C2D	a spread of those with children under 10 yrs and those with children 10–16 yrs will be obtained in each group
Empty nesters children leaving/ left home		BC1* C2D	it is unlikely, in the UK, that people aged 45 + will be first-time entrants into the housing market
Retiring/retired		BC1 C2D	Often a time when couples move areas of capitalize their home asset

Note:
*Mixed sex groups; all other groups are male.

effective since the amount of unstructured information obtained becomes difficult to handle by an ordinary human brain. Qualitative practitioners can only assimilate a certain amount. They are not computers although several practitioners have tried to make use of high-tech approaches to aid analysis and interpretation.

Sample methodology

Until now we have concentrated on two questions: *Who* to interview? and *What size* should the sample be? The next question to consider, which although third in this chapter should really be considered alongside the other two, is:

How should the sample be interviewed? Chapter 1 outlines all the methodological approaches currently in use. Consideration of which one or ones to use depends on the research objectives and subject matter. There are no hard and fast rules to follow; each research design is very dependent on personal judgement.

There are only two basic methodologies available to qualitative researchers: the group interview and the individual interview. A third possibility which becoming more widely used is the integrated group and individual approach.

The checklist below is an attempt to help research designers to decide on which of the three basic approaches to use. Once the basic methodology is decided, a wide number of variants currently exist within each basic approach. By systematically running through the checklist below, it should be possible to determine which approach best suits the problem and subject matter.

'Bearing in mind the research objectives and subject matter, do I want . . ?'

to encourage consumer creativity ☐	detailed individual case histories ☐
an opportunity for the group to be observed ☐	a sense of perspective (quasi-numerical) ☐
to use a wide range of projective techniques ☐	to cover a lot of small but important consumer segments ☐
the expression of socially normative attitudes ☐	individual differences rather than similarities ☐
an opportunity to expose a lot of advertising, packaging or new product ideas ☐	to discuss an intimate matter or financial details that someone may not want to share with unknown people ☐
to explore 'route' and 'direction' not execution ☐	to assess communication of an advertisement or pack design ☐
a 'dipstick' feel for consumer temperature ☐	to understand a complex process of decision-making ☐
to use innovative stimulus material ☐	to avoid 'hothousing' reactions to a creative execution or a new product ☐
information as quickly as possible ☐	to explore a strategy change which is likely to be alien and easily rejected by consumers ☐
to talk to downmarket consumers ☐	to talk to people who may be difficult to find or less willing to participate in market research ☐

to avoid threatening an individual by the subject matter or interviewing techniques ☐	to minimize 'bravado' behaviour: e.g. businessman playing marketing directors, men denying emotional reasons for behaviour, women admitting 'cutting corners' with families/children ☐
to interview children or adolescents ☐	

An examination of the checklist distribution should indicate whether or not a group, individual or integrated approach will be most appropriate. If the ticks fall mainly on the left, a group approach is indicated; mainly on the right indicates an individual approach, and an equal distribution between right and left suggests the need for both group and individual methodologies.

A few other points need to be borne in mind in refining a research design. It is at this stage that common sense is the most valuable attribute the designer can have! For example, a group which mixes consumers by age, class and brand usage will not easily allow for analysis to detect differences between users of different brands.

Certain types of consumers tend, irrespective of the research objectives, to be best interviewed in a certain way. Young people for example are better interviewed in groups or paired depths, businessmen are often more forthcoming on a one-to-one basis.

It is also important to consider the nature of the target sample in terms of life stage (pre-children, young parents, established parents, 'empty nesters', grandparents), rather than chronological age alone.

Examples

1. Sample: C1C2 women 18–24 years
                 Users of moisturisers
    Question: Does it make any sense to mix pre-child women
                 with young mums when discussing cosmetics?

2. Sample: C1C2 men 35–55 years
                 Package-holiday takers
    Question: Since this tends to be a joint male/female decision,
                 does it make sense to have a single sex group?

As discussed, the best designed samples often include a mixture of interview methods which clearly reflect a structure designed with the research objectives in mind. However, the realities of the project can never be ignored. Thus, such issues as the type of stimulus material must also be considered. Will that age or social class group be able to deal with the material? Does it lend itself to groups rather than depths?

One also cannot ignore the costs involved. Group discussions are essentially cheaper than depth interviews. They are also a quicker way of contacting a larger number of people where fast turn-round is needed particularly when clients want to watch. Clearly these considerations cannot be ignored but neither must they become the only determining factor, otherwise the real value of good qualitative research design will not be obtained.

Other issues

Having decided upon a basic structure for the sample, there are other issues to be considered.

Type of group or individual interview

The starting point will be a decision that groups, depths or a combination of both is most appropriate. The next step is to decide on the type – extended, standard, re-convened or mini groups; individual, paired, couple depths. Be open-minded and consider all the possibilities each time (see Chapter 1).

Interviewing location

Where respondents feel most comfortable is usually the best venue. Hostess homes in the same area as the respondent lives or hotel rooms for businessmen are usually preferable. Sometimes it is advantageous to interview people in their own environment. This applies when asking people to report upon aspects of their own homes (decorating, DIY, furniture), and helps to provide a realistic context.

The UK has had a very different history regarding consumer laboratories or viewing rooms which are almost *de rigueur* in Europe and the USA. There is an unsubstantiated belief that viewing rooms, with their modern decor and less realistic (than someone's front room) proportions, interfere with the validity of consumer response. These rooms are thought either to intimidate respondents or to create an artificial response. Where the viewing facilities are obviously part of a client company (manufacturing or advertising agency), this knowledge may affect the tone of consumer response (though in exactly what way or which direction, no one has proved). Where the viewing facility is offered by an independent research organization, this type of bias is removed.

For a fuller discussion of the one-way mirror see Chapter 9.

Incentives

Thought should be given to the type of incentive offered (money or a gift) and whether or not babysitting expenses will be offered on recruitment. Different qualitative companies have different policies but incentives do increase the likelihood of fuller attendance.

Scheduling

The considerations for scheduling of fieldwork must take the following points into account:

- whether the sample can be interviewed during the day or in the evening and how this can be fitted around respondents' normal activities, e.g. around school times for mums etc.
- if more than one researcher is involved, the logistics of dealing with one set of materials must also be allowed for. Travelling time for out-of-city work also needs to be taken into account.
- if clients wish to attend groups, dates and times need to be cleared and slotted into the main fieldwork schedule.

NOTES

1. Socio-economic classification or social class. The stratification of society for the purposes of market research, based principally on the occupation of the head of household.

Social grade	% of Adult Population	Head of Household Occupation
A	3	Higher managerial administrative or professional
B	14	Middle managerial, administrative or professional
C1	22	Supervisory or clerical, junior managerial
C2	31	Skilled manual workers
D	19	Semi- and unskilled manual workers
E	11	State pensioners, casual or lowest-grade workers, unemployed

3 Group Discussions: Philosophy, Mechanics and Process

GROUP PROCESSES

Sooner or later every researcher and research user faces the problem of deepening and strengthening his understanding of experiences in groups. What factors influence what people say and how they behave? How may I know which answers to accept at face value? Which aspects are merely effects of this situation we find ourselves in, and which others reflect more fundamentally held views and opinions?

No matter how experienced you are in group discussion work, you will find yourself occasionally, if not frequently, perplexed by this sort of question. This chapter is the result of our having worked through many of these things before, and we hope it will help you to increase your understanding and ability to work with the factors that influence groups. In a little while we'll go on to describe the various types of group experiences, but for a moment let us consider the more general picture of the nature of the group discussion itself and its position among the different forms of learning environment that we have found ourselves in. For that, after all, is essentially what qualitative research is — a learning experience, where the researcher tries to learn about, and hopefully understand, the perspectives, viewpoints and feelings of his or her informants.

For most of us there are three main types of learning experience:

1. *Formal teaching*: where an agreed, or relatively agreed, body of knowledge is passed on by an 'expert', be he a teacher, professor, practitioner, whatever.
2. *The acquisition of skills*: this often has a strong experiential element, but differs from the true group discussion in that the onus of the learning is upon 'getting it right'. Examples here include driving a car, fly fishing, typing, computing.
3. *Experiential learning*: much of the information in group discussions comes

in this way. The unique aspect of this type of learning is that we use *ourselves* and our experience as part of the learning process. We introspect on the nature of our sensations and reactions and upon the reported experiences of the other group members as the means of increasing our appreciation of what is happening. [In a market research group it's not *necessary* that all the participants should introspect on their experiences in the group, although it might be desirable that they do so, but it is *essential* that the moderator undergoes this experience of opening herself up as a source of knowledge and interpretation.]

The basis of our ability to open ourselves up to the group experience goes back to our childhood. Unfortunately not only did we learn how to be open, we also learned how to close ourselves up from the group and to fight with other members. And so while most of us have been participating in groups ever since we were born, we've seldom developed practical models of the processes that govern them, except at the intuitive level. *Process*, as it is used here, is a name used to describe the phases or stages that the group goes through. *Dynamics* refers to the forces and tensions that exist between participants in the group, including the moderator. Later in the next chapter we shall return to the subject of group dynamics and describe one model of these derived from the area of group pyschotherapy that you may use practically to increase your understanding of market research groups.

We are not confusing market research with psychotherapy here; it's simply that the processes of groups themselves are the central subject of therapeutic groups and we may learn from and adapt the theories that have been developed there. In modern market research there are two commonly held points of view about what constitutes a group discussion. These viewpoints prevail irrespective of size or length of the group and they represent two radically different ideas about what is going on.

The first notion we have entitled *The Question and Answer Group Session*, which is construed as the collection of a series of opinions from individuals who are gathered together at one time for convenience or because of commonalities in behaviour or attitude.

The second is the *Psycho-dynamic Market Research Group*, in which the group forces become an integral part of the procedure. They are taken account of, used as part of the experience and the data base. Our aim in studying group processes is to provide us with the skills and ability to run this latter type of group *in which we conduct a planned endeavour to develop the forces that lead to smoothly running co-operative activity.*

(i)   *The Question and Answer Group Session* is the simpler and more basic of the two perspectives. Some fact-finding projects prefer to view groups in this fashion. The essence of such groups is that respondents' comments are accepted as valid, factual expressions of their point of view. We would argue that the 'facts' that you receive in a group situation are *always* heavily contaminated by process factors. We are as, or more, likely to respond to a situation *in terms of our experience of the group*, the moderator and the other people in it as to any other influences. During a group what I feel about what that man has just said at that moment for me *is* the truth and constitutes the basis of my experience. How I portray or disguise my feelings from the group at large depends upon my current and former strategies for coping with such a situation. Pretending that utterances are 'facts', free from contamination, merely blinds us to these influences rather than enabling us to work with them. We are not suggesting for a moment that respondents are deliberately lying; only that their experience is always affected by the situation and those around them. And since this experience constructs their perception of what is going on around them, they respond in accord with this particular picture of 'reality'.

(ii) *The Psychodynamic Market Research Group* — in which the group forces become an integral part of the procedure — describes the second point of view. These forces are taken account of and used as part of the experience and the data base. Increasingly our market research groups have adopted this second perspective rather than the first. We aim to take account of the group processes rather than ignore them.

The authors have noticed that some colleagues make this transformation from individual question and answer sessions in a group to properly formed group discussions easily, whereas others have a great struggle. We believe that underlying this problem for both researcher and clients, indeed for each individual, there exist two basic and conflicting drives in each of us; on the one hand there is the desire to be *unique and separate*, and on the other hand *the wish to be part of the group*. Both these desires are always present, though not necessarily in equal amounts. The existence of these two opposing drives is well demonstrated by the conflicting attitudes towards group discussions that one meets in our profession. One view is that membership of the group is only achieved as a result of surrendering individuality, and *is thus inimical to the expression of personal truth*. The opposing viewpoint tends to regard the group as a rational debate suitable for solving or discussing *any* problem from abortion to health foods, and assumes that individual viewpoints expressed during the group may be taken literally as undistorted expressions of personal truth.

Both these attitudes contain an element of truth and taken together reflect some of the powerful underlying, different feelings and beliefs about group forces. The authors would like to express their philosophy on this matter. We believe:

Each member of the group, though he may continue to behave in ways which are characteristic of him, is influenced by the behaviour of each of the other members and by the atmosphere or climate prevailing in the group at the time. This climate is something to which each member contributes but over which none has control.

So that if one is to understand the behaviour of a particular person in a group at any one time, an exhaustive knowledge of that individual is not enough; one must also look to the processes operating in the group which will have played a part in shaping that behaviour. These processes are not normally within the conscious awareness of participating members but may be more readily apparent to the trained moderator.

THE IMPORTANCE OF EARLY EXPERIENCE IN GROUPS

The earliest influence upon us is usually our family and it is from this source that we derive our earliest personal model of group behaviour. You may have a typical or atypical family, but in any event *it will not be the same* as any other family that has ever lived. Consequently every person's model of group behaviour is slightly different and each of us is destined to be different in style as a moderator or informant, to interpret events differently and to experience different aspects of the group. *This in our view is the great strength of qualitative group work, not its weakness.* This richness and diversity gives rise to new insights, revelations and understandings in a way that no other standard investigative procedure can.

After our family and their immediate friends, for the majority of us the next group of people we found ourselves among was at school. In some ways the 'first day at school' is the most accurate real-life reflection of the market research group. There you are, gathered with a group of strangers with whom you may or may not have some things in common, about to embark upon an agenda about which you know nothing, but of whose importance attempts have been made to convince you. How did you feel on that first day at school? Introspect on that for a moment, because it is most likely to be some distant reflection of your emotions that day that underpin your feelings when you come to moderate or participate in market research groups. Were you happy, excited, frightened, anxious, angry with your mother for leaving you? Perhaps a mixture of several or all of these things. Equally obviously we all experienced them slightly differently, and transferring this to the market research situation in later life we can see that no two respondents will ever bring quite the same set of experiences, anxieties and values to the group.

As you possibly remember, over the first few weeks at school the group that was to become your class was *formed*. Personalities emerged, roles and styles were developed that for some of us characterize aspects of ourselves that are with us still. Market research groups, unlike schoolroom ones, can only last a couple of hours or so, but during that time our past experience of group behaviour leads the respondents and moderator to replicate, if only for a short while, the processes of natural groups.

The components of groups

All group discussions have three basic components:

1. Structure
2. Content
3. Process

So far we have concentrated on bringing the importance of group processes to the fore, but now we shall examine process among its fellow components.

Structure

This is the first of the two components that rest firmly in the control of the market research elements of the situation. Structural factors include things like:

- the time and place for the group discussion.
- the duration of the discussion.
- the demographic qualifications of the respondents.
- the number of respondents.
- commonalities or differences in usership and behaviour between respondents.
- the seating type, disposition and ambience of the venue.
- the position and arrangement of respondents and moderator in the room.
- the choice of moderator.
- the presence or absence of observers, clients, trainees.
- the hardware, technical equipment including tape recorders, videos, one-way mirrors, microphones, artbags full of concept boards, etc.

Structural considerations are important, especially since for many respondents they constitute the 'hard facts' of the experience – will the coffee be drinkable, will they stick to the length of time they said, how will I get home if it's raining? – and they should not be distorted or abused without consultation with the respondents, since this has negative implications for the future of our voluntary contact with the public.

Content

This includes all of the components that form the subject matter, order, techniques (projectives, role plays, etc.) of the group discussion itself. It is normally agreed beforehand with the client as representing the best means of enabling respondents to provide answers to his 'questions' or brief. It may, in part or whole, be formalized as a discussion guide or interview format. Like structure, content is controlled by the researcher.

There are several important considerations here; firstly, that the content is known to the researchers but not known to the respondents. We are generally in favour of making this 'hidden agenda' more open to informants as early as possible in the group. While it is hidden it represents, going back to our classroom analogy for a while, the 'test' questions that the teacher or 'expert' is going to spring on the class. This cannot help but heighten respondents' anxiety.

Secondly, the various aspects of the content, the *verbal* questions, the *televised* commercials, the *written* concepts, as we progress from one to another will effect transformations in the content *type* of discussions. Wherever possible you should allow responses to mirror the content type of the stimulus, permitting or encouraging visual responses to visual material, auditory to music and words — even if only in terms of discussing something of a similar type of sensory experience to that contained in the stimulus. For example,

'Does that music remind you of anything you've *heard* before?'

or

'I'd like you to *sketch* your impression of what you've just *seen*.'

Thirdly, the very possession of this control over the content in the form of the discussion guide or expert knowledge may reinforce the moderator's need for control and omnipotence over the group. This often results in clinging (by the moderator) to the content or schedule and according it more importance than the informants' answers or the group's mood: a sort of 'It's my group, you can't have it', type of attitude. This is rapidly picked up by the group as the moderator being more interested in himself (his bits of paper, video or whatever) than in them or what they're saying. This almost invariably produces task defences amongst the group which ensure that they will *avoid* the task of conducting the discussion as openly and honestly as possible.

Fourthly, and in connection with the last point, while the moderator may retain control of the overall content for the purpose of facilitating the group's completion of the task, she should wherever possible encourage *the group itself* to structure the content of their responses. Having set the outlines of the task, it is quite laudable to allow the group to direct the pace and flow of its own responses to the stimulus material. We shall provide some further suggestions on this topic when we discuss the position and role of the moderator in the chapter on interviewing skills (see Chapter 5).

Process

Process refers to the sequence of stages that the group passes through *simply as a result of its existence as a group of people* trying to communicate with each other. Most of this aspect of the group's behaviour will take place outside the conscious awareness of the participants, but the moderator should learn and develop his appreciation of these stages so that he may work with them to facilitate the completion of the task rather than against them or in spite of them. A good moderator must know what stage his group has reached in order to know when it is possible to introduce new material, invite disclosures, close up or finish the group in a satisfactory manner.

The simplest and most memorable method of describing the stages of the group's process are the five rhyming key words:

1.   Forming
2.   Storming
3.   Norming
4.   Performing
5.   Mourning

and this is the usual order in which they occur. Each stage is typified by different needs and anxieties among the group members and we shall briefly describe each of them.

Forming   If the group is to run as a co-operative activity in which the group forces contribute to the completion of the task, then forming is very important. This is the stage of *inclusion* and it is vitally important that all the members should say something during it. Moreover, each should speak within the first few (five) minutes of the group – leaving people any longer than this is likely to heighten their anxiety rather than reduce it. Thoughts like: 'Why doesn't she ask me something – she obviously doesn't think I've got anything worthwhile to say.' or 'What *am* I going to say when it comes to my turn? They've already said everything I can think of.' are commonplace experiences for respondents who are left on the outside through virtue of not having spoken during the first five or ten minutes.

Forming can also set patterns for communication later in the group. If forming is done by the moderator in a sequential round-the-group question and answer fashion, then whenever it's uncertain the group will revert to this mode of operation and wait for the moderator to seek their opinions in turn.

So that you may establish a pattern of the group discussing matters with each other, including listening to what each other member is saying (as well as to the moderator), forming is often best accomplished by asking each person to introduce himself to his neighbour and tell them a little about themselves and perhaps a few details about the topic area – like brand usage, frequency of use or whatever. Then ask the members of a pair to introduce *their partner* to another pair of group members. That way four people have now spoken to each other without the moderator's interference. In an eight-person group one foursome may now introduce themselves to the other. Where pairs are not possible because of odd numbers, trios or a mixture of trios may be used.

This forming process takes ten minutes, but at the end the result is a properly formed group, capable of exchanging information and viewpoints and of listening to each other without direct pressure or coercion from the moderator. If you wish to make attitudes or feelings a slightly more prominent part of this process, ask the pairs to introduce themselves to their neighbours and tell them what they feel or think about washing up or pets or whatever the subject might be. Then introduce their partners, together with their viewpoints, to the next pair and so on.

Another problem that rapidly arises from the failure to include everyone in the forming process is a feeling of rejection in the excluded participants which may quickly produce a group defence of rescuing the injured party or dissociating from her. Quite often moderators will avoid including a respondent they feel to be dodgy in some way. He may be too old. You may have seen her before and the temptation is to 'ignore' her in case she reveals something. This is not the best way to proceed. She knows that she knows you and the rest of the group may sense it too, and the result will be an unspoken collusion at dishonesty. After that, anything goes. It is generally much better to acknowledge problems like acquaintance – ask when you last met and, if on market research matters, what the topic was. If the rules have been broken you may have to explain this and ask the respondent if she would mind leaving, offering to pay her for her 'participation'. After reforming and running the remainder of the group, take the issue up with the person responsible for the fieldwork. Recruiters will quickly stop cheating if they are always found out. It's embarrassing for them with both you *and* the respondents.

If the rules have only been bent slightly, you may decide to proceed, depending upon the particular situation.

Storming   It sounds terrible but it happens in every group and refers to the group's working out the issues of *power* and *control*. People want to know who knows what, who is assertive, who compliant, and how the moderator will respond to the manifestation of tensions or struggle. Do other respondents have similar levels of experience or expertise as themselves? Can they parade their latest status symbol without being rejected from the group – or, worse still, being outgunned by someone with a bigger one?

Some members will storm the minute they have the chance, others will wait until they see the size of the 'competition'. Some may out-assert others, another may choose a tactic of silent aloofness or discounting along the lines of: 'I've never taken much notice of commercials for margarine, actually. I've got better things to spend my time on.'

Storming is simply the group discovering both the nature and the means of their relating to each other. It helps the group set boundaries or limits and leads towards the establishment of norms. One slightly alarming aspect is that storming can break out at several points during the group. Particularly when any new topic, or more specifically, *new form* of stimulus is introduced.

Norming If storming is typified by changes of pace, sporadic activity and a general feeling of tension, norming has begun when acceptance and agreement begin to pervade the atmosphere. People begin to find that they have things in common, even if one is bigger or newer than another's. Or they may accept a difference and find a shared perspective as a result of this: 'I'd never thought of it that way. I can see it in a different light now.'

Body language settles, becomes more peaceful and calm. There is more mirroring of each other's language, posture and gesture. Proferring of cigarettes, sharing of spoons, agreeing on the weather, moving up to allow more space to another – all are commonplace examples of small acts used to signify group membership, and provide useful indications for the moderator. Occasionally the storm may rekindle for an instant but it quickly abates. The atmosphere of peaceful conciliation makes it tempting for the moderator to linger in this pleasant ambience. Resist this. The group is now ready to perform the task for which it convened. Now is the time to present – or represent – the primary task.

Performing This is when the real work of the group is done – it may be described as task-oriented co-operative activity in which both assent and dissent are permissible. The group will be bent on the task, leaning forward with interest, signalling evaluation (see Chapter 7) and the moderator will feel swept along in the process. Revelations and insights will appear and a feeling of constructive activity will pervade the room. The group will usually enjoy this phase as much as the moderator and client, and will be prepared to revisit this process after a short period of relaxation. The introduction of new stimulus material will normally rekindle storming, new norms must be established and then the group may perform again. Diagrammatically, the process looks like this:

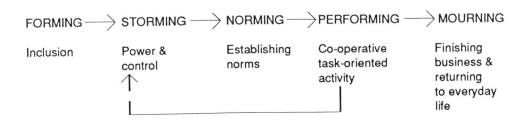

Mourning Market research groups often dismiss or omit this vital stage – or at least the moderator does; the respondents are most unlikely to forget that they have children to collect, meals to prepare or dentists to visit. Usually about 20 minutes from the end of the allotted time the first time-conscious signal or question will appear, especially if the moderator has neither revealed nor stuck firmly to his schedule. It is good practice at this time to acknowledge that the group has reached a point where it must consider winding up and to ask for extra work or time if you need it. Not less than five minutes from the end you should ideally allow respondents to recap their experience in the group, and ask them:

1.   If they felt they had said anything they didn't mean.
2.   If they had left unsaid something that was important to them.
3.   If they had any final remarks.

Resist the temptation to leave tape recorders switched on while you 'pop out to the loo' five minutes from the end, and don't allow clients the chance to deluge individuals with questions as the group breaks up. If you can't prevent this, do point out that people who are anxious to leave are quite likely to agree to anything and that you'd rather take these questions on to the next group and present them with due regard to process. It's quite acceptable for clients to ask questions in the last ten minutes of the group while it is still formed, although in our experience this usually produces storming which makes the responses to the questions less than reliable.

In general, it really is better to take observers' questions on into the next session if possible.

4 Group Dynamics

We wish now to examine the occurrences in groups from a different standpoint. In the last chapter we described how an understanding of process is a necessary and desirable acquisition for a research practitioner or observer. Now it is time to turn our attention towards that most difficult and complex of areas: the forces and tensions generated within the group itself, including the effects of spoken or unspoken psychological material, emotions, desires, needs, which we shall collect together under the heading of group dynamics. We will tackle this subject using examples as we go along, so let's begin our enquiry with a typical situation.

It has become almost ritualistic for the moderator to comment, just after the last respondent has left:

'That was a really good group, I wish they all went like that.'

or, alternatively:

'That was terrible, it was like pushing water uphill. They seemed to resist everything.'

In the trade, it has become lamentably commonplace to accept that a study will contain a proportion of 'good' groups coupled with a proportion of 'bad' ones. This in turn leads to the strengthening of the 'You mustn't judge the results by what you hear in one group' type of defensiveness, used by researchers to ward off anxious or uncertain clients. Why shouldn't every group be representative of some aspect of the results? Why is a 'bad' group less representative than a 'good' group?

Of course, both types of group are representative of something — but of what? It's tempting to assume that client and researcher are using the term 'representative' to mean the same thing, but often they aren't: the client is wondering if the group was representative of the results; the researcher usually orients his use of the word more towards the group dynamics — meaning that the group wasn't representative of a task-oriented group which got on with discussing the subject in an open, yet focussed, manner — and that therefore the results aren't necessarily what they seemed to be.

Going one step further, then, from a researcher's point of view, what do we mean by good and bad groups? In what sense are they good or bad?

Although he may never consciously have discussed the topic, every researcher knows the power of the good task-oriented group; it is vital, vigorous, focussed, humorous, supportive, and the level of co-operation is great. Such a group is capable of learning by experience, even of dramatic change in perspective in response to the needs of the members or the subject being worked on. *The key feature of the good group is that it accepts that the perspectives of the group will develop as a result of the interventions and opinions of its members;* it does not rely upon the advent of 'magic' perpetrated either by the moderator or by the inventiveness of the creative team. The atmosphere is harmonious, dissent is accepted as a valid development of perspective, the body language is forward and positive.

By contrast a 'bad' group is riven with defensiveness, tension and unspoken hostility. So much so that the moderator feels that an unspoken contract exists between the members to work against him. They may seem to be colluding, working together on the lines of some contract of evasion, almost as if they had rehearsed it. Sometimes you feel 'ashamed' to introduce a new stimulus for discussion into such a setting. Very often these atmospheres appear very early in the group, are replaced by some other form of negativity, only to reappear later. No matter what you do – in fact, the more you do the worse things seem to get – the group remains impregnably defended against getting on with the task.

A 'bad' group hates learning by experience, all suggestions of a rational alternative or practical nature are discounted ('I've tried that – I didn't like it'), and most usually an atmosphere of suspicion or hopelessness pervades the room, interspersed with odd 'What are we here for?' or 'What's next?' aggressive remarks. Body language is closed, tight and leaning away from the centre, but nobody ever suggests an alternative way forward – not even leaving or bringing the session to an end! It all sounds terribly familiar, but before we can make suggestions about how to overcome it we must understand a little more clearly how it arises, and what it's all based on.

There are two major contributors to the creation of dynamic forces and tensions in groups. They are:

1. The material – past experiences, thoughts and feelings – that people bring with them to the group.
2. The group experience itself.

Both these aspects may contribute to either 'good' or 'bad' group outcomes and we shall discuss them below. The common element underlying the 'bad' group which we wish to avoid seems to be the generation of *anxiety*. The most basic component of the good group seems to be *trust*.

MATERIAL BROUGHT TO THE GROUP

Often respondents arrive for the group in a flustered, tense condition, with very little knowledge about what to expect of the experience. Just as the moderator experiences pre-group nerves, anxiety and resistance (trying to find excuses not to go, deliberately delaying) so do the respondents and the recruiter. In a recent national survey *the number one fear* of the ordinary people interviewed was 'speaking in public'.

On their way to the group it becomes apparent to respondents that they've volunteered to do what they most dread – and on an unprepared topic! (Later in the chapter we describe the defensive tactic of bringing pre-prepared material along).

With his irritation sparked by the tension created by his own task defences,[1] as the moderator arrives he finds the recruiter busily engaged in last-minute displacement activity, glaring anxiously at the sky as if in search of weather reports or omens, muttering like an anxious bride who is uncertain whether the groom will show up. Even if they manage some pseudo-relaxed pleasantries between them, make no mistake about it, this is a fraught, tense situation.

So the respondents arrive into this charged atmosphere having answered a few questions at recruitment without knowing what they mean. Each one of them has at the very least to cope with the following things that accompany her to the group:

(i)   All her anxieties about being in a group of strangers.

(ii)   Her insecurities about the worth of her own opinions.

(iii)   The uncertainty about who the others will be and what they will think of her. If she uses guilt-inducing amounts of convenience food – what if they don't – better keep quiet about that!

(iv)   Her doubts about whether she'll be able to answer the questions – this is a 'survey', isn't it?

(v)   Keeping to her own schedule (kids to fetch, meals to cook, shopping to do).

THE GROUP EXPERIENCE

Suddenly she's arrived; she's had a cup of instant coffee thrust into her hand and now she's sitting among a group of people who look more relaxed than she feels – because of course these torments don't show. Can they spot that she's petrified – better not say too much. What's more, everyone else is experiencing much the same; no wonder that the group falls back on defence mechanisms that they've developed over the years to cope in such 'exposed' situations. And since they are all in the same situation, these defences tend to manifest themselves as group rather than individual responses. After all, that's what they came to, isn't it – a group experience?

Far from being in an open, trusting, frank and informal atmosphere, the typical group starts from a 'bad' atmosphere: anxiety and tension are rife and the group has already assumed an essentially defensive group mentality; stony silence prevails. Firstly, the moderator must use his knowledge of process to get things rolling; help everyone to speak, perhaps disclose the agenda or a substantial part of it, point out that there are no right or wrong answers, that we're here to share opinions. But the tensions may persist, the dynamics are still working to frustrate open discussion. What is the basis of this resistance? Can we work it out from what's happened so far?

Thinking back to our description of the bad opening situation for the group, what's the most likely escape route for people who are anxious and defensive? The most obvious answer is to wait for someone else to do something first. And all the group knows that it was the moderator who convened the whole experience. The result is a group of expectant, childlike expressions turned towards the moderator, their 'leader', waiting for instructions; someone must exist who will provide security for all these uncertain, insecure people?

The dependent group[2]

Acceptance of this desire by the group to be led by the moderator produces the most common form of 'bad' market research group – the dependent group. The group concentrates at first on establishing this idea of leader and followers as firmly as it can, concentrating on topics, waiting for prompts and using expressions that will support the omniscience of the moderator to the exclusion of all else. The group falls silent when the moderator does not instruct them, pretends to be helpless, that its opinions are worthless, or behaves in an infantile fashion.

Amazingly, at the same time the group will let the moderator know that he is not such a good leader as he thinks he is. To return to a real situation as an example, a man doing groups on a 'female' subject like washing – if he accepts the role of leader – will quickly find the group testing his competence and sneering at this leadership with remarks like:

'I bet you don't have much time for washing at home!'

or

'You should ask your wife what she thinks!'

or

'What sort of washing machine have you got?' (Expecting him not to know)

or

'What programme do you use for coloureds?' (Expecting him not to know)

All of these have been asked of the male author during his early experience. Each 'question' undermines his leadership without directly challenging it, in that it is likely to expose his lack of familiarity or expertise. The point here is that the group doesn't want to overthrow him unless a new leader has proffered herself since that would terminate their comfortable dependent status, but they do want him to be sure that they know that he doesn't really know enough about washing to lead them anywhere. Stalemate.

In a dependent group, opinions or development don't seem to originate from the group, but from the leader alone. Respondents *feel that they are participating only when talking to the moderator.* This leads to a sense – the more unpleasant since it is associated with getting too much and giving too little – of feeling neglected, ignored or starved. Any relief that might be obtained from feeling that the moderator cares for individuals or their opinions is undermined in a group who are meeting for such a short length of time and whose underlying purpose is obviously concerned with selling things to people. Indeed it might be suspected that the notion of caring about the people themselves in any market research group is eroded at a deep level by the 'selling' aspects of the situation, including the presence of advertising material and products themselves and the payments to respondents.

The essential feature of discomforts of this kind is that they arise *as a direct result of the dependent nature of the group itself* and this point must always be mentioned and demonstrated by the moderator if the pattern is to be broken.

The group engaged in fight or flight

After dependence is broken, or as an alternative, the next most common assumption of the whole group leading to evasion tactics is that, since nobody seems to know what to do or say, *the very existence of the group itself is threatened.* Even a one-and-a-half hour market research group can generate a huge unspoken anxiety about the uncertainty of its continued existence.

All kinds of factors may contribute; for example only the moderator knows the structure and how long it will last, other respondents may express their intentions to leave early on arrival, the moderator may be called to the telephone and so on. The group's response to this threat is to engage in fight or flight, either to fight off the imaginary source of termination, or to fly from it.

In our jargon the most frequent form of fight response is the *dominant respondent.* This is not always a leadership type of ploy at all. Often the dominant respondent doesn't wish to lead the others; she wishes to fight with them and the moderator as a means of preserving the group. She is fighting on the group's behalf. This is why dominant respondents are so difficult to get rid of; if they are of this type the rest of the group collude in their domineering because while the group is locked in struggle its survival is ensured. If challenged as to why she is monopolizing, this type of respondent will usually answer: 'But I thought you wanted to hear *our* opinions.' – thus subtly admitting her behaviour is on the group's behalf and that it is with their support that she is engaged in the struggle (for survival). Domineering is actually a challenge to the leadership and will only occur if the moderator has set himself up as a contender for the leadership himself. So we may see that domineering is usually a *fight*-type response dedicated towards prolonging the survival of the group. Other commonplace types of fighting include competitiveness, boasting, status signalling and distorting events (so that we may argue about whether the advertisement said one thing or another).

There are two very common forms of *flight* that exist in the market research group; the first can be difficult to spot if you are not on the lookout for rigid, repetitive, monotonic tones and forms of speech, and concerns *adherence to a pre-prepared statement or point of view*. This offers a fine ruse for preventing development of open discussion in the group, especially since a respondent can feel a sense of self-satisfaction for having 'thought the matter through beforehand', for having done unpaid work, if you like. A further consequence of arriving with a prepared stance is that respondents feel they need talk only when the subject and manner of discussion fit their own choosing; all other material may be legitimately avoided as not within their domain.

The moderator must not respond by being prepared to interact with their pre-prepared private material in public, otherwise he will quickly find himself involved in pairing with the protagonist watched over by the rest of the group. He must instantly offer the material to the whole group for comment.

The other common form of flight is the indulgence of frank or extended discussion of irrelevant or anecdotal material. The best example of this we can offer occurred during a group whose task was to discuss the relationship between a certain type of margarine and butter. The following exchange occurred between respondents:

> 'I used it when I was roasting in tin foil the other day.'
> 'Oh, what were you cooking?'
> 'Roast badger.'

The group was astonished and delighted. Here was an anecdote worthy of pursuit:

> Where had the badger come from?
> What did it taste like?
> Who had eaten it?
> How was it prepared for the oven?
> . . . and so on.

The moderator was left by himself to wonder what to make of the official task or subject from which the group was running; knowing that his client was interested in margarine and would not thank him for a discourse on badger cookery!

Both fight and flight must be pointed out to the group and offered as subjects for commentary:

'We seem to be wandering off the point a lot. What does the group think about this?'

or

'There seems to be a lot of aggression in the atmosphere. Can the group comment on this?'

The paired group

A third form of defence to which the whole group subscribes is when two members *pair up* in some kind of alliance. This *pairing* is watched by the remainder of the group in the hope that the group has spawned a new potent relationship which will give birth to a new idea or meaning for the group. In that pairing always has a covert sexual nature (it most frequently manifests itself between men and women but can occur between members of the same sex, two smokers, two childless people, two of almost anything), it is doomed to failure since the overt sexual behaviour is inadmissible in a group. Yet the group may watch the courtship (e.g. the elaborate proffering of cigarettes, sitting together to share ashtrays, comparing brands) with great attention. The most common manifestation of pairing is undoubtedly flirting between moderator and respondents.

These then are the three basic assumptions[3] that the group will operate upon as defences against anxiety and, in that much of their anxiety focusses around their imagined inability to complete the task satisfactorily, they must be seen as task defences:

(i)   Dependency
(ii)   Fight and Flight
(iii) Pairing

Each manifests itself as an emotional climate in the group *which the moderator must not avoid* by pretending that it doesn't exist. If the moderator herself demonstrates a propensity to ignore reality in this way, this merely provides greater licence for the fantasies underlying these assumptions about the nature of the group situation to proliferate. The moderator must respond to the emotional climate as if it were real — as indeed he will experience it as being — and he must then create permission for the group to overcome it by facing up to it when, hopefully like all fantasies, it will disappear. The best means of doing this is to describe it briefly then offer it to the group for comment.

Our attempts to clarify this complex area of group dynamics must, unfortunately, appear as lacking in detail and length until one bears in mind the real-life situation; here it is more usual for what is going on in the group to appear complicated and confused. It is only momentarily that clarity emerges.

Usually the unspoken operations of the group mentality and the emotional involvement of the moderator herself make clear-headedness difficult, but we make no apology for trying to throw light on factors like defensiveness that are usually dismissed as random occurrences, in the good group/bad group mythology. They are not random; they occur according to patterns and we have made some suggestions for recognizing and overcoming them.

In the next chapter we shall consider some specific suggestions for overcoming process and dynamic problems as and when they occur *in situ*.

It may surprise readers that the authors should cling so tenaciously to their determination to discuss group problems and processes in terms of *group perspectives* with no resorting to the more usual individualistic 'troublemakers', 'ringleaders', 'passive' or 'timid' types of classification and argument. Through the years we have noticed over and over again that we experience our groups *as* groups. We cannot help but do so since this is how they manifest themselves. We have never had an individual leave because he was bored, threatened, disillusioned or fed-up in over 8,000 groups between us, but we have witnessed almost every conceivable form of group defence, resistance and denial mechanism.

The reason for this perseverance of the group seems obvious in retrospect; respondents are recruited and invited to participate in a market research group discussion. In other words, from their point of view they are justified in the basic assumption that their primary task is to be a member of the group. Bearing this in mind, it comes as rather less of a surprise, therefore, that they will engage willy-nilly in tactics designed to protect or save the group from threat of extinction, either real or imaginary, since at the most fundamental level they may construe this as preserving their principal function. From this we may see that for market research group discussions individual psychology really must be viewed in terms of group psychology.

NOTES

1. 'Task defences' are strategies employed, usually outside the level of awareness, to avoid getting the task done — like forgetting the tape recorder or tapes.
2. The theoretical model of the types of group instances that is developed in this chapter borrows heavily from the work of W. R. Bion and we acknowledge our debt to him.
3. The theory of 'basic assumptions' is brilliantly described by W. R. Bion in his book *Experiences in Groups and other papers*, Tavistock Publications, 1961.

5 Interviewing – Getting Better

Some of the important considerations leading to general good practice include the development of moderating skills through:

(a) Practice
(b) Listening
(c) Creating rapport
(d) Using silence
(e) Learning what to do when it goes wrong
(f) Understanding the role of the moderator
(g) Trading disclosures

We will describe and illustrate these practices and skills as we move through this chapter. Although we shall move on to a description of more advanced techniques, we shall not make the mistake of overlooking the area of how you might get from being an absolute beginner to a position where you might hope to practise some of the more difficult skills.

It is often underestimated just how long it takes to train inexperienced researchers merely to feel relatively comfortable, competent and collected in the interviewing situation. In our experience we have found that two years is an absolute minimum from setting out as a novice to attaining a thorough grounding in both group and individual interviewing skills. It takes this amount of time, doing or sitting in on interviews and groups in the first place – for there is, as we have explained, a large experiential component to learning this kind of skill – just to become able to put the interview guide aside for long enough to be able to really look at and listen to what's going on in an open, receptive manner.

There are differences through the very nature of the situation between depth interviews and groups here. Because of the one-to-one aspect of the depth interview, the researcher *must* obtain permission from both client and respondent for a trainee to sit in. This is advisable practice for groups too, though not essential.

Most beginners are more comfortable with depths at first. They feel less threatened by the one-to-one situation. This has several aspects which are worth mentioning:

(a)   They are less daunted by an individual than by the sheer size of the group and, as it mushrooms correspondingly, the task.
(b)   They have less anxiety, about what both the respondents and the outside observers will think of what they say and do. They're less worried about performance skills.
(c)   They don't have to worry so much about the social niceties and etiquette demands of entertaining a large group of strangers (eight or nine would for most of us constitute a larger dinner party than usual).
(d)   Me-and-you is a different structure from me-and-them; the former is potentially intimate, the latter is risky and exposed.

Underlying this last point is, we believe, the crux of the matter; when doing individual interviews you don't have to make the transformation from an individual to a group-centred orientation. This shift sounds simple enough, but describes an elusive and difficult transition which we have found some trainee researchers actually unable to make. We are not talking here about asking individuals questions in a group, that is individual-centred and not what we understand as a group discussion: we are talking about co-operative structured activity which harnesses the forces within the group itself and brings them to bear upon the task. The group dynamics are harnessed, as well as the opinions of individuals, and in this way the understanding of the effects of the group on individuals and vice versa is optimized.

The role of the moderator in all of this is crucial, and we will come on to describe that; but for now, we suggest that you practise thinking about your respondents as a group, and direct your questions and your observations to the group as a whole as in: 'I'd like to hear the group's views on lager', rather than 'Would (each of) you tell me why you drink lager?'. The former question allows the respondents to structure the response, the latter already assumes the existence of a reason or hierarchy of reasons which may or may not be true, either for individuals or for the group as a whole.

Even more powerfully, when you note a change of atmosphere, energy level, postures, pace or mood, you may observe: 'There seems to be a change of atmosphere in the room. How does the group feel about that?' or if you have been discussing 'things' rather than 'feelings' a better follow-up might be: 'What does the group think about that?'.

Try to form in your mind's eye a space in the centre of the group, into which you 'put' the questions. Both of us will occasionally use a low table for this purpose when we know that the establishment of this space or group matrix, as it is sometimes called, is going to be important or difficult. You may then use the low table to place stimuli on later in the discussion, and the group will *know* they are to discuss it as a group since it 'occupies' part of the matrix.

Here then, are a series of general rules and tips about being in groups, starting from the beginning.

THE BASIC CONTRACT

Just as you will have left your office or some other place, so will your informants have disrupted their normal routine to come to your interview or group session. They may have been anticipating it excitedly or anxiously for days, alternatively they may have remembered it only five minutes before they were due to leave. Whichever is the case, other events in their lives will most certainly have moved on since they agreed to come, and new circumstances may well dominate their thoughts. These can take the form of anything from the banal – having forgotten to get the meat for the evening meal, to the profound – loss of employment, an accident or illness. In any event, they will seem of pressing importance to the individuals concerned.

There are two main points here: firstly, that we, the researchers, cannot make assumptions about the mental state or preoccupations of our respondents, and secondly, that in order to facilitate and optimize the chances of their concentrating on our session, we should clearly set out how long it will last and what we hope to achieve. Just as you need a briefing to understand your client's concerns, a brief, honest description of your research task will help your informants to help you *and*, knowing when they will be leaving will enable them to relax more during the time they are there. A simple introduction has been used with great success by one of our researchers:

> I'd like to welcome you to this market research group discussion. In this type of research we spend about an hour and a half really trying to get to grips with people's thoughts and feelings about products, advertisements or issues. Today's subject is . . .
>
> One thing to remember is that in this type of work we talk only to a relatively small number of people, in several groups like this, and so the views expressed here in a sense represent those of a much larger audience. So it's important to say what you really think, and express your real feelings and, just as the whole population would have a wide variety of views on a topic, so may members of this group. Don't be afraid to speak out if you agree or disagree: we're as interested in the variety of opinions as anything else. Remember, too, that there are no right or wrong answers. We're interested in *your* opinions.
>
> Now I'd like to introduce you to the topic and tell you what we're trying to achieve . . .

At this early stage it is very important to look after your respondents like a nurturing parent. Make sure they are comfortable, offer coffee or some other form of refreshment, let the atmosphere calm down and allow people to take in their surroundings. If what you plan includes anything unusual like role playing or experimental creative work, ensure that you have time to explain things properly.

All of the above, apart from hopefully setting up an open communicative atmosphere, denotes your awareness of their point of view and a willingness to see things from their perspective. The most fundamental mistake that beginners make in this area is to pay more attention to their own needs and equipment — tape machines, videos *and clients*, than to the respondents. This instantly signifies to the respondents which is of greater concern to you and in this case the message that comes across is that you are more worried about your things than theirs. It really does help to give yourself 20–30 minutes to set up before they arrive.

GETTING STARTED

Often those first few questions feel like pushing off from the shore with a group of passengers you hardly know in a vessel about whose seaworthiness you are unsure. The inexperienced moderator often experiences these first few minutes as full of empty silences, jerky conversation and contradictory remarks. A natural enough response to all this is to 'try to get into the brief' and the air becomes blue with questions as the moderator tries to get on with his task.

In our view, it is vital to be relaxed and relatively unhurried in these first few minutes. 'Warming up' refers to the process of starting slowly and helping things to get going. Above all, you should demonstrate your *willingness to listen* during this period. If someone says something interesting, invite a perspective from the rest of the group and refrain from offering your own viewpoint unless no one else will. Show that you are *comfortable with silence*, while people organize their responses.

Allow people to express or 'dump' any previously held viewpoints or convictions that they have brought along with them. After learning everyone's name it is quite a good lead-in to start with something like 'Let's hear what *you* all expected to happen here today. What do you think all of this is about?' Or: 'Did anyone have any thoughts about the group before she came along?' Absolutely invaluable material bearing on people's preconceptions may arise out of this, as well as a further indication of our interest in *their* point of view. Someone may think the whole subject 'a waste of time' either genuinely or because she is anxious that she won't be able to think of anything to say about it. Since she has agreed to come to a discussion and may know, at least in general terms, the overall subject area(s), it's more likely to be her anxiety than a genuine disinterest in the topic that underlies her apparent discounting of the subject's importance.

Creating Rapport

Apart from using the correct forming and questioning procedures, it is advisable to create rapport with your informants in depths or groups. Here is a series of suggestions offering techniques for doing just that.

Mirroring

This involves the adoption by the interviewer of similar or identical behaviour to the respondents. You may mirror posture or body language, words, syntax or manner of speech. A famous ad-man is once reported to have won an account by practising the regional accent of the marketing director who controlled the account; knowing him to be fanatical about his birthplace, he was then able to claim he was from the next town! Whether this apocryphal story is true or not, the point is well made. Be wary though, we don't advise following our ad-man's risky and dishonest practice – but you can use identical words and phrases, and pass these back and forth between the respondents and yourself, thus creating a feeling that 'We're using the same language'.

Much easier is to mirror expressions, posture and gesture, since we tend to do this anyway. The old adage about old married couples growing to look like each other is based upon just such mirroring of each other's behaviour, expression and movement over many years.

One of the most noticeable examples of mirroring in everyday group discussions is the rash of cigarette smoking in a group when the first brave soul lights up. There is an instant scrambling for ashtrays and a sense of relief among smokers which, these days, is often accompanied by mutually disapproving glances from the non-smokers. Both sub-groups have their sense of rapport with their own kind enhanced, together with an increase in their sense of ostracism or isolation from their counterparts.

The moderator should observe these sub-groupings, whether in terms of opinions expressed, body language or behaviour, since she may need to use them to aid her analysis of events at a later stage.

Another useful technique for creating rapport is *trading disclosures*. For example, if you are talking to a new mum about baby food, it may be a good idea briefly to confess your own uncertainty and confusion when you had your first baby; or as a non-parent, to admit your total bewilderment about the subject. If it's your first group discussion on this topic, tell the respondents this and they'll be much more supportive and forthcoming. If something is confusing, admit your own confusion. Above all, try to see things from their point of view; at the very least it'll stop you being paranoid about your own feelings and ideas, or the lack of them!

Adopt a 'listening' rather than a 'questioning' orientation from the outset. Indicate your willingness to listen by allowing silences, not filling them with a battery of questions.

If you get a silence, offer it to the group:

'Can anyone build on this?/Take this on a bit?'

'Does anyone have a comment or experience that fits in here?'
'Has this provoked any thoughts or feelings?'

You may also offer up the silence itself for comment:

'That seems to have stopped us dead in our tracks. Any thoughts about why?'

Remember that respondents themselves will have many different prejudices and anxieties resulting from their own former experiences in groups. Work with this differences, don't try to ignore them or pretend they don't exist.

Just as you will have your own feelings about each of the group members, so will they about each other. If good forming technique doesn't help to overcome tensions, you may have to bring them into the open during the group, as in:

'We seem to have a difference of opinion here. Let's discuss it together.'

Whenever outright hostility is ruining things, you may refer to the tension between two or more individuals and ask them what they think about it. Surprisingly, often they will be relieved to be given a chance to sort things out.

KEEPING THINGS GOING

A good researcher is one who answers all the questions in the brief, not necessarily one who asks them. Try to internalize the questions that need answering and then pose them or reframe them in a manner that suits the pace and stage of the group. Don't stick rigidly to a form of questioning that irritates or offends the group, or adhere to a style of expression that seems out of tune with the group. Most of all, when you have evidence of shared values and attitudes among the group, avoid devaluing or contradicting these values by your insensitive questioning. For example, among a group of ecology-minded conservationists don't bluntly ask: 'Would you be prepared to pay more for high performance petrol?' – even though that's what your client may wish for guidance on. Reframe the question along the lines of: 'We have taken environmental factors into account and managed to come up with a high performance petrol. Would that be useful to you?'

Practise observing the group stages and dynamics described in the last two chapters. Once you have learnt to spot them, be careful not to introduce tasks at inappropriate times. Don't introduce stimulus material while *storming* is going on – it will either be used as a weapon in the fight or tossed out of the ring altogether. Once a mistake like this has occurred, the appearance of stimulus material at any time may become associated with storming behaviour and as soon as you introduce anything, arguments may break out anew.

Once *norming* is established and people are finding shared experiences and viewpoints, then you may ask: 'Is the group ready to have a look at something now?' And, hopefully, move smoothly into an explanation (if necessary) or presentation of your material.

The introduction of any new material will often reintroduce storming as the group struggles to find out who knows or feels anything about the stimulus, and whose expertise or viewpoint will prevail. Be patient, the storming will subside and the group will move into constructive discussion.

Don't fill your head with questions, keep your mind open and clear, and allow respondents to structure the order and pace of the material, except where this is preordained by experimental design.

When you are confused, don't resort to a barrage of questions to try to throw more light on your confusion. The chances are you already have enough information to resolve your uncertainty – you just don't know how to arrange or rearrange it. One thing is for sure, if you're already confused, a whole lot more information arising from new questions is likely to muddle things further. In the silences and pauses listen to the thoughts inside your own head and try to isolate the source of your confusion; or failing that, try to recall the moment at which you became confused. Then you may return to that experience later and perhaps form a different perspective as described in our chapter on analysis and interpretation (See Chapter 10). For example, you might say:

> 'Some time ago Bill said (X, Y or Z) and I found myself feeling that I didn't understand (whatever it was). What was going on for other members of the group at that moment? Can anyone recall it for us?'

ADVANCED SKILLS

Listening inside your mind

Now that things are underway and we have cleared our heads of the interminable list of questions in the interview guide, we may turn our attention to the development of more advanced skills. Firstly, we must learn to listen at more than one level. Let us hypothesize for a moment that there are three levels; the first thing to do is to name and describe them.

The manifest level

This is the level of actual utterances and their conventional meaning. It includes everything which actually gets said in the interview, and the technique for handling this kind of material is best called *reportage* – meaning straight replay of what was said. As we can all tell from our daily newspapers, even this is subject to huge distortion via the technique of *editing*. Please resist the temptation to fall back on the defence of 'I'm only telling you what they said' to your clients; this is neither a sincere nor a responsible position.

The intentional level

This is a more complex level of communication where what was *meant* is more important than, or even contradictory to, what was said. Much of the communication between respondents and interviewers in qualitative work is of this type. Body language or tone of voice may discount what is actually being said.

Verbal agreement may be proferred in order to hurry things along, gloss something over, or avoid uncomfortable areas. You may point this out if it seems like a suitable moment, along the lines of:

> 'You're saying "Yes", but I feel that your posture is telling me that you don't really agree with it. Do you have a mixed point of view about this or something?'

Or, more openly:

> 'Can anyone (or the group) take a completely different standpoint on this subject? Just for argument's sake, say?'

In our experience, once the intentional or correct meaning is acknowledged, it usually rises rapidly to the surface and adds a new perspective to the group's response, which often overwhelms the original one. A very common example of this occurs when people say polite, relevant things about a commercial which they experience as utterly boring. Often you may get a clue to this from the increasing amount of fidgeting and looking distracted which goes on as the niceties proliferate.

In our view, although slightly more obscure, this 'intentional level' is of greater importance than the 'manifest', since feelings and emotions are being brought into play here – even if only to suppress their true shape – and these are far more likely to influence behaviour in the marketplace than the conventions of chit-chat.

The subconscious (hidden levels of meaning)

The fleeting expression of our deepest hopes, desires and wishes occasionally bubbles to the surface and often it appears as excitement, empathy, joy, anxiety, anger – a true emotional response. What makes it so complex is that it is not always temporally congruent with the experience that generated it. Sometimes it froths up several minutes later, apparently in response to something else. Listening to this train of emotional responses is the hardest technique of all, and to have any hope at all of succeeding, the moderator must bring his own deepest level of experience – his or her subconscious into play.

Imagine for a moment that there is a pool deep inside you, a dark, quiet place where the waters are occasionally disturbed by something – anything – that happens. You are lying with your eyes closed, beside the pool, listening for any disturbances. In a state of reverie, you wait there, ready to receive whatever transpires when the waters are disturbed. Suddenly something makes the surface stir or ripple and you are roused. Just before it sinks below the surface can you glimpse the form and nature of the thing that lighted upon the water? Turn your head and look. Examples of this include the sudden appearance of unusual or trigger words or gestures. 'Disgusting', 'brainwashed', 'outrageous', for example, are usually verbal cues to the presence of deep or hidden feelings.

Although it may sound ephemeral and elusive, do practise this way of listening in reverie or your own analogous method for achieving it. Here lies the true gold dust for the qualitative worker – the element of insight from your respondents in order to understand their way of seeing and experiencing things more clearly. It is extremely difficult to achieve the threefold listening state without considerable practice and, we must say, it is much inhibited by the presence of observers or extraneous participants. Ideally, the moderator is able to pass from one to the other, especially from the manifest to the intentional, whilst keeping his inner ear and eye cocked for the hidden levels.

Listening for patterns

Listening in reverie is particularly good for spotting patterns of significance that are deleted from the intentional and manifest levels of conversation. For example, words like 'irritated' or 'annoyed' may occur several times within a ten-minute period. Even though they are manifestly being used about different things or topics, there's often a veil or disguise being used in such an instance to ward off the moderator's suspicion that they don't like his 'brand' or her 'commercial'. Pulling these two words together in a question like "Now I'd like us to try to find something which might *irritate* or *annoy* us about brand X" will often help these suppressed aspects to surface.

In a more general sense listening for patterns may help you to cross-check and develop a rolling analysis of the import of what is being said. Many remarks and answers offered in qualitative sessions are the result of phenomena beyond the brand, advertising or task issues. They may be made as *ritualistic* responses: these are preordained automatic utterances which comprise endless variations on the 'Hello, how are you?' 'I'm fine, thank you. How are you?' banal theme, and researchers have come to recognize many research-specific responses of this order. They *may* mean what they appear to mean but very often they do not. Examples include:

'I don't watch much TV these days.'
'We're all into health foods now.'
'I never watch ITV.'
'I like the cartoons best.'
'I don't use convenience foods.'

'I always buy on price.'

If you are uncertain about the sincerity of a remark you may sometimes check it by asking a respondent to recall it later; very often throw-away remarks are completely forgotten or recalled only with difficulty.

As another aspect of patterns, be aware of the patterns of interactions between the informants themselves and between respondents and the moderator. Does someone always respond in a typical way after someone else has spoken or after you have spoken? This may well be a result of personality attractions or social class issues rather than of heartfelt views being honestly expressed. It is quite permissible to draw attention to this phenomenon and ask the participants to comment.

Anchoring

The name 'anchoring'[1] was given to the practice of conditioning a response in an individual or group setting by the NLP theorists. The advantage of this is that should you subsequently want to return to that state in the group, you may do so by invoking the anchor as a stimulus. Since so many groups get bogged down in negativity or over-critical posturing, I usually try to anchor a positive mood at the earliest opportunity. My favourite anchor in a group setting is a clap of my hands which calls the instant attention of everybody as an involuntary shock response – followed by my saying the word 'Good!'. I do this after the first emergence of a positive group mentality. At later points in the group, I may reinvoke a positive frame of mind by clapping my hands and saying 'Good! Now we're going to look at . . .'.

You can anchor all sorts of group behaviours. Some useful ones are:

Attentiveness
Humour (to lighten the atmosphere)
Relevance
The primary task of the group

It is extremely important to practise anchoring so that you may establish anchors which work successfully for *you*. We often use leaning forward and listening very carefully to anchor a response from a passive informant. The very first time such an informant makes a spontaneous and prompted response we will sit forward and nod gently as she speaks. Later in the session at a time when you require a response from the person, leaning forward and nodding gently will often produce one. You may also use touch as an anchor with particularly reluctant people. Going over to them and touching them on the shoulder or arm and saying 'Well done' will anchor their responsiveness, and touching them later, or simply gesturing that you intend to touch them by reaching out for the anchor point, will often produce a response.

Utilizing non-verbal communication (NVC) as well as applying and analysing projective and enabling techniques are all part of getting better. But these are such important topics that they warrant separate chapters of their own and are tackled later in the book (Chapters 7 and 8).

WHAT TO DO WHEN THINGS GO WRONG

No matter how experienced you are and how you perform on the day, things are going to go wrong from time to time, particularly in group discussions. In depth interviews the problems are less critical since in one-to-one encounters you may usually own up to a mistake and ask the informant to go over something again with you. In a group, however, most often events will appear to be completely beyond your control.

In the left-hand column of the figure below we list some of the most common problems and on the righthand we make some suggestions about dealing with them. Remember, these are only suggestions. Be flexible and find the means that best suit the hour and your style.

Problem	*Means of coping*
Leadership – rivalry – participants taking the group off their topic.	Politely remind the informants of the group purpose and task.
Leadership – rivalry – constant disagreeing.	This is a 'game'[2]. Pass it out to other group members and ask the group how it feels about this. 'We seem to have a row brewing here – how shall we cope with this?'
Leadership – domination	Employ an ascending scale of techniques to diminish dominance: — withdrawal of eye contact; — withdrawal of NVC; — completely turning away; — give verbal indication of desire to interrupt – transfer questioning – remind the group of the primary task and then ask the group to go on to a new aspect of the discussion, starting with 'Now, let's hear the rest of the group's views on . . .'.
Fight – aggression between participants.	This is part of storming and includes power, control and leadership issues. Don't worry, it's not such a bad thing. You can always stop the fight by asking

Problem	Means of coping
	others in the group for their views and allowing them to express them. Try not to run away. The fight will only recur if you don't allow a resolution *by the group as a whole*. Indicate that the group can live with *differences* as well as with agreements.
Flight – withdrawal	Nurturing – look after and take personal interest in the informant. Offer a gift (e.g. more coffee) or a compliment or other form of acknowledgement. Use supportive body language. *Don't* play Rescuer though; this reinforces the possibility of the respondents playing victim, and can lead to a game.[3]
Spurious conformity	Introduce an alternative notion of conformity: for example 'We were talking to some other people who thought . . .' and ask the group to comment.
Freezing – group going dead.	Energizing – introduce laughter or some other stimulus to raise energy levels, or acknowledge the silence and ask the group about it.
Sub-group formation and alliances.	This is a real group phenomenon, known as 'pairing'. The group behaves as if two members have paired up to challenge for leadership of the group. The fantasized hope is that they'll create a new (as yet unborn) leader. As soon as the leader is 'born' hope dies in that the 'Messiah' doesn't lead them free of frustration, anxiety or distrust. You may offer the pair the opportunity to 'take over the group'. Ask the group if it would prefer that. You may then witness the destruction of the fantasized hope as the new leader threatens actually to be born!
Going off the topic/idle/chatting.	Best be straightforward. Remind the group of the purpose of the session,

Problem	Means of coping
	but don't be too hasty; 'leaking out' often occurs here and the group is relaxing too.
Age or class rivalry.	A sub-section of interpersonal conflict, power and control. Some storming should be allowed in order for workable norms to be established.
Rationalizing.	Use 'reverie' type listening and try to listen for the subconscious content and then distract or change direction.
Masks, posturing, lies.	Alternative means involve either capitalization upon the masks or postures with an invitation to role play or gentle exposure of the mask or posture by counter-posturing.

These seem to us the main sorts of moment-to-moment problems and phenomena that occur during groups. The other types of problem are based upon the setting, lay-out and structure of the groups themselves.

NOTE

1. For a fuller description of anchoring see *Frogs into Princes* by Richard Bandler and John Grinder.
2. We call this particular game, 'Whatever you can do, I can do better'.
3. The favourite game in these circumstances is 'Nobody ever takes any notice of me', which of course leads to everyone taking *very special* notice of them and evoking the negative payoff of embarrassment at being in the spotlight.

6 The Individual 'Depth' Interview

We have defined qualitative research in an earlier chapter and have stressed that it is centrally concerned with understanding issues rather than measuring them. Qualitative information provides and adds to our understanding of the nature and elements of the universe we are seeking to know and interpret; quantitative information tells us about its size and shape and the proportion and incidence of its characteristics.

Although this definition may seem obvious, it is all too often taken for granted or ignored and the definition of qualitative research is described by methodology. Qualitative research today is almost synonymous with the group discussion/group interview/focussed group method. It is far less frequently defined by the individual 'depth' interview method, which is seriously underrated and often misused in contemporary practice.

One of the reasons for the poor image of the individual depth interview and for its low profile, is the fact that a great deal of confusion surrounds its definition and role. The individual depth interview comes in many guises. The word 'interview' may be prefixed by any of the following – unstructured, 'unstructured direct' (or indirect), 'executive', 'professional', 'semi-structured', 'open-ended', 'mini-depth', 'communication check', 'paired depth', 'couple depth', 'non-directive', 'friendship pairs'.

A few minutes thought about the wide variety of terms used for the depth interview suggests that there are a number of concepts implicit in the definition.

1. The type of questioning used ('unstructured', 'indirect', 'open-ended').
2. The length of time taken for the interview ('depth interview', 'mini-depth' interview).
3. The skill of the interviewer ('executive interview').
4. The objective of the survey ('communication check', 'accompanied shopping', 'observation').
5. The nature of the unit selected for interview ('individual', 'couple-depth', 'friendship pair').

THE TYPE OF QUESTIONING USED

The pursuit of understanding is a complex 'searching' type of procedure which cannot be rigid or standardized. Both the individual depth interview and the group discussion are characterized by a flexible interviewing structure which changes for each interview. Based on his knowledge of the research objectives, previous experience of the field of enquiry and the nature of the social interaction taking place, the researcher will select which parts or points in the dialogue with the respondent to pickup and explore further, which to ignore, and which to return to later in the interview.

Flexibility does not mean that the interview will take any direction the respondent may choose. There is a task in hand, a hidden contractual agreement between interviewer and respondent which is understood by both parties. The respondent has implicitly agreed, by acceptance of an incentive, to provide the interviewer with information on a particular issue or topic. The quality or relevance of this information may vary enormously but at face value it is related to the area of enquiry. The interviewer has an agenda in mind (the research objectives, the issues to be discussed) and is continually trying to understand both rational and emotional components of the respondent's reported attitudes and behaviour.

The terms 'unstructured' or 'non-directive' refer to the form of the questions used in a depth interview. The actual question is not written down in black and white with careful instructions about when to probe and when to prompt; instead the depth interviewer has an interview guide which outlines the agreed agenda of issues to be explored and indicates at which points the stimulus material or projective techniques can be introduced. The questions used in consecutive depth interviews and those used by the same interviewer or between different interviewers on the same research project are different. This is because the open-ended questions extensively used in the qualitative interview allow respondents to express their thoughts and feelings, describe their behaviour, formulate their attitudes and give indications of their motivations *in their own terms*, using their own unique vocabulary as opposed to that pre-set by the researcher, before the project began.

Not only is the depth interview flexible, it is also evolutionary in nature. The interview content (that is, the areas covered and the order in which this is done), as well as the questions used by the interviewer, change in response to growing understanding.

It is a commonly expressed view that individual interviews are easier to conduct and by implication require less expertise than group discussions. Thus, buyers often do not insist on a particular researcher conducting the depths but are extremely choosy when it comes to moderators for their group discussions. This has led to the practice of allowing young qualitative researchers to be let loose, without supervision and training, on individual depth interviews before being initiated into the supposed finer art of moderating group discussions.

This practice sadly undervalues the skill and art involved in depth interviewing. As we discuss later in this chapter, people are more often defensive when interviewed alone than they are in groups. Sometimes more skill, not less, is needed for meaningful responses to be achieved. Without the ability to use projective techniques with skill and ease and without a sophisticated under-standing of body language, the depth interview will not be deep! At best it will provide the same type of information yielded by many quantitative questionnaires, without the benefit of numerical measurement.

THE LENGTH OF TIME TAKEN FOR THE INTERVIEW

There is an unfortunate tendency in the minds of many practitioners and buyers of qualitative research to equate time with quality. In relation to the individual interview, the longer it takes is often assumed to be an indication of maximum depth.

We contend that this is misconceived and naive. As indicated earlier, an interviewer unskilled in the use of projective techniques may well interview a respondent for an hour and a half but a skilled interviewer may uncover crucial attitudes, behaviour and motivations in half that time. Conversely, if a research task is to evaluate what an advertisement is communicating, it is destructive to make the interview last longer than half an hour since the respondent is likely to become so overtly conscious of the fine details of the advertisement that both interviewer and respondent lose sight of the original objective. In the latter case, the interviewer is seeking to understand, 'gut-level' responses to a finished (or near-finished) advertisement, and these are likely to operate at an emotional rather than rational level. The longer the interview lasts, the more likely the responses will be rationalized.

However it is true that a depth interview which is being conducted to explore the relationship of an individual to a product category and the brands within it, requires time. Time is necessary to:

- set down parameters for the interview;
- establish rapport;
- conduct the interview at the respondent's own pace;
- establish a facilitative atmosphere which is relaxed, conversational and encourages free-ranging responses;
- introduce and complete projective tasks;
- complete the interview in such a way that the respondent does not feel exploited.

Some of these are worth discussing in a little more detail.

Setting down parameters

Assuming that the recruiter has performed her role satisfactorily, the interviewer and respondent meet for the first time. As with any social interaction with which we are all familiar, both parties begin a process of instant judgements. The interviewer makes assumptions on the basis of age, accent, style of dress and body language whilst the respondent does the same. In addition the respondent may well be masking feelings of anxiety, embarrassment and uncertainty about the nature of the interview (see Gordon & Robson 1982) and particularly about what is expected of him.

The establishment of parameters is therefore a crucial first stage of the interview. The respondent, by virtue of his presence and acceptance of the incentive, is indicating a willingness to be interviewed but has very little idea of how his views will be used or indeed whether they will be used against him. The interviewer must painstakingly explain market research, perhaps giving a few general examples of types of survey conducted in the past. The tape recorder must be explained and, more importantly, the respondent must be encouraged to feel free to express his opinions, whether they are positive or negative in relation to the topic being discussed. Reassurance on the confidentiality of the information is essential, particularly concerning the way in which the taperecording will be used. Finally, the interviewer should briefly outline the structure of the interview, for example:

> 'I'd like to talk to you about your views on meal planning, then I am going to show you an advertisement and a new product and finally I'd like you to have a little taste of a product I've brought with me.'

or

> 'We are conducting a survey to find out how people feel about owning, looking after and feeding a dog nowadays. I'd like to ask you about all the dogs you've ever owned, starting from your first one . . .'

The respondent must understand that the interviewer is not expecting him to answer in a certain way, and that he can be as variable as he likes in the opinions he expresses.

If this procedure is followed, the respondent may feel somewhat reassured on those particular issues but is still likely to feel defensive and anxious about the interview. This feeling may continue throughout the interview if it is not understood as an integral dynamic of the one-to-one interview situation and not dealt with by establishing trust and rapport.

Previous research into the individual interview experience (Gordon and Robson, 1982) suggests that respondents *are* anxious and their anxiety relates to a number of different aspects of the situation.

- whether or not the given answers are correct and please the interviewer;

- worries about self-image – whether or not the respondent appears stupid to the interviewer;
- anger at the interviewer for perceived repetitive or pointless questioning (which may make the respondent feel that it is his responses that are at fault rather than the interviewer's questions);
- irritation with the process of market research (for example, 'This is ridiculous, the packaging doesn't matter as long as the product remains the same').

Some of these reflect a basic human need, which is, to present ourselves to others in the best possible light.

On the other hand, the interview can also be experienced positively – the situation itself is enjoyable and interesting, the opportunity to give opinions is appreciated, there is relief that the experience is not as bad as expected and feelings of sympathy towards market research and a desire to co-operate with the interviewer can and do emerge.

It is these latent good feelings that need to be nurtured in a depth interview whilst all the anxious feelings require strenuous effort and attention to reduce their presence.

Establishing rapport

This is a cliché that frequently turns up as the first item on a discussion guide. The implication is that it is a process that happens in the first five minutes of a depth interview, after which both interviewer and respondent happily stride off into the sunset for the remainder of the interview with no barriers between them.

This is simply not the case. Rapport continues to build, from the time of setting the parameters to the conclusion of the interview. Interviewers have personal methods of establishing rapport, so it is difficult to spell out a step-by-step procedure. Instead a number of guidelines are given.

Dress

As stated earlier, respondents are making assumptions about the interviewer as well as vice versa. It is advisable not to be too dissonant with the respondent – for example, wearing a smart and obviously expensive suit or dress and accessories for a downmarket respondent, or jeans and contemporary 'scruffiness' for a businessman. Occasionally misjudgements occur. This does not ruin the interview – it simply makes the establishment of rapport more difficult.

Share

If the interviewer is prepared to share personal or even intimate aspects of himself with the respondent, the latter is more likely to be open (less defensive) in return. An interviewer does not merge into the background nor act as a *tabula rasa* on which the respondent projects his innermost feelings. In the world of social interaction, 'tit-for-tat' is a strongly present dynamic. If I, as interviewer, let you (respondent) get some insight into me as a person, then you may do the same in return.

This does not mean that the interviewer needs to tell the respondent how he feels about the subject under discussion, although this can be a useful means of encouraging the respondent to disagree. Other personal characteristics can be shared at different or key parts of the interview.

What is important is that the interviewer chooses how to relate to the respondent with *self-conscious awareness* and, since each encounter is unique, the effect of the interviewer 'opening up' to a respondent will differ from person to person (See Sue Jones' Depth Interviewing 1985).

For the practitioner, it is worth experimenting a little in order to see which types of personal admission seem to encourage reciprocation, and which do not.

Body language

The way in which an interviewer sits, gestures, his tone of voice, frequency and intensity of eye contact create or discourage rapport. As interviewers, we can communicate interest, encouragement or warmth to the respondent, or disinterest, aloofness, boredom or anger. Obviously, the more positive support that is given to the respondent, particularly when he may be expressing a heartfelt response, the more likely he is to express such a thought again.

Techniques

A facilitative atmosphere is relaxed and conversational and is based on good rapport between the interviewer and the respondent. Some practitioners have developed techniques which are used to intensify trust between the two parties. These often involve a physical activity such as the interviewer leading a blind-folded respondent round the house and then the process reversed. Odd or eccentric as this may seem, there are problems which require establishment of extraordinary levels of rapport and where a fun procedure between the two people involved can do so quickly and efficiently. Mirroring is another technique discussed in the previous chapter.

Administering projective techniques

Although much has been written about projective techniques (see Braithwaite and Lunn 1985), very little is written to aid the novice practitioner on how to administer them, particularly in an individual interview. They *do* take time. For example, if asking a respondent to draw his feelings about travelling on the Underground, the initial response will be one of self-conscious terror accompanied by many excuses relating to drawing skills, particularly a lack thereof! The situation mirrors childhood experiences such as being picked on by a teacher, or figure of authority, when unprepared.

With all projective techniques, it is crucial not to pose them as tests of any description which require an intellectual or physical skill. Returning to the time issue, a respondent being interviewed alone needs to practise before he is given the real task. Thus both interviewer and respondent may draw their feelings on a general issue or subject (for example, unemployment or butter) before attempting the subject or brand under enquiry.

Some projective techniques take longer to administer than others and some are unsuited to the individual interview. Word association, sentence completion, bubble cartoons, personification and mapping, all require very little practice, are not particularly threatening and are therefore suitable. Others such as psychodrawing, role playing and 'words and pictures' do not only take time but require reassurance, continual encouragement and practice.

Completing the interview

At a particular point in time, the interviewer usually knows, without any doubt at all, that the usefulness of the dialogue with a particular individual has come to an end. It is tempting, particularly if the next respondent has arrived and is waiting, to be very abrupt and bring the interview to a sudden close. This is experienced as dismissive to the respondent who may still feel that his comments and views are going to be as interesting as the ones he expressed earlier on. When this point occurs it is wise for the interviewer to start giving 'close' signals such as 'There are one or two last things I'd like to ask you' or 'Before we finish talking I'd like to show you this/ask you to taste this'. The respondent then has time to add anything else he wishes to say and to leave the interview feeling that he has made a contribution rather than feeling discarded like a well-wrung dishcloth!

THE SKILL OF THE DEPTH INTERVIEWER

In contemporary commercial research it is generally accepted that the cost per interview is based on the level of skill of the interviewer. There are generally three types of interviewers:

- An interviewer from a standard field-force (quantitative).
- A semi-structured or depth interviewer (usually an ex-quantitative interviewer who has been specially trained).

- A qualitative researcher (who moderates group discussions as well as depth interviews).

Buyers are well advised to establish the level and type of skills and training of the interviewer(s) when buying a sample of depth interviews, since the first two will not be providing depth at all, although the product may well be called by that name.

A standard fieldforce interviewer is trained to administer questionnaires in a certain way. She will also be trained to use 'probes' and 'prompts', for example: 'Can you tell me anything more?', 'Is there anything else?', 'What exactly do you mean?', 'Why do you feel like that?', and so on. These probes are usually predetermined by the researcher designing the study and are not left to the interviewer's discretion.

A specially trained depth interviewer is usually an ex-quantitative interviewer who has shown a special aptitude for open-ended types of question. She is trained in the approaches and some of the techniques of the depth interview but does so *mechanistically* rather than conceptually. She will know how to put a respondent at ease, to establish a relaxed pace, to avoid expressing her own personality or views so as not to lead the respondent in any way, to use certain projective questions (such as 'What do you think other people may feel about toy advertisements aimed at children?') and will be able to encourage the respondent to develop points.

This type of depth interview is widely used for industrial research (such as interviewing machinery manufacturers) or for specialist research projects in the medical area (for example health visitors, dentists, opticians). The advantages of these depth interviews are:

- a relatively large number can be conducted (100–150) at a reasonable price;
- that a *description* of current behaviour and attitudes is exactly what the client wishes to know. Little interpretation is required;
- the questionnaires can be analysed by a researcher who has been well briefed on the background and objectives of the study but may not have done any interviews personally.

The main difference between this type of depth interviewer and the qualitative researcher conducting depth interviews is that the former does not usually meet the client buyer, and the latter always does. If the buyer is not able to brief the interviewer directly by explaining the full background to the problem, the current research objectives and the types of decisions that will need to be made, the interviewer cannot incorporate this knowledge into his questioning framework, with the result that the information may be descriptively useful but is unlikely to offer the subtle psychological and motivational insights that provide diagnostic guidance.

A qualitative researcher, particularly one successfully operating in the tough commercial world of the 1980s, brings a unique set of skills to the marketplace. No two qualitative researchers have an identical background and approach and that is why sophisticated and experienced buyers of qualitative research purchase one particular individual. Qualitative research is widely accepted as a people business – buyers buy researcher X for her knowledge and experience of advertising research, and researcher Y for his psychoanalytical orientation in understanding basic consumer motivation. Different types of client buyers relate to different qualitative researchers, and different research problems require different sets of skills. Thus a single buyer may choose researcher X for one project and researcher Y for the next.

What skills are necessary in a qualitative depth interviewer? The list can be awesome. The Qualitative Research Study Group (1979)[1] suggested that a good qualitative interviewer needs, besides experience and training, a wide and often disparate set of personal abilities, such as:

- intellectual ability plus common sense.
- imagination plus logic.
- conceptual ability plus eye for detail.
- detachedness plus involvement.
- 'neutral' self-projection plus 'instant' empathy.
- non-stereotypical thinking plus capacity to identify the typical.
- expertise with words plus good listener.
- literary flair/style plus capacity to summarize concisely
- analytical thinking plus tolerance of disorder.

Obviously no-one can have all these qualities, but they do provide some guidelines for assessing and comparing the performance of different researchers.

We also suggest that in addition to some of the personal qualities described by the Study Group, good qualitative interviewers need to have:

- an academic background or orientation.
- practical experience in an associated field.

In the 1980s qualitative researchers are increasingly finding it essential to understand some of the concepts which stem from other disciplines such as transactional analysis (TA), semiotics, Freudian theory, humanistic psychology, linguistic structuralism and so on. An eclectic and considered application of some of these to specific types of problem can prove extremely useful in contributing to the insight required from qualitative research. The application of transactional analysis to new product development using individual interviews has been described by Blackstone and Holmes (1983). The relationship between the consumer and a new brand (via its advertising) is a transaction that can be understood using the TA model of complementary or crossed transactions.

Finally, the practical experience of qualitative researchers in advertising, marketing, manufacturing or retailing cannot be overemphasized. Buyers of research who function in the world of advertising are unlikely to trust the conclusions and recommendations of a qualitative researcher who is ignorant of the creative development process. Similarly a marketing manager is likely to hold a qualitative researcher in very low esteem if he does not understand elementary marketing concepts, such as the pressure of own-label brands or the particular problems of a number of brands in the current retail environment.

Good qualitative interviewers have a reputation and also confidence in their background and experience. A buyer should ask questions directly, if using someone for the first time, about the individual's past experience and orientation (academic and pragmatic) as well as following up references or asking such organizations as AQRP/MRS (Association of Qualitative Research Practitioners/Market Research Society) for published details of a company or individual.

OBJECTIVES OF THE SURVEY

Individual depth interviews are chosen for the five major types of study discussed in Chapter 1:

Broad market/exploratory studies
New product development
Creative development (including pack design)
Diagnostic studies
Tactical research projects

In the context of a broad market (or exploratory) study, individual interviews may be used to:

- understand a complex purchase process: for example, how does a person decide which car to buy or which holiday to book?
- search for a gap for a new product by understanding in detail how individuals currently behave in relation to a product category and where the potential may lie for a new entrant into the market;
- understand the psychological or sociological reasons underlying the behaviour of a particular segment of consumers, for example 'the health aware' or 'advertising-sophisticated consumers'.

A depth interview will nearly always be chosen instead of a group discussion approach if the subject of the interview is intimate/personal (such as sanitary protection/contraception) or when longitudinal information is required (such as a house purchasing history).

For new product development, depth interviews are particularly advantageous when

- a few test products are available for placement prior to the interview;
- information is required about how each member of the family reacted to the product(s);

- the strengths and weaknesses of the product(s) need to be evaluated prior to reformulation or production of a larger number of samples;
- 'mock' packaging has been designed and the positioning of the product requires clarification or understanding.

These depth interviews may be *focussed* and therefore both shorter in length and more economical in cost. Often the research proposal may recommend mini-depths for these types of problem and may or may not include self-completion questionnaires or diaries to provide a focus for subsequent discussion.

With regard to creative development research, including pack design research, it is at the later stage of the developmental process that depth interviews are most appropriate and indeed offer advantages over the group discussion method.

Communication, whether via advertising or packaging, is an individual process. A commercial either entertains or it does not, the humour appeals or it falls flat, the message comes across loud and clear or it does not. A pack either positions the product in the desired product segment (for example, a quality tea) or it does not. These aspects of communication are best assessed individually since immediacy of emotional response is the most useful means of evaluation. These focussed depths (that is, focussed on communication effectiveness) are sometimes called 'communication checks'. Usually a skilled qualitative depth interviewer can evaluate the communication in a half-hour interview using projective techniques to reach below rationalized responses.

The choice of interviewing method for diagnostic or tactical studies depends very much on the complexity of the problem, the ease or difficulty in finding appropriate people to interview (for example, triallists of a newly launched brand might be few and far between), whether or not the problem will be clarified by consumers 'sparking off' one another or whether the answers will come from painstaking sleuth work from a number of consecutive interviews.

THE NATURE OF THE 'UNIT' SELECTED FOR A DEPTH INTERVIEW

Some problems or subjects require an understanding of the dynamics between two or more people in relation to a purchase process, for example:

Mother and child – confectionery, toys.
Families – leisure, finance.
Husband and wife – major durables (buying a fridge, decorating the home).
Two friends – eating out, choice of entertainment venue, buying clothes.

It makes sense to interview the pair together to observe how each influences the attitudes and behaviour of the other.

It is very helpful to interview children or adolescents in pairs instead of alone, even if the subject matter does not seem to indicate the need. These younger age groups find the one-to-one interview with a strange adult both intimidating and anxiety-provoking, with the result that respondents tend to freeze (that is, withdraw or withhold). The 'two of us to one of you' dynamic seems to be more reassuring, with the resultant increase in richness of information.

These interviews are sometimes called 'couple depths', 'paired depths' or 'friendship pairs'.

As discussed earlier, triangular interviews also have a role to play as a 'unit' for depth interviews, particularly when differing perspectives on a brand are required.

LOCATION

With individual interviews, the issue of where the respondent should be interviewed needs careful consideration. There are four widely-used options:

- Own home.
- Recruiter's home.
- Central interviewing facility, e.g. hotel.
- Viewing room (one-way mirror).

Interviewing in the respondent's own home has advantages in that it allows the moderator to experience the home environment — the geographic area, the neighbourhood, the street, the house, the interior, all of which form as important a part of understanding the individual as the content of the interview itself.

The disadvantages are entirely practical. Firstly, only a few interviews can be accomplished in one day with in-between travelling and, secondly, the interview is easily disrupted by doorbell, telephone or children.

The decision whether or not to interview at the respondent's home depends on the subject matter (DIY, decorating), the distribution of respondents (scattered or clustered) or the 'unit' interviewed, (e.g. couple, mother and child).

Often, individual interviews conducted in the recruiter's home are organized like a doctor's appointment list — hourly or half-hourly. The advantages are that the moderator can complete more interviews per day as no travelling is required, and that video playback equipment can be used. Generally speaking all types of individual interview can be arranged in this way, even those with businessmen, although the latter are often more responsive in central facilities such as upmarket hotels, where refreshments are served and the atmosphere is both impersonal and business orientated.

The use of one-way mirrors is discussed in Chapter 9.

Like everything else in market research, each survey needs to be considered. There are no hard and fast rules — only common sense and forethought.

NOTE

1. Market Research Society, R & D Society Sub-Committee on Qualitative Research (1979), 'Qualitative Research – a Summary of the Concepts Involved'.

7 Non-verbal Communication

INTRODUCTION

No matter how we may later construe or interpret it, we are fated to experience the world, the things and the people in it through our bodies. More than this, our bodies are the main means of projection of our own intentions, actions, drives and needs as well as the route to their satisfaction.

Consequently the expressions and gestures we use have deep biological as well as social significance. And so, in the sense that we all employ it, speak it if you like, we're all already experts in body language. But so much of it is unconscious and operates outside of our awareness that it's almost like having to learn a foreign language. As with any foreign language, one of the keys to mastering it is practice. So, while you're reading, become aware of your own body, its changes of posture and expression, its involuntary movements. Allow yourself to introspect on the meaning of any signalling functions these phenomena might have.

Modern qualitative research is very much a doing/activity oriented process with a strong experiential component. Describing what happened in a group discussion presents all sorts of theoretical and practical problems. At what level of detail do I describe it — second by second, movement by movement or subject by subject? No, most of these are too microscopic; we generally offer a broader sketch of what happened *that seemed significant* and highlight intimate details to emphasize or dramatise turning points or decision moments on our journey through the experience. Very rarely can we face the music and own up to the fact that it may have been an event lasting no more than a second that put us on the trail of something that led to a change of view, a deeper understanding — even a moment of enlightenment. Yet, in actuality, it is usually some change in posture, a gesture or an expression that heralds such a discovery. We must be alert to it, yet it probably won't feature in our final description, analysis and report at all.

Since in our profession the main means of reportage is 'verbal description' we tend to constrain our analysis to that level — if necessary portraying a respondent by what he said, perhaps using his own dialect, vocabulary and syntax to illustrate the point. But seldom, if ever, do we portray the gesture or postural shift that let us know that something was afoot.

Notwithstanding this, non-verbal communication (NVC) is of crucial importance in qualitative research. One of the problems of interviewing generally is that people often don't say what they feel. Very often they experience conflicting — even contradictory — emotions about what has been shown or what someone else has said. For many respondents, one of the best ways of not making a fool of themselves or getting into a hassle may be to keep quiet in these sorts of circumstance. But all kinds of non-verbal signals, which we call *minimal* cues, will give you, the moderator, evidence of the presence of conflict.

For us researchers, facilitating the expressing of a complex negative or positive emotion may be of critical importance to the brief. For example, it's no good accepting a rational agreement that Japanese cars represent good value as an indication of willingness to purchase if this overlays a deep xenophobic hatred of the Japanese which the informant is too ashamed or scared to reveal.

How then may we become aware of hidden conflict or emotion, be it in response to test material, or to other group members, or to the interviewer? Of course it's not always possible to discern it — indeed in many cases the deep level at which it exists may prove irrelevant to consumption of biscuits or whatever — but often it's just below the surface and is of great importance to behaviour and will leak out non-verbally by means of a gesture, facial expression or change of posture or demeanour.

INTERNAL (PERSONAL) AND EXTERNAL (SOCIAL) BODY LANGUAGE

We have then this stream of movement which we must take into consideration. Is it *all* relevant to qualitative research? Must the interviewer watch respondents like a hawk to detect the significance of every twitch? Of course not. Much bodily communication, like language, is internal inner communication. Just as you may hear voices in your head when you think, so a constant exchange of NVC takes place on the subject of bodily business.

'I'm hungry,'	says the stomach.
'I'm stiff,'	says your back.
'I'm sore,'	says your backside.
'Why don't you stroke me?'	says your aching calf.

Further, one may get 'Tired from just thinking about it', just as one may 'Ache for a change'. This internal communication is not just to do with biological needs: it may just as easily be emotionally inspired. It can erupt spontaneously, too. What researchers must learn is to distinguish the NVC that is relevant to the research task and to respond to it as distinct from the constant stream of movement that is bodily business.

One vital clue is of paramount importance here; NVC that is intended for you or another group member or a concept board *will nearly always be directed specifically toward or away from the target object*. Broadening this view slightly, we can observe that the four most common forms of relevant movement are towards, away from, around or aside. It's *socially directed* NVC that we're most interested in as qualitative researchers, though if a wonderfully appetitive food commercial makes someone's tummy rumble that seems relevant too!

Before we pass on to describing NVC in more detail, we should apologize for the fact that writing about NVC is a bit like a wood turner trying to write a description of a particular flick of his wrist and its significance on the final shape of the thing he is making. The best solution to this problem is to practise *observation and discussion* of NVC with your colleagues and any tolerant friends you may have.

PROCEDURAL CONSIDERATIONS

At the simplest level we use NVC to help us move the interview or group along in response to the needs of the informants as well as to the brief. We must learn the following cues and constantly be on the lookout for new additions to our repertoire.

(i)   To recognize someone's desire to speak as indicated by any of the following:

> finger raised
> head nodding
> direct eye contact with moderator
> sitting or 'perking' up.

(ii)   To recognize signs of withdrawal or boredom:

> yawning
> repeated gestures (slow foot tapping)
> looking away
> vacant stares
> involuntary 'starts'.

(iii)   To recognize suppressed anger or hostility:

> stiffening of the posture
> clutching of the fists
> tightening of the lips and jaw
> turning pointedly away from another
> expelling air through the nose.

(iv)   To recognize shyness as indicated by any of the following:

       blushing
       hesitancy/stuttering
       lowering eyes
       shrinking.

(v)   To recognize the signals of discomfort, either specific or general:

       restlessness
       looking at watch
       gross rearrangement of sitting position/posture.

(vi)   To make a note of unspoken assent or dissent. The taped record won't necessarily contain this data and we should note it as we proceed.

(vii)   To respond to signals of desire to leave/break flow.

(viii)   To recognize a desire to interrupt another speaker from the occurrence of:

       triple head-nods or other impatient gestures (tapping the fingers, etc.) Often accompanied by verbal signals like 'Yes', 'But' or 'Well'.

Recognizing and responding to these and other indicators of the presence of some active form of thoughts or experience will help keep the flow of your interviews and discussions going.

You may use your own body language to help things along too. *Mirroring* others' posture will often help create rapport with them. Contradicting the posture of an over-intrusive respondent will express your disapproval and, if you contradict at an extremely different speed, this will heighten the effectiveness of your action.

Pacing is another useful technique. Very often good pacing will help a respondent verbalize and give expression to thoughts and feelings which are at the edge of her awareness. Pacing simply refers to the art of matching the speed of someone else's NVC. You may pace *any* aspect of NVC in order to increase someone's feeling that you are in tune with them. Good examples are:

- Rate of breathing.
- Eye blink rate.
- Finger or foot tapping.
- Postural punctuation of speech.
- Speed of speaking.

You get maximum effect by combining mirroring and pacing.

As a further sophistication you may practise and develop the art of cross-over pacing. You can pace something going on in one sensory mechanism in a different one. For example, you could pace breathing rate with hand tapping, or eye blink with foot tapping. Practise by pacing your completion of each of the sentences you are reading with some form of non-verbal signal.

NVC IN ANALYSIS OF MEANING AND INTERPRETATION

At this level things are somewhat more complicated. All participants in qualitative research are aware of the fact that quite often the non-verbal signals contradict the verbal ones, and that often the non-verbal response is more important than the other. The mere fact that someone has difficulty in expressing something verbally may in itself constitute a finding of paramount importance. Every experienced moderator will be familiar with the feeling that the group is not saying what it feels.

Given for a moment that all NVC represents potential data, how then can we know what it means? The first and most important thing to remember is that non-verbal signals can give you vital information about the *form* of someone's thought processes but not about the *content*. Imagining that you know what they are thinking is an unhelpful fantasy of your own. You must always check it out with the informants themselves.

An example here is that of someone stroking their chin or face, or adopting the tilted head of what we call the 'telephone postures'. This is invariably an indication that someone is having an internal dialogue – talking to themselves. An observant interviewer may follow this up with a probe, perhaps along the lines of:

'You look like you're having an interesting thought. Would you like to share it with us?'

If you can't follow up verbally then a determination of what was being thought may only be hypothesized by carefully comparing the specific non-verbal cues with the specific statements that the person has already made.

Neuro Linguistic Programming[1] and Accessing Cues

As an interview proceeds, informants will be asked to respond to things that we show them or questions that we ask them. Things like: 'Is there anything it reminds you of?' or 'Can you think of the brand most similar to this?' In order to answer questions like this and thousands of others, respondents must access information from their memories or past experience. When you watch someone trying to remember something, if you observe them closely you will notice a specific pattern of movement and changes in the person's physiology which are specific to the process of remembering. Think now about the two examples described below.

1. Aileen fidgeted in her seat, her feet tapping; 'I don't know' she said, 'I feel confused about it.'
    She encircled her knees with her hands as if to still them. Then, looking downwards and to the right she said 'It doesn't feel right, there's something missing. It doesn't grab me.'

Just by listening to her language, we may realize that Aileen is into her feelings but there is another very specific piece of information that she has offered us, given *just by her eyes alone*.

2. 'It's not clear to me what they're getting at' said Mike.
    'What is it that's not clear?' asked the moderator.
    Tilting his head backwards and looking up towards the ceiling, Mike reflected 'Let me see now . . .'

Mike's words and actions provide one immediate and vital piece of information; he is somehow searching 'visually' for information. Again, just as informative as the words chosen is the direction of his eye movements.

Back in the mid 1970s Richard Bandler and John Grinder (1979) studied the pattern of people's eye movements as they thought and spoke. They noticed that certain directions of eye movements were very closely related to the *type* of information being retrieved and these patterns of eye movement they called 'occular accessing cues'.

In essence:

*   *Upward* eye movements are connected to *visual recall* or construction (of new images).
*   *Sideways* eye movements are connected with *verbal or auditory* recall or construction (putting things into words).
*   *Downward* eye movements are associated with *kinesthetic* memories and derived emotions or feelings, and with internal dialogue.
*   *Defocussed eyes*, often experienced as 'looking through you' is another recall or construction technique which is practised in face to face conversations when it is impolite not to make eye-level contact with your co-conversation-alist. Usually it is indicative of visualization of other forms of remembered or constructed material.
*   *Closed eyes* are particularly associated with recalling tastes or smells.

When assembled, these patterns are grouped to form what is called the 'accessing cues schematic' (see Fig. 7.1, p. 84). Directions may well be reversed for a left-handed or partially sinistral person.

It has been the author's experience that when interviewing people with dominant visual systems you first become aware of their eyes: these are often wide open and aware. Auditory people tend to look from side to side more and tilt their heads in the 'telephone postures'. Kinesthetically dominated people tend to look downwards, often they will encircle their knees with their hands. Check for these cues and tendencies among your friends and colleagues.

In the interviewing situation, familiarity with the ocular accessing cues will help you to create rapport with your informants by enabling you to use the appropriate leads for the system being used by the respondent, for example:

	Follow up
For people using visual access:	'It's *clear* to me that . . .'
	'Have you managed to *picture* something?'
	'It's *apparent* that you're searching for something. Can we help?'
For people using auditory/verbal access:	'I *hear* what you're saying, can you . . .'
	'Would you share what you *heard* with us?'
	'Is that *speaking* your language?'
	'Can you *relate* to that?'
For people using kinesthetic/emotional access:	'What do you *understand* about . . .'.
	'What sort of *vibes* does this give off?'
	'Does that *connect/resonate* with anything for you?'
	'How do you *feel* about . . .'.

It will also provide you with all sorts of additional cues about who to follow up with (based upon the occurrence of accessing cues) and what kind of question to ask them.

On a general practical basis, the first application of NVC to analysis and interpretation should probably be a consideration by the moderator of the overall level of movement and gesture in the interview and whether this had a positive, involved character, or was disinterested and slack. At which moments did things get lively? When were people inactive and distracted? Which of the advertisements or concepts generated the greatest movement and was this, by and large:

Positive:	Leaning forward and looking intently − general increase in body tone and muscular activity.
Confusing/unresolved:	Moving to the side looking about for clues, avoiding eye contact.
Negative:	Leaning backwards, looking away, crossing arms, pushing away with hands.
Disinterested:	Vacant facial expressions, low levels of activity, yawning.

Figure 7.1   Eye and head movements

Following up from a basic assessment of the level and variation in interest, one may watch out for more specific cues.

Here is a description of some common NVC that occurs in qualitative groups or interviews, together with a brief indication of its usual meaning. Remember that things aren't always the way they seem, and you should follow up the non-verbal signals by checking things verbally. We have put the meaning first because some things are commonly communicated by more than one gesture or signal.

Opening up:	General expanding and opening of the posture.
	Figure 4 leg crossing.
	Parting or uncrossing of arms or legs.
Closing up:	Shrinking or diminishing in posture.
	Folding arms or crossing legs.
	Parallel leg folding.
Entrenchment:	Re-establishing a 'set' early posture.
	Sitting straight up.
	Folding arms.
Boredom:	Vacant staring.
	Not hearing.
	Yawning.
Interest:	Forward leaning.
	Touching the face.
	Spontaneous involuntary movements.
	Pursing of the lips.
Disinterest:	Shrugging shoulders.
	Examining hands.
	Clenching and unclenching fist.
	Examining the ground, lower legs or feet.
Dissent/Rejection:	Head tossing.
	Pushing away with hands.
	Brushing off from clothes.
Irritation:	Active backward leaning.
	Tutting.
Evaluation/Undecided:	Hand on or around chin/face.
	Drawing down of eyebrows.
	Forefinger between lips.
	Hand linked beneath arm.
	Scratching ear/back of head.
Positive resolution of evaluation:	Leaning forward.
	Head nodding (even if only just visible).
	Palms turning upwards.
Negative resolution of evaluation:	Leaning back.
	Side to side head movements.
	Palm turned downwards on lap.

| Trying to see things more clearly: | Raising the head and gaze. Putting on/polishing spectacles. |
| Anxiety: | Tense posture. Clutching chair. Rapid audible breathing/deep-lung smoking. |

This is by no means an exhaustive list, but it should help. We would suggest that you use it as a starting point and develop your understanding further. If you adopt any of these postures or gestures as you read you will find it hard not to experience the prevalent mode of thought that normally accompanies them.

It is vital that you not only practise the ability to interpret and use the flow of information contained in NVC, but that *you become more sensitive to it generally*. This is often overlooked once practitioners have embarked on an erudite discussion of the meaning of non-verbal cues. In this context it helps to remember that the peripheral areas of your eyes are much more sensitive to movement than the central, foveal area. This is extremely useful in group discussions since it means that while engaging someone who is speaking with a direct gaze, we may watch out for bodily reactions from other group members 'out of the corners of our eyes'. It is of inestimable value to practise this skill. Here are a couple of suggestions for doing this. If you work often with other people about you, practise becoming aware of their movements whilst you are engaged in another task like talking into the telephone or report writing. If you get the opportunity and you feel that you have understood the significance of a movement someone has made, check it out with them.

Another exercise involves standing directly in front of someone with your gaze in direct contact with theirs at a distance of about four or five feet. Now try to become aware of the position of their hands. Are they clenched or open, occupied with anything or hanging loosely? Now ask them to change the position of their hands and their mode of articulation. You must try to spot the change without lowering your gaze. You will find that, if you practise, your degree of sensitivity to movement outside your direct gaze will increase enormously and, correspondingly, you will expand your awareness.

Although it's a fine dividing line, there is some difference between body language that indicates general presence of feelings which might arise in response to stimulus material and that which denotes a reaction to other members of the group, including the moderator.

As a rule, opening up or relaxing of the posture indicates an emphatic positive response to stimulus material, whereas closing up indicates disagreement, reserve, or even disapproval. Inactivity usually connotes uninterest, whether in stimulus material or another's point of view. Mirroring *each other* indicates the existence of rapport (which is not necessarily the same as agreement but may suggest it) whereas restlessness of the whole body and particularly the hands usually suggests flight of some kind. Here is a list of a few more examples.

- Reaching out to others as well as leaning towards them suggests interest or intimacy.
- Exposure of parts of the body, especially the areas containing the sexual organs, can be a prelude to sexual invitation, and may precede 'pairing' – a phenomenon fully described in Chapter 4.
- Expansiveness is normally accompanied by large gestures.
- Emphasis is often accompanied by a precise tone of voice.
- Reclusiveness is often accompanied by 'tiny' precise movements, flickering gestures and quietly voiced opinions.

Reassuringly for many of us, Estes (1937) found that artistic and literary people were good at matching films of people's movements and descriptions of their personalities, while university teachers and professional psychologists were poor at it!

Attempting to draw these various threads together, we have devised a simple system for describing how you are likely to experience another, based on a simple combination of postural cues and non-verbal signals. Posture (and this does not mean deportment) is one of the most relevant cues in NVC, and the most important dimension appears to be whether the posture is basically tense or relaxed. So, we have:

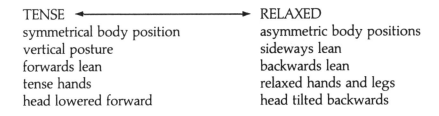

TENSE ←—————————→	RELAXED
symmetrical body position	asymmetric body positions
vertical posture	sideways lean
forwards lean	backwards lean
tense hands	relaxed hands and legs
head lowered forward	head tilted backwards

In terms of the *signs* people use, the most important dimension seems to be whether they are open or closed. In this respect we have:

OPEN ←—————————→	CLOSED
legs akimbo	legs crossed
arms at sides	arms folded across body
hands open and relaxed	turning away
maintaining eye contact	avoiding eye contact

Putting these together we have produced a synthesis of how you are most likely to experience the attitude or personality of people in each of the four quadrants.

This is by no means a definitive picture, nor is it meant to preclude exceptions to these categories. Remember that your own internal state will materially

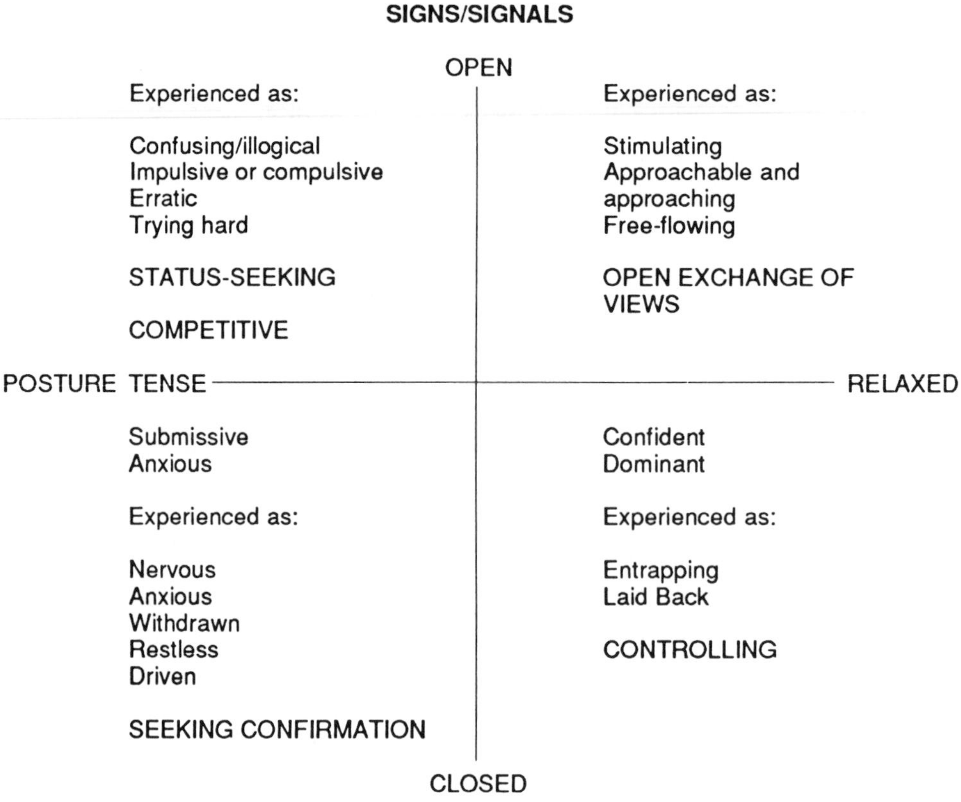

SIGNS/SIGNALS

OPEN

Experienced as:		Experienced as:
Confusing/illogical Impulsive or compulsive Erratic Trying hard		Stimulating Approachable and approaching Free-flowing
STATUS-SEEKING		OPEN EXCHANGE OF VIEWS
COMPETITIVE		

POSTURE TENSE ———————————————————— RELAXED

Submissive Anxious		Confident Dominant
Experienced as:		Experienced as:
Nervous Anxious Withdrawn Restless Driven		Entrapping Laid Back
		CONTROLLING
SEEKING CONFIRMATION		

CLOSED

Figure 7.2

affect how you perceive others at any given moment. But it does provide a useful model of how we've experienced respondents' personalities, and it relates this to their signs and postures.

NOTES

1. Neuro Linguistic Programming (NLP) is a series of principles and practices which aim to improve and increase the effectiveness of communication. An illuminating introduction to the subject may be found in 'Frogs into Princes' by Richard Bandler and John Grinder [Real People Press 1979].

8 Projective and Enabling Techniques

In our experience, much of what has been written and discussed about projective techniques has been weighty, theoretical and serious, in contrast to the way in which respondents relate to projective techniques in real life qualitative market research situations. Respondents enjoy projective techniques as much as moderators have fun in administering them. They create new energy in a group discussion and lighten the mood or tone of the proceedings. This light-hearted and sometimes child-like delight with projective techniques should not undermine the importance we attach to their role in qualitative research and in no way trivializes the theoretical sources from which they stem. This chapter discusses projective techniques in a manner which we hope will make them more accessible to practitioners and end-users. They are not psychological mumbo-jumbo but an invaluable aid to reaching below superficial, rationalized responses in a way that is perfectly acceptable to respondents themselves.

In our view, the use of projective as opposed to enabling techniques in market research represents a false distinction. They are identical in that their main aim is to facilitate a deeper exploration of a person's feelings about a situation, product or type of activity. If there is any difference it is that with a projective technique a respondent will usually be asked to create some-thing. In 'enabling', they're usually asked to *do* something which often has facilitating but no interpretive value.

Before going on to describe the development and use of projective tests in market research, let us start with a more general description of the nature and purposes of such tests. Looking backwards we can quickly see that like many other aspects of psychological theory, projective testing has had a turbulent history.

If there was ever an argument between qualitative and quantitative methods in market research, then it was a mere squabble compared to the rumblings and thunderings of controversy that have surrounded the development and use of projective techniques in clinical and experimental psychology. Once again, though, the basic argument separates those who believe in, or accept, the introspections of themselves and others as a kind of 'evidence' in building an assessment or understanding, from those who see such means as unreliable, unscientific or imprecise. Once again we are faced with a technique about which virtually everyone who has ever heard of it is curious, not to say intrigued. The central premise – that we project or reveal our innermost feelings by our words and actions – seems to make sense at such a deep 'intuitive' level, yet many are critical of such testing methods to the point of denouncing them as chicanery.

Of course, in the strictest sense, such antiquarian practices as 'reading' the pattern of tea leaves, the insides of dead animals or birds, or the meaning signified by the order of cards are experiments with a strong projective element, involving the interaction between tester (or fortune teller) and testee (or client), and responses to material which is abstract to varying degrees. No wonder the whizz kids of twentieth century science are against it. Viewed like this, the whole thing smacks of voodoo, witchcraft or mere tomfoolery.

Notwithstanding the risk of being burned at the stake of modern science, our work with projective techniques over the past twenty years has convinced us of their value. Quite simply, we feel that projective techniques help us enter the private world of the individual. Our purpose in using them is not therapeutic – although in that people obviously enjoy participating once they feel confident, they often do cheer people up; we use them for descriptive and diagnostic reasons. Just as we would not presume to be clinical diagnosticians, neither would we make any use of projective material or perform 'analysis' upon it without our informants' consent. Nowadays in our normal practice the entire generation, use and analysis of the projective material is carried out in the informants' presence, usually by the informants themselves. Occasionally, at the interpretation stage, we will collect together a series of projections that seem to us to illustrate a point, or in a presentation we may retell a story that seemed particularly pertinent (see Figure 8.1) But our main purpose in using these methods is to bring the inner perspective of our informants out into the open in a way that they feel comfortable and happy with.

So that you may have an example of the use of this method in your mind as we progress, we will describe a basic application we sometimes use as an enabling technique. At the very simplest level, we might use such a technique to encourage informants to become aware of their inner perspective and its potential bearing on our investigation. One such technique, derived from gestalt groups, which has proved useful starts with the group leader or moderator outlining what is going to be involved in the task. As always, we do not encourage the onset of anxiety by sending respondents off on a task or excursion which has not been explained to them. We might introduce the task in this way.

> I'd like to join in a game with you that we can play in a group. It involves trying to remember something from your past which you share with the other group members. I'm suggesting that we play it in order to be aware that it's things that are *inside* your mind that we're interested in discussing together as well as the events that happen here today. In a way, sharing this experience gives

Figure 8.1 **A collection of projections describing a very positive attitude to advertising.**

us all permission to talk about inner thoughts to each other. Are you happy to give it a try?

Providing the group feels comfortable, the moderator may then proceed:

So that we can relax and concentrate at the same time, I suggest that everyone closes their eyes like I've closed mine. (Moderator closes eyes.) I'd like you to think back to your home when you were a child – choose whichever period in your childhood comes to mind. Now imagine you're inside your childhood home. Look around you. You're looking for your favourite toy. Go and look for it. (Pause.)

Have you found it? Nod when you've got it. (Moderator opens eyes and waits until everyone has nodded.)

Now if you can, pick it up and look at it. Or just look at it. What do you feel? I'll now ask everyone in turn to talk about their personal experience of the situation, to describe the toy and how they felt holding or looking at it. So don't forget.

This simple technique for recalling loved possessions and childhood thoughts has all sorts of valuable spin-offs for the group and its process – although the material it produces is simply the shared 'confidences' or private thoughts of the group members with no specific marketing orientation.

Firstly, it demonstrates to group members that they may share or trade disclosures with each other about quite intimate aspects of their lives without anything horrible happening. People do not guffaw with laughter because you turn out to have a 'Teddy Bear' too. The feelings of cohesion as everyone discloses these relationships between themselves and their childhood toys is quite palpable. As a result of this, people feel less exposed about revealing their feelings to each other when it comes to discussing how they feel about products or advertisements.

Secondly, it encourages people to talk about what is going on mentally so that later, when the group leader asks, 'What do the rest of you think (or feel) about that?', people do not respond as if they were not listening or paying attention. They have been given permission to listen to the 'feelings' of other group members and to express their own. You should remember that in 'polite' society, especially among groups of strangers, etiquette demands that one should pretend one has not heard things that are personal or that transgress the rules of 'nice' behaviour. Every experienced moderator has had to cope with the social anxiety and furtive glances associated with the tummy rumblings of an anxious informant. Until the perpetrator owns up or someone else intervenes on his/her behalf and helps to make things OK, the entire group may 'freeze' with half its energy directed into a communal cocked ear which is listening out for that taboo noise again.

Thirdly, perhaps more subtly, by closing their eyes in public, informants have acknowledged the existence of their own inner space – and that of others – within the research discussion context.

Fourthly, this kind of enabling technique may have a more specific project-orientated application when the focus of a study is the kind of product or service that constitutes an experience which the informants might be invited to enter or re-enter in their own mind's eye. Good examples of subject material that is amenable to this kind of projection includes studies of banks, shops/supermarkets or restaurants. The moderator can obtain all sorts of useful data from the projections people describe about, say, a visit to a bank. Were they treated well? Did they have to wait long? Become uncomfortable? What did they want or need during their visit? Did the staff recognize or know them? What was the tone of their interaction? As our economy becomes more service oriented, studies of our experience of these everyday interactions is likely to assume increasing importance.

By now the reader, especially if she is an inexperienced moderator, or even if she is not, may be dreading the apparently preposterous suggestion that one should ask a group of men containing a rugby forward and a policeman to recall their favourite toy and describe it. Structure the task to suit the situation. It is the *inner perspective* that is important, the specific details matter little. You may ask them to recall the first time they went to a pub, their first fight, their first date with a girl, their best night out with the lads, instead.

Much useful specific material about either the informants or the subject of the project may emerge but, the technique provides the inestimable benefit of teaching respondents by example that their private inner voices are of interest to you.

And so, at the simplest level, we might make use of an enabling technique for describing a real or fantasized memory which allows informants to project fantasy material (about toys, parents, whatever) if they wish, or just straightforwardly to describe a past event. But what, properly, are projective tests or techniques? How may we define them? What are their strengths and weaknesses?

THE DEFINITION OF PROJECTIVE TECHNIQUE

Starting with the easiest part, the noun root of the name, it is appropriate to say that most psychologists and projectivists would be happier with the description 'techniques', rather than the alternative, 'tests'. The word 'test' is used to describe phenomena of widely varying degrees of precision, but in the pyschological sciences the word 'test' is usually confined to events in which some attempt at measurement is made. We may then go on to ask, 'What is being measured?, or 'What is being tested?'. In projective work there is no straightforward answer, and correspondingly we feel happier with the word 'technique'.

So techniques it is, then; but what of 'projection'? In classical psychoanalytic literature, and most brilliantly described by Melanie Klein, projection is viewed as a defence mechanism with which the ego protects itself from anxiety by externalizing unpleasant feelings or elements of one's experience – often ascribing them directly to others. The colloquialism 'The pot calling the kettle black' sums it up most eloquently. It is as if, by seeing bad things as outside oneself, one denies their existence within. Very often in cases of rape or sexual assault the assailant will project his own irresistible desires on to his victim by swearing that she gave him the 'come on', the eye, or whatever. 'She made me do it. She *wanted* me to!' Thinking about it for a moment, if this were the sense in which we market researchers defined the word, then the material produced by our own projective techniques would actually be *undesirable and atypical* (at least consciously) of an informant's normal feelings. So this is not the definition we seek. What we are looking for is something more in line with the old adage 'We put something of ourselves into everything we do', a much more commonsensical, if pedestrian, notion. So, taking this as our basis, let us suggest a working definition of projection now:

> The tendency to imbue objects or events with characteristics or meanings which are derived from our subconscious desires, wishes or feelings.

For the true projectionists, the word 'subconscious', or its alternative 'unconscious', is of prime importance. We are much less confident in our own market research work of the influence of subconscious desires on our material. It does creep in, sometimes obviously, but most usually the projections in market research may be viewed as a way for people to talk about themselves more freely, with the occasional insight into a deeper level.

Much more importantly, from our point of view, is that whether he knows he is doing it or not, a means must exist whereby the meaning or importance of a respondent's behaviour can be communicated to the observer. In clinical tests this is partly accomplished by scoring the material. In market research it's wholly dependent on observation of the material and the subject's subsequent description of its import and meaning for him. *It is vitally important that the informant him or herself does the description or interpretation of the response.* One of the main, and in our view justifiable, criticisms of projective analysis in the past is that the 'result' is just as likely to be based upon the projections of the tester in response to the material as on the intentions of the testee in producing it.

Even in clinical applications it is being recognized that the interpersonal relationships in a projective situation are just as important as the test material, and that they profoundly influence what is being communicated. Often regarded as a weakness, we feel this is one of the principal strengths of the use of these techniques in market research. Handled properly, they can deepen and strengthen the relationship between researcher and informants.

And so we suggest that working from the definition above, projective techniques should be utilized when suitable, but should be regarded as a whole

– including non-verbals like frowning, head scratching, nodding, crossing out and non-specific verbals like sighing and tut-tutting.

So, based on the underlying theory that the way an individual perceives, interprets, or structures the test material will reflect fundamental aspects of his psychological functioning, what are the *features* of projective techniques?

1. Perhaps the simplest definition of the central feature of projective techniques might be that of 'taking something at more than face value'.
2. They should constitute a relatively unstructured task. The idea here is to permit the widest possible variety of responses. In market research applications, we wish to focus the task a little more closely. After all, we are not usually trying to discover whether an informant hates his mother or not, but rather how his psychological make-up influences his perception of, say, a make of car or a brand of breakfast cereal.
3. They should permit an opportunity for the respondent to describe, explain or just talk about his response to the interviewer.
4. There may be a considerable practice effect. People tend to be more comfortable with them after their first 'bash'.

Having briefly described the principal features of projective techniques, let us have a look at some of the *types*: there are 5 main procedures:

1. Association
2. Completion
3. Construction
4. Expressive
5. Choice-ordering.

ASSOCIATION PROCEDURES

Word association

Examples of these are *word association* and the famous *Rorschach* ink blot test. Word association was first systematically described by Galton in 1879 – a series of unrelated words is presented to which the subject/respondent responds with the first word that comes to mind. (The early experimental psychologists saw in such tests a tool for the exploration of the thinking processes.)

The clinical application of *word association* tests was stimulated by the psychoanalytic movement. Jung selected stimulus words to represent common 'emotional complexes'. Responses were analysed with reference to reaction-time and content. Overt expressions, for example laughing, flushing, hand movements, were also noted. The test would then be readministered, the subject being asked to recall his responses; changes in these and other features of re-test behaviour were noted.

Word association tests were also used in connection with crime and lie detection (the polygraph) – words linked with the crime are used, and physiological as well as verbal responses are recorded.

In market research, word association is typically used in conjunction with potential brand names (are responses favourable, unfavourable or neutral?) and also in connection with products, product attributes and brand images.

The trigger word is introduced verbally and is responded to either verbally or non-verbally:

Tell me the first thing that comes to mind when I say corn flakes.

or

Write down the first thing that comes to mind when I say Heinz.

Answers, either written or spoken, will give the researcher a variety of consumer vocabulary associated with the brand or product. Top-of-mind thought associations will be helpful in discovering brand imagery, product attributes and the like. So, for cornflakes we might get answers like: family, Kellogg's, sunshine, British, boring, children, etc.

As well as products and brands, people can be used in word associations, for example, when an advertiser is planning to do testimonial advertising. Respondents' associations with the personality will illustrate the extent to which he/she is liked/disliked, familiar/unfamilar, and what the person means to consumers generally. In other words, polarized responses will emerge from using the technique.

Word association is involving. It elicits a lot of giggling and energy in group discussions, and is viewed as fun by most. If respondents write their word associations down, they do so anonymously – no name is attached to their answer. So, knowing their thoughts can be disowned, they feel free to be uninhibited. The technique is very useful as a way of 'warming up' respondents, preparing them to play other projective 'games' in the group discussion or interview.

The *Rorschach* test consists of ten ink blot cards; subjects are asked to describe what the blots look like or remind them of. It is a visual form of association test. Originally the Rorschach was administered to different psychiatric groups, and the reponse characteristics that differentiated the various psychiatric syndromes were gradually incorporated into the scoring system. This scoring system appears to be an extremely complex procedure involving a verbatim record, the timing of the responses; the positions the cards are held in, and so on. The problem of scoring/interpretation, as we shall see later, has always been the *bête noire* of the projective movement. To date the ink-blot test has not been adapted for use in market research.

Brand personalities

In order to understand brand personalities, consumers are asked to project personalities on to brands by imagining them as people and thereby using their association skills. It is a game which respondents can find difficult to play. The manner in which it is introduced is therefore vital. Respondents must feel relaxed and comfortable in the group or interview situation before being asked to participate. When administered successfully, the technique evokes rich data and imagery about brands and is extremely helpful.

Respondents are asked to think of a brand and to imagine it as a person. They then describe the person to the moderator. Brands become people who dress in a certain way, have particular personality traits, drive cars, etc. Consumer imagery of brands is projected into these people and the brands come alive.

For example, respondents asked to personify Domestos described the brand as:

A knight in shining white armour to come and clean out all the bad from the world.

Like a policeman, male, strong, fighting off the baddies and winning.

Strong and dependable, caring, bright and cheerful person like my mother.

Respondents can also be asked to imagine brands as other objects, like cars, shops or animals. Again, useful imagery is attached to brands by using the process of analogy.

Respondents find brand personification extremely easy if they are given a little visual help. By using visual collages of different types of people, houses or interiors of homes, respondents are able to translate the brand into a person with a clear lifestyle. Abstract collages (visual) also help the analogy process. When shown a collage of objects (for example, iron, wooden stool, flowers, coloured cushions, a 'ghettoblaster', a colourful buffet of food, an oldfashioned horse and cart and so on) respondents are able to describe emotional differences between brands. Thus Kelloggs might be personified by the different coloured cushions representing range and enjoyment whilst Alpen may be represented by the flowers (naturalness and health). Visual collages of cars or types of drink may also be used. One brand may be seen as a BMW and described by consumers as young and successful whilst a competitive brand may be seen as a Rolls Royce — established and traditional. Again, it is the group's explanation of the reason for choice of car that is significant not the interpretative guesses of the moderator.

Words and pictures

Another associative technique uses visual and verbal prompts. Respondents are given a pile of words and pictures cut out of magazines. They are asked to choose ones which they associate with a brand or product. When the task is completed, respondents are asked to explain their choice of words and pictures.

This exercise allows the researcher to discover the more emotional responses to brands and their imagery. Respondents choose words and pictures that demonstrate their beliefs and feelings about a brand which would otherwise be difficult to articulate. It is crucial that they are given the opportunity to explain their choice. Our interpretation might be completely contradictory to their reason for choosing something. A respondent may choose a very bright blue picture, and we might think that it illustrates a bright, lively view of the brand, but it may well be the respondent's pet colour hate.

Consistency of words and pictures chosen across the sample will illustrate a clear and consistent brand image. Users and non-users often have different images of a brand, and the words and pictures exercise helps us to discover these imagery differences.

We have found the words and pictures exercises to be invaluable, not only in our interpretation of findings, but also in giving our clients textural feedback from groups. The exercise is particularly useful for discovering:

1. Brand imagery
2. Brand personality
3. Product category imagery
4. Imagery of people (for example in testimonial campaigns).

The technique offers creative stimulus from respondents. It can be used by consumers to generate a visual and verbal advertising concept for a new product, and thereby sheds light on perceptions and expectations of the product. Words and pictures have proved to be exceptionally valuable as a starting point for advertising agencies in the development of early creative ideas. It also sheds light on the effects of advertising at a more emotional level, since words and pictures consumers choose reflect their own inner feelings about brands and products. By looking at a collage of words and pictures, creative teams are able to understand visual imagery of brands and products rather than only being exposed to an entirely intellectual and verbal analysis of the problem.

COMPLETION PROCEDURES

Examples of these are the respondent being required to complete sentences, stories, arguments or conversations.

Again, in psychology such techniques have mainly been used with abnormal/ maladjusted subjects (to test their degree of maladjustment).

Some examples the text books give are along the following lines:

Complete sentences with such beginnings as
I feel . . .
What annoys me . . .
Women . . .

Whether these are actually *projective* appears (to us) to be dubious. A 'stem' such as 'people who smoke filter cigarettes are . . .' is obviously more projective in that the respondent can (on a conscious level) disassociate *him* from the answer and hence his conscious and subconscious defences are more likely to be relaxed and allow a more revealing answer.

The Rosenweig Picture–Frustration Study consists of a series of cartoons each depicting a frustrating situation with two word bubbles; one word bubble has words in it, the other is empty, to be filled in by the respondent. An example is a man in a car saying 'I'm very sorry we splashed your clothing just now though we tried hard to avoid the puddle', and a man on the pavement with a blank bubble above his head. This test is supposed to measure the direction of someone's aggression (extra-punitive, intro-punitive, impunitive); the assumption is that the subject identifies with the person associated with the blank bubble. An example is given in Figure 8.2 of a similar technique applied to market research.

Sentence completion

Sentence completion is often used in quantitative research, when the interviewer is trying to get responses that lie just below the surface. It is often used in self-completion questionnaires, and sometimes in semi-structured depth interviewing, but seldom in group discussions because the technique does not provide as many insights as other projective techniques, and is primarily useful when time is limited but depth of feeling still needs to be tapped.

The technique is a simple one, and involves asking respondents to complete a sentence that has already been started. The completion added to the beginning of the sentence is thus projected by the respondent and insights are gained about the topic of interest.

People who are concerned about additives and preservatives in food are . . .

● Health faddy and cranky
● Doing the best for their families.

I think women who buy frozen pastry are probably . . .

● Lazy and quite extravagant
● Making better use of their time.

Figure 8.2   Completion test

Brand mapping

This is a completion technique which is widely used in the industry. A variety of competitive brands are presented to respondents, who are asked to group them into categories of those they see as being similar. This provides a useful interval in the group, when respondents can get off their chairs and physically move the products into categories on the table or floor. More importantly, it allows the researcher (and ultimately the client) to discover the consumers' segmentation of a particular market. (See Figure 8.3)

Brand mapping is a particularly useful technique for new product research. It enables the marketeer to find gaps in a market, and to understand how consumers view the market. It also permits the development of a perspective on whether gaps could usefully be filled by new products or best left alone. The criteria used by respondents to differentiate between products and group them into categories may well be different to preconceptions held by the manufacturer or advertiser.

The technique's flexibility is also very useful. Having grouped products according to certain dimensions, respondents can be asked to group them according to others. Or they may, after further discussion, discover other dimensions themselves.

Crowded marketplaces can be represented by brand mapping in group discussions, and perceived differences and similarities between brands and products help in understanding a brand's positioning. A brand may have a dual positioning and float between categories. Or having mapped the market in a particular way, respondents can be invited to change the mapping after they have seen advertising and this helps in understanding where and how the advertising is seen to position the brand.

It would be extremely difficult for people to do a brand mapping exercise verbally, without physical product props. Having products for consumers to see and handle facilitates segmentations which reflect reality much more closely than discussions alone about the market would do.

CONSTRUCTION PROCEDURES

These require more complex and controlled intellectual activities on the part of the subject. The best known is Murray's Thematic Apperception Test (TAT) which consists of nineteen cards containing vague pictures in black and white, and one blank card. For each card, the subject is required to construct a story including what led up to the situation depicted, what is happening, and what will occur in the future. In the case of the blank card, the picture itself also has to be imagined. In interpreting the TAT, the examiner determines who is the 'hero' of each story and, on the assumption that the subject identifies with her, analyses the content in terms of 'needs' (for example achievement/

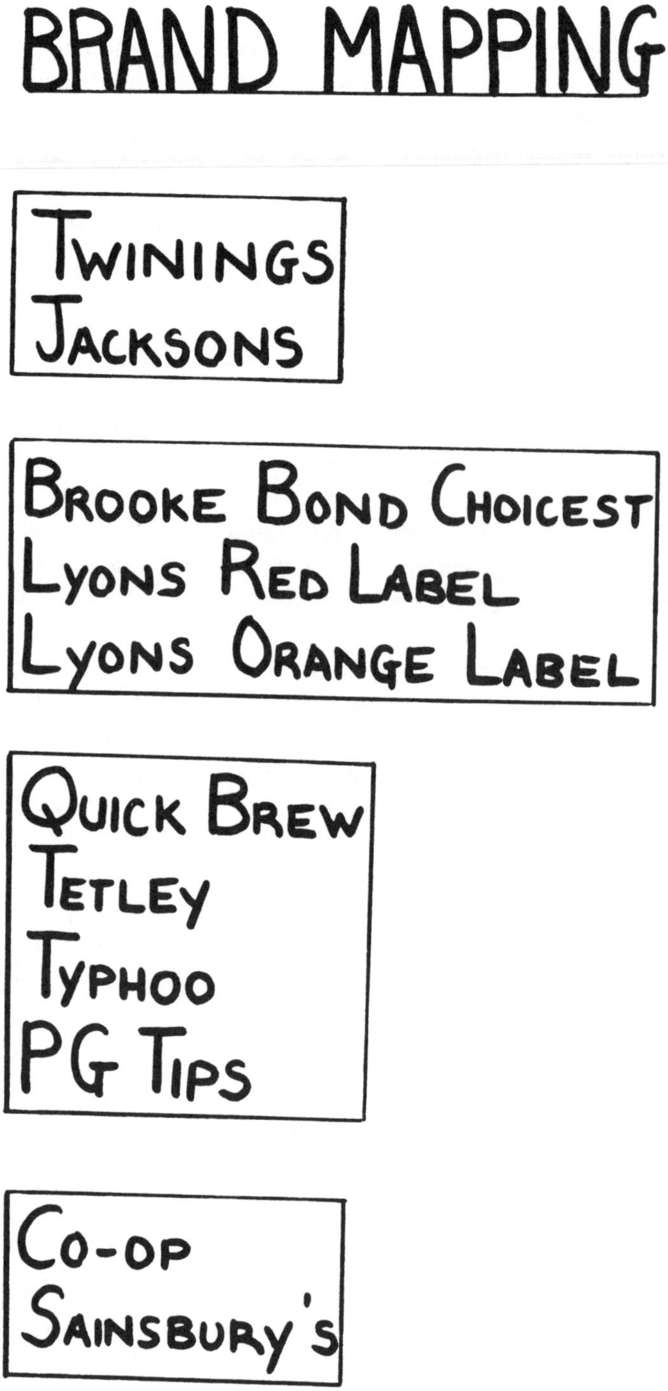

BRAND MAPPING

TWININGS
JACKSONS

BROOKE BOND CHOICEST
LYONS RED LABEL
LYONS ORANGE LABEL

QUICK BREW
TETLEY
TYPHOO
PG TIPS

CO-OP
SAINSBURY'S

Figure 8.3   A brand map

nurturance/sex) and responses to environmental forces that may facilitate or interfere with the satisfaction of needs – for example, being comforted or being in a shipwreck.

In market research typical construction techniques might be simple third-person questions ('What would your neighbour/the average person/most businessmen think of X') or the requirement to fill in a word or 'think bubble' in a drawing relevant to the product area (see Figure 8.4). Or respondents might be given such a drawing without a thought bubble and asked to make up a story around it (what led up to the situation, who are the characters, how do the characters feel about each other, how will it all end?) or they might be presented with a set of purchases/activities of a hypothetical individual, and asked to describe that individual's personality and interests – the theory being that a respondent's feelings towards the items on the list will be reflected in his or her description of the owner. The respondent then describes why he has allotted various characteristics to the imaginary purchaser. Let us examine each of these individually.

Projective questioning

Projective questioning is frequently used in market research. It is a way of allowing respondents to be 'let off the hook', and is also a useful method for the moderator to test hypotheses.

> What do you think the average person is most worried about when asking for a loan?

Answers to this question will usually reflect respondents' own fears about asking for a loan, without causing them any discomfort or embarrassment at having to overtly express their own feelings.

> Other women I was speaking to yesterday told me that they thought this pack looked a bit garish. Why do you think they said that?

> In a previous group, some men I was talking to said that if they were to order a sherry in a pub, people would think they were a bit odd. Why do you think they said that?

Questions such as these are helpful in two ways: first, they expose issues that respondents may not have thought about, allowing the moderator to test a hypothesis, or client's concern. Secondly, they reassure respondents by giving the statement 'other people' credibility, and thereby allowing them to feel less self-conscious about holding an opinion that they might otherwise have feared to be eccentric or atypical. Projective questioning essentially draws out beliefs and opinions that might have been withheld and thereby reveals deeper emotional layers while re-enforcing respondents' feelings of safety while answering the questions.

Figure 8.4   Example of a construction procedure

'Thought' Tapes and 'Talkie' Tapes are a form of indirect research stimuli based on this technique (see pp 227). Instead of the moderator asking the question, a tape recording of a mock interview or group discussion is played to the respondents who then respond naturally and easily.

Stereotypes

Stereotypes enable the researcher to understand typical user profiles. Respondents are presented with a selection (two to five) of descriptions of stereotypical families or people. Underneath the descriptions respondents write down, for example, the typical family's shopping list. The answers provide useful information about perceptions of brand and product usership.

Examples of stereotype families are:

Family A: Both are about 30 years of age with two young children and are very much concerned about owning things. They desperately want a better lifestyle, so he works hard, often for overtime pay, in order to be able to achieve this. She is planning to return to work, part-time, as soon as possible. They spent time furnishing and decorating their home as they are very house-proud. When it comes to buying things, they are more influenced by looks than anything else. They watch TV and read an average amount and tend to follow trends once these have already become fashionable. They think of themselves as modern and up-to-date, but are really quite conventional with regard to family life. They fall into the medium income bracket.

Family B: Husband and wife are in their early fifties with one married son and a 19-year-old-daughter. Mr B works at a boring job and is grateful for the money, which pays for the basic necessities of life. Mrs B does not work, so they do not do much in their leisure time because they cannot afford it. He enjoys football and gambling; she bingo. They watch TV a great deal. They feel that life is hard nowadays, and owe a lot of money. The recession has hit hard. They buy on price − the cheapest possible. Their attitude to their family is traditional, and so are their political and social views. 'British is best' in their minds − they are suspicious of all things foreign.

If a particular brand keeps occurring in one family's shopping list, the brand's user imagery can be more closely understood. For example, in a study on breakfast cereals, Alpen emerged as a trendy, 'trying to keep up with the Joneses' product, which was young, modern and unconventional, like the family that bought it. Kellogg's Corn Flakes, on the other hand, was seen as conservative traditional, home-oriented and safe.

The technique can be used in reverse as well. Respondents are given a shopping list and are asked to describe the type of family or person that would be most likely to buy the products or brands on the list. This is an extension of brand personalities and highlights consumer perceptions of usership.

Bubble drawings

Respondents enjoy this technique, and it is often enthusiastically received in group discussions. It is also successfully used in quantitative research to offer a greater depth of feel and below the surface understanding of consumer behaviour (see Figure 8.5).

Respondents are presented with the drawing of a situation in which there are people. The drawing reflects an aspect of the topic under discussion. So, for example, a drawing might show a woman standing at the fridge, about to take out a carton of orange juice, with an empty bubble coming out of her mouth. Respondents then write down the presumed thought of the woman in question. The completed thought bubbles are anonymous once they have been collected, so that freedom of response is assured.

Bubble drawings are usually specifically devised for individual projects. The variety of situations that can be drawn is therefore very wide. Often what had merely been a passing comment in general discussion emerges as a distinctive product attribute, and consistent bubble completions give weight to something which might otherwise have been dismissed as of no great importance.

Figure 8.6 is an example which we suggest you fill in.

EXPRESSIVE PROCEDURES

If construction techniques focus on the product of the subject, expressive techniques put emphasis on the manner in which something is constructed by the subject, rather than *what* this is. In psychiatry, expressive techniques can serve as therapeutic as well as diagnostic devices – in addition to revealing his difficulties, the individual may relive them. This category includes drawing, modelling and painting, play activities and psychodrama.

An example here is the Machover Draw-a-Person Test. The subject is asked to draw first one sex then the opposite and while he does so his comments and the sequence of drawing of different points are noted. This is followed by the subject making up a story or answering questions about the person he has drawn. Scoring is qualitative and involves preparation of a composite personality description. The interpretative guide is said to 'abound with sweeping generalisations – for example 'the sex which is given the larger head is the sex accorded more intellectual and social authority'. Evidence for this is believed to be non-existent!!

Psychodrama (Moreno)[1] uses the acting out of scenarios often derived from patients' own problem areas and may employ outside actors, a director, other themes, role reversals and so on.

Figure 8.5   Example of a bubble drawing

Figure 8.6   A thought bubble

Psychodrawing

A commonly used expressive technique is 'psychodrawing'. Respondents are encouraged to draw a brand (that is, a well known one) in order to explore which graphic elements make up its identity or to draw their feelings about a particular product category, service or brand (see Figures 8.7 , 8.8 and 8.9).

Role playing and enactment

These are both expressive techniques which we use to facilitate the expression of feelings about a brand or a commercial without having to resort to a written or oral question and answer framework. Let us describe quickly two such applications and give a few indications about how they work and what you might expect.

'Playing in' the brand is a technique where the respondents are asked to choose *one each* from the main brands in the market and to talk to a potential customer in the manner, tone of voice and language that the brand might use. So, for example, we might postulate a customer who is a young housewife whose first child is just starting to toddle and who is worried about cleanliness, hygiene, safety, and meeting with others' approval as she seeks a new toilet cleaner for her new house. Each respondent talks to her as the brand and is constantly reminded that they are role playing the brand by being referred to as 'Domestos' or 'Frish' or 'Vortex' by name. They are encouraged to stress their benefits and the competitor's weaknesses, and the consumer may ask each brand questions as it talks to her. After hearing them all she feeds back her responses to the group and the moderator. How did she feel about the 'people' she had just met? If she met them on the street, what would they look like and what would they be wearing? How would they address her?

This kind of technique works particularly well for personal products — perfumes and cosmetics, health foods, analgesics, toothpaste, toiletries and shampoo, where the end user often has some fantasized end result that may guide or determine her purchasing, but about which she dare not speak rationally. As with role playing, it is advisable to warn people of it some time before asking them to do it and most importantly of all:

1. To give them time to *practise* the role, either singly or together, just as one would rehearse for a stage performance, for at least five minutes before having to role play.
2. Wherever possible, to link the role play with a low-risk commonplace activity — call it charades in the above example; in the one below we usually introduce it as a variation on the TV game 'Give Us A Clue'.

All too often we assume the existence of brand personalities with no real evidence whatsoever. 'Give Us A Clue' is a technique that we use not only to establish the reality (or lack of it) of a brand personality, but also to throw

Figure 8.7   Cleaning your teeth: before

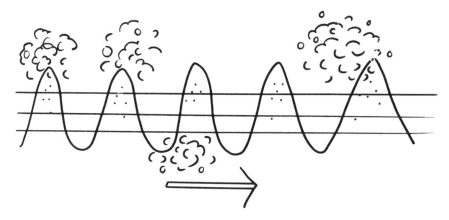

Figure 8.8   Cleaning your teeth: during

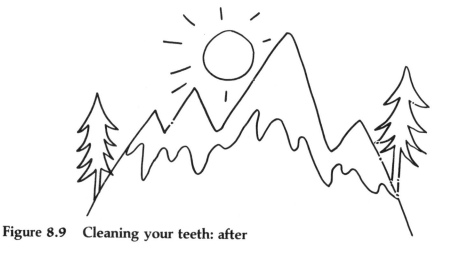

Figure 8.9   Cleaning your teeth: after

light on the nature and character of that personality. Let us imagine that we were trying to establish the brand personality of Bold washing power. The theoretical problem here is a slightly complicated one, remember that the role players will be *users* of washing powders, *not the powders themselves*. To get around this, we get two members of the group to role play the *users* of the brand under consideration and the rest of the group tries to guess the product used by these players. The role players may not mention the brand name during their role play and it may be desirable to prohibit them from talking about washing altogether. If they succeed we may ask on what basis they reached their conclusion — that is, what is it about Bold users that 'singles them out'? If they fail, or in any event, we may ask the role players what aspects of the particular women they had played related to their usage of Bold. Thus we may extrapolate from the user personality back to the brand itself. Here is how the play might work in action:

> *Moderator*: Now, we're going to have a game of Give Us A Clue. Two of us are going to act out the personalities of a typical user of a brand of washing powder and the rest of us are going to try to guess which brand it is and why.
> Who'd like to have a go at acting out? (*Pick two, if no one agrees, and send the rest away for 10–15 minutes.*)
> Then, to the two protagonists say: I'm going to show you a commercial for Bold. I'd like you to invent a 5-minute conversation between two women who might use this powder. The conversation can take place anywhere you like and you may indicate this, *but you must not mention washing or washing powder in the first couple of minutes*. The aim is to help them guess it as soon as possible. At no time may you use the brand name of the powder.

> Think about it for a moment and then let's rehearse together until we've got it right.
> After their rehearsal you may call the others back to watch the enactment.

There are all sorts of opportunities to learn at all the points along the line in this type of exercise. Do they find the idea of a Bold user conceivable in the first place? What are the key ingredients of such a user's personality? Where would she be? What would they be talking about? Do they discuss housework, holidays, divorce, romance or what? How easy is it for the others to recognise the Bold user? What gives it away — words, key phrases, body language, dress, postures, manner, prejudices. etc? What other brands/user personalities are confused with Bold? What factors separate them?

CHOICE ORDERING PROCEDURES

These involve the choice or arrangement of items that best fit given criteria like 'attractiveness' or 'meaningfulness'. This necessarily involves the presentation of more highly structured stimulus material calling forth simpler responses from the subject than most projective techniques, and lends itself best to quantitative procedures.

However, such a procedure is used almost automatically in qualitative projects. As moderators we often ask respondents to explain which things are 'most important' or 'least important' or to 'categorize', 'group', 'order' or 'rank' certain aspects of a problem, brand or service. An example of choosing appropriate words that apply to a brand of soap is included in Figure 8.10.

SOME GUIDELINES FOR THE USE OF PROJECTIVE TECHNIQUES IN MARKET RESEARCH

After our discussion we need to describe how we use projective techniques in our qualitative work. There are four main aspects to consider:

1. The suitability of various research situations for the use of projectives.
2. The method of administration of the techniques.
3. The design and structure of the techniques themselves.
4. Interpretation and analysis of results.

When to use projectives: the suitability of the situation

One of the most commonplace problems experienced by qualitative executives within our own organizations seems to centre on the decision to use projectives or not. Will they be useful or waste time? Will the client accept them? Will they produce interpretable material? Are they relevant? All of these are questions which we have faced many times. Once again, we usually try to deal with them as unique enquiries each time they occur. We try to avoid the creation of rules for applying this kind of research technique. Many factors will contribute to their appropriateness or lack of it. Not the least of these will be the researcher's own degree of comfort with the techniques and their application. As an observation based on experience, researchers work much better with projective material they have designed themselves than with material that is handed down to them.

A general rule here is the more structured the technique itself, the less formal are the rules governing its use. Word *underlining* (Figure 8.10), for example, may be used entirely informally as a pre-group warm up, as may brand associations. Projective drawing as in 'I'd like you to draw a situation in which you might use one of these' (brand or product) can work well in groups or individual interviews given a short period of warm-up and encouragement, including a chance for informants to ask questions so that they may allay their anxieties about their performance.

Where a very rich, detailed or complex *sequential* response is required as

HERE ARE SOME WORDS THAT MIGHT APPLY TO A BRAND OF TOILET SOAP. PLEASE UNDERLINE ANY THAT YOU THINK APPLY TO LUX.

LUX

SOFT
CREAMY
HARSH
GENTLE
KIND
FEMININE

MASCULINE
CHILD
OLD FASHIONED
MODERN
TRADITIONAL
PURE

ARTIFICIAL
SCENTED
SLIMY
HIGH QUALITY
BLAND
EXPENSIVE

Figure 8.10   Choosing words that apply to Lux

in open-ended responses to a series of pictures then the technique invariably functions better in one-to-one interviews. The distractions of the group situation are too great and the social conditioning is usually too strong to permit a trip into fantasy land and, hopefully, towards formerly unexpressed wishes and desires.

Both of the present writers will happily use a series of pictures with a slightly more structured task like *caption writing* and word or thought bubble completion in group discussions, but we are both aware of the distractions and the effect of the structured forms of the stimulus, (usually negative) on the quality of response. However, we judge the general energy-raising and facilitating effect of the exercise on overall group dynamics and performance to be well worth the risk in most cases.

Three dimensional techniques like object-sorting and plastecine or clay modelling, obviously contain less contamination when used in single interviews, but their play and participative value is so great that they, too, are often used in groups.

As a guide it is perhaps sensible to remember that clinical practitioners generally insist on quiet, intimate, private, one-to-one applications of projectives and this must, in some ways, represent the ideal. But we should remember that our aim is *not* the same as a clinician's; we are not going in search of unconscious material with the end aim of providing therapy for the sick or maladjusted. We may wish to make a 'diagnosis' of the responses of sorts, but we have a serious ethical responsibility to our informants not to cause them embarrassment or distress, nor to make use of interpretations of their responses without their permission. Whenever possible you should check that interpretation with them too.

Consequently, we feel relatively happy with the application of most of these techniques in groups. We are aware that we lose some degree of depth this way, potentially both in the informants' responses and in our ability to encourage his and our own interpretation of them, but we judge that in many cases the overall beneficial effects are well worth it. We have even used simple projectives like the one below at the recruiting stage too. This one has been used as part of a screening process for creativity:

> Here is a face on the left, and next to it are four blanks. We'd like you to complete each of the blank diagrams to represent a different facial expression.
> (Time limit – one minute. See Figure 8.11)

In an individual interview it is wise to try a few dummy run projectives before the real ones. The interviewer and respondent *both* do a psychodrawing or exchange thought bubbles before the respondent does the projectives most relevant for the research. Used in this way projectives work both in their own right and as facilitators in the production of rapport in the interview.

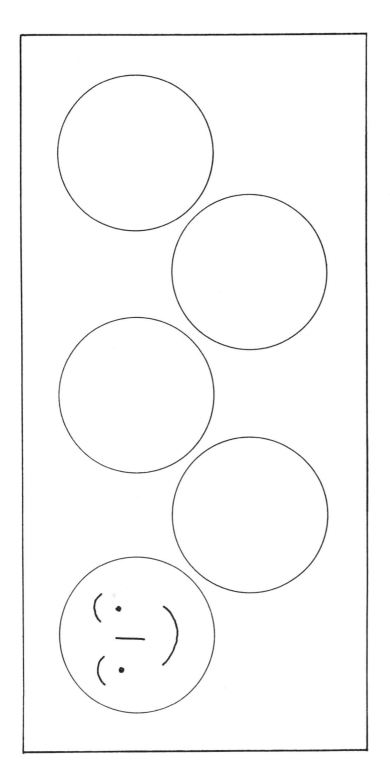

Figure 8.11 A simple creativity test – creating facial expressions

Methods of administration

Again we find ourselves referring to clinical practice for our basic guidelines and then modifying these to suit market research application. In their efforts to develop reliability and a degree of precision or at least comparability, clinicians have evolved fixed and definite methods of administration for their techniques – the more 'test' like the technique, the more rigid the rules of application. We are much more flexible than that. Generally you should remember:

(a) That it is not possible to make hard and fast rules about using projective and enabling techniques in groups. Recalling a maxim we describe elsewhere, you must work with the group so that they feel comfortable about undertaking what for them is a risky business. Why do we feel that the affair is risky? It is simple enough to understand if you relate to the potential experience from the respondent's point of view for a moment.

Most informants in market research surveys are not qualified psychologists. They are ordinary people, and for ordinary folk their experience of question and answer situations has usually been focused around producing the right, most accurate or most flattering answer. To give some examples: typical situations encountered include school lessons where the right answer was important; the doctor's surgery where an accurate description was desirable; or the job interview where a relatively flattering assessment of one's capabilities seemed like a good idea. In other words, respondents bring to bear a certain anxiety about the correctness of their answers when responding to interviewers.

(b) To tell respondents precisely what is expected from them in terms of procedure and performance. Tell them there is no right answer and that you are trying to enable them to express their feelings as well as to describe what they may do or say. Show them examples of projective drawings (using stick figures) to demonstrate that it is not a drawing test. Reassure them about spelling; that it is not important. Give them an idea of the time limit for the task (generally, not more than five minutes). Do not leave them feeling abandoned in the face of difficulty. Respond to the non-verbal signals of distress or confusion with encouragement and direction, but *do not* direct the projective material. No response from an informant is preferable to moderator-inspired projections.

(c) To try to do your projectives at a relatively uncontaminated moment. Do not let the entire group discuss washing up for ten minutes and then ask for projective drawings of it.

(d) To keep calm, do not manifest anxiety, flap or hassle. Organize the material before the group. Quite often when there's projective drawing to be done we give the drawing materials to informants during the group forming warm-up process. They keep it on their knee or nearby and feel familiar with it when the time comes to use it.

(e) As a rule *do not* use stop watches, rulers, numerical rotations or other forms of test type equipment.

(f) Keep instructions and materials simple; pencils, four or five colours at most – except where colour choice is a basic component of the projection.

(g) Remember the steep beginning of the learning curve. If the response is poor first time round, do not be disheartened. Try again with something else later in the interview or group, or regard the first attempts as a practice and encourage the participants to have another shot at it.

(h) Keep as quiet as possible during the performance. Do the task yourself if it helps you to aid them.

(i) Watch your non-verbal signals. Do not sit like an anxious teacher; relax, do not become tense with expectancy. They will become afraid of disappointing you.

(j) Avoid the temptation to peer at or inspect their efforts. *Do not* walk around behind them.

(k) Gently, after the right time, stop the exercise and then after a few seconds' pause ask someone who has seemed reasonably confident in the group to describe what they have done to you and the others. Then go to everyone else in turn and ask them to describe their efforts and explain what they mean. You can invite responses and comparisons from the group as a whole.

(l) Practise them yourselves. Do your own projections and then analyse them with your colleagues.

After completion of projection, the respondent-interviewer interaction is of vital importance. *Each respondent must own and describe her projection* to the interviewer and others present. Questions are quite permissable but attempts to 'force' or 'suggest' interpretations should be avoided.

Design and structure of the tests themselves

We have already described the basic types of techniques and their classification. We invariably design specific stimuli for different projects and this is often straightforward as, for example, with word lists, and sometimes more complicated and a little more costly in the case of pictures to be used for word bubble completion. When we design stimuli we try to keep them simple, excluding extraneous and misleading cues whenever possible. We usually try to exclude class or role stereotypes, except where these are germane to the study. In essence, the golden rule is *keep the material simple* and avoid too much detail or stylization.

An example of a design we evolved in a particular project might prove useful to illustrate the way in which successful projection may be developed. We were attempting to help a brand of cat food whose market share had been steadily declining. In the absence of any project or packaging improvements the brief was to search for a new, more relevant and motivating positioning for the brand in advertising terms. Given that a major competitor had covered virtually every straightforward claim in a long series of owner testimonial commercials, we felt compelled to explore the *owner/pet relationship itself* to look for other important properties that might have a bearing on feeding. After all, in human terms the relationship between food and love is well understood.

Initially we fiddled about with a series of drawings of owners and pets in various 'typical' situations. We put word bubbles in our drawings *emanating from the owners' mouths* and gave these to informants to fill in their own words (see Figure 8.12).

By far the majority of the responses were of the rather unhelpful 'Here kitty-kitty' or 'nice pussy' type. We retired to think again. It was while looking at his own cat at home that inspiration come to one of the researchers. Introspecting about his own thoughts or feelings during those seconds of staring at the cat, he realized that he was not wondering about what was going through his own mind - he *knew* that: he was wondering what was going through the cat's head. What was the cat thinking about him? Somehow he felt sure that the cat was thinking about him, it seemed to be gazing at him so intently!

And so we amended our projective design and made the thought bubbles come from the cats. Lo and behold, the response rate doubled, and the richness of the material quadrupled. We rapidly became aware that owners' relationships with their cats ran the whole gauntlet of feelings from mother-parent-lover-playmate, and that the telling similarity between all the relationships was their intensity. The cats themselves seemed to be open-ended stimuli of the greatest strength, on to which owners might in turn project their desired, needed or longed-for relationship. It was intensity of these relationships, manifested by the projections of the cats' thoughts and feelings, that surprised us (see Figures 8.13 and 8.14).

From our analysis of the richness of this pet-owner relationship we were able to work with copywriters and art directors on a series of scripts that built a 'true love' relationship between a 10-year-old boy and his kitten. This was a permanent relationship that was planned to develop in complexity as the cat and the boy grew older.

Analysis and interpretation

The analysis and interpretation of projective techniques is no different from the procedures involved for qualitative research in general (see chapter 10). There are no systems of scoring or tabulation. Instead the descriptions and explanations of the projections given by respondents themselves form the data base which then requires ordering and interpretation. We search for common themes, we note dialogue and language, structure, situations, colour, mood and tone.

Figure 8.12   The cat owner's thought bubble

Figure 8.13   The cat's thought bubble

Figure 8.14   The cat's thought bubble

One of the primary advantages of projective techniques is that they bring the 'unsaid' into the open.

For many people, it is impolite to make racist comments, derogatory remarks about 'poufters' or references to 'the working class' in a situation where any one of the members of the group may be insulted, so by disowning the thoughts through the medium of the projection, it surfaces as a topic for discussion in a safe way. In many of the new product development projects we have conducted, where new alcoholic drinks are being designed for young singles, the masculinity of the drinker is often called into question (see Figures 8.15, 8.16 and 8.17).

Another example where an interpretation of the projectives can help is in understanding the key elements that make up a brands' identity. In a recent study on Atora, a famous brand of suet, we asked respondents to draw the pack from memory. Their drawings clearly showed that the three horizontal bands of colour together with the confidence and dominance of the graphic style in which the brand name was shown, were the most crucial parts of the brands' identity. Modifications were made to the pack which did not interfere with these elements.

When using projectives in a group discussion, the simplest way to find out whether the projections are relevant is to ask the group, in a projective way! For example, 'if you were the manufacturer of Whizzo and you had seen these words and pictures which you have created, how would you feel? Would you feel happy about the public's view on Whizzo? Would anything worry you?

What we are saying is that we advocate a straightforward, verbal, descriptive method for analysing projectives.

Having said this, there are occasions on which more subtle clues leak out. Where you notice them (factors like proximity – distance, accompanied – aloneness, active – passive, harrassed – calm, tidy – untidy, can all provide the basis for useful probes) gently ask the informant about them, without leading. We would recommend that in no circumstances should you attempt to play psychiatrist. You are not qualified to do so, have not been invited or asked to do so, nor have you sufficient knowledge of the informants' lives to tamper with them by making pronouncements which they may take seriously.

Counting the number of occurrences of a particular posture, scene or product may be useful. Frequency of mention is always an indication that the particular response is worth further consideration.

In depth interviews the situation is slightly different (see Chapter 6). The one-to-one relationship focusses much more interviewer attention on the respondents and vice versa. This makes for a slightly tenser feeling, where respondents often feel they are under close scrutiny. Consequently, defences rise, and one is unable to encourage an open exchange of opinions and feelings. We've often found that trading disclosures is one of the best ways of overcoming this mutual suspicion.

Figure 8.15   The masculinity of the young male drinker

Figure 8.16   The masculinity of the young male drinker

Figure 8.17 The femininity of the young female drinker

IN CONCLUSION

If you feel that we have not *told* you what projective technique to use in what situation, then you have misread us. They are experimental procedures which trade potential insights for a degree of risk-taking. You must make your own decisions about whether and when to use them and design material according to our ground rules, but with which *you* feel comfortable.

NOTE

1   Lewis Yablonsky, *Psychodrama*, Gardner Press, 1981.

9 One-way mirror

The use of facilities with a one-way mirror is normal practice in the US, and is becoming increasingly popular in Europe and the UK. In such facilities observers may watch the group discussions or interviews whilst concealed behind a one-way mirror. They may see the interviewer and respondents but may not themselves be seen. The appeal is seemingly straightforward since it opens up the qualitative arena to a much broader spectrum of spectators. No longer does the client have to take it in turns to see and listen to his consumers – he, or more typically they, can witness the event first-hand. More attractive still is that the mirror allows the marketing and research departments, agency account people, creators and planners to view together and quite often discuss the implications, if not at the time, at least soon after. Quite simply then, the one-way mirror seems to offer everyone involved in the product or advertising the opporunity to get closer to the consumer – but does it really?

To regard the one-way mirror as a simple and desirable fact of life in the qualitative process is a beguiling notion, but a misguided one. The truth is that the presence of the mirror colours and affects *everyone's* perceptions of what exactly is going on. By everyone, we mean of course the respondents, but also the moderator and the viewers too. Thus, we should carefully consider exactly how and why the one-way mirror affects the qualitative experience.

THE RESPONDENTS

First the respondents. The truth is that even if it is not explained away or made light of by the moderator, respondents realize that the mirror on the wall opposite them does not simply exist as an aid to vanity. Modern rational thought dictates that most things are there for a reason – especially when the situation is so obviously contrived as the market research group. So, the respondent of even the most average intelligence knows that there is likely to be someone behind that mirror. Who, how many and why, he can only speculate. Even when the moderator appears to come clean and admits the presence of a few close friends or colleagues – is his or her suspicion really allayed? Why should he or she trust this stranger who, although trying hard to be friendly and encourage conversation is only really disclosing what is necessary? Worse still, the moderator is obviously the only person in the room who really knows the purpose of the meeting, and who will to some extent control the course of events.

This obviously contrived and rather dishonest situation intimidates even the most confident individual. If the moderator does not admit to the purpose of the mirror early on, you can bet that the most aggressive, or the archetypal dominant respondent, will confront the issue about half an hour into the group, when his confidence has built up and his position or role in the group is established, if not secure.

The point is that, on the whole, a well-behaved group plays along with the game, keeps a conspiracy of silence, and appears not to be aware of the mirror. They often even use the mirror for its legitimate purpose – smoothing the hair, fixing smudged make-up, or practising that winning smile or nonchalant pose – all, of course, to the delight of the spectators behind the mirror. But everybody knows that the mirror is there and is to some extent suspicious of the unknown behind it. Respondents might forget over time and lose them-selves in a particularly lively debate or interesting point of view, but at moments of stress, boredom and tension, that awareness is likely to resurface. These are often the critical points of a group discussion, when a respondent hesitates about disclosing a real personal view, or a less than rational feeling about a brand or product. At this point he knows he is going to be judged by his peers – i.e. the group and the moderator – but suddenly the mirror resurfaces as does the question 'Who is behind that mirror and what might they think of me?' A huge question-mark rests on this issue. It is at this critical point that the presence of the mirror might inhibit, suppress or exaggerate a true reaction.

This leads us to another fact of life – respondents come into the group and are likely to play out roles or acts until they find out what's going on. And they may, of course, switch roles at any point during the session.

On the whole, people in market research groups play 'good' respondents – they seek to please, to win the approval of both the other group members, and most importantly, of the moderator. A childish game to be played by rational adults discussing adult things perhaps – but just how often do you hear the questions 'Well, how did we do?' or 'Were we any good?' at the end of a group? Thus, 'good' respondents seek approval, as might a good pupil in school. The same analogy holds for 'bad' respondents. Like his school-child equivalent, he seeks attention from both the moderator and the group – the more attention the better. Hardly profound, but in a viewed group discussion we introduce a new but unpredictable variable. Without the presence of the mirror, both the 'good' or 'bad' respondent can assess his performance easily and accurately. He either wins the support, approval or attention of the group and moderator or he doesn't.

The feedback is immediate. Once we have a mirror and the possible presence of unspecified others, he or she can never really be sure of the reaction to his comment or opinion.

'If someone or some people are behind it, are they laughing at me, admiring me, or despising me? What should I say or do which would impress, shock or please them? What do they want from me? The respondent cannot answer his question and neither the moderator or viewers know if indeed he is asking it, or if he reaches any conclusion.

In this way, the mirror introduces a new element of uncertainty into the situation for the respondent, which might change or affect his behaviour within it. The important point for the users of his views and reactions is that with the mirror we have introduced a variable into the research, of which the consequences and effects are difficult to predict, understand or even observe.

THE OBSERVERS BEHIND THE MIRROR

Behind the mirror a different game is being played out. Very often the cast of characters behind the mirror contains people with very different, even opposing viewpoints as well as one or two casual or disinterested observers. Apart from anything else an awful lot of displacement activity goes on behind the mirror to help offset the boredom of the scene. Eating and drinking (often too much) are the norm as are respondent baiting and criticizing the moderator. The observers are usually action- or decision-oriented people who are unaccustomed to sitting silently listening to others in the semi-darkness.

Selective perception − hearing or seeing what one wants and ignoring the rest − is commonplace. Observers find themselves unable to concentrate and dip in and out of the process, often missing critical points and issues, contradictions and rationalizations.

THE MODERATOR

The moderator has the worst position of all. He or she is performing for at least two audiences, one behind, one in front of the mirror. He may feel torn between sharing with his respondents and protecting the creator's material or the client's product. What should he do? The increase in anxiety often blocks and lowers his sensitivity. He longs for the ordeal to finish.

And then, when it's all over, the moderator has to re-enter that group behind the mirror that has formed and stormed without him and, without any knowledge of that group's view he may be pressed for an interpretation and asked to justify a line of questioning. No wonder many moderators fear the mirror!

In our view it is perfectly acceptable, even desirable, for moderators to decline to produce an on-the-spot analysis. Very often these only lead to dissent among tired protagonists of one view or another. Far better to wait until the debrief when (hopefully) there has been proper time for reflection and examination or at worst to wait until the following day when a night's sleep has let the mind sort some of its impressions, fantasies and concepts.

DOES THE MIRROR INFLUENCE THE REALISM OF THE FINDINGS?

For many years it was argued in the UK that the research facility with its one-way mirror produced atypical results because of the unfamiliarity of the setting when compared to the standard UK living-room venue. After many years of agonizing both with and without the mirror, the present authors came down largely in favour of it, providing that the extra stresses and strains described above are acknowledged and considered. In our experience only the very best and most experienced moderators can cope with the added discipline of the mirror. If has taken us five years to get used to it including, in both our cases, considerable experience in the USA where the mirror is commonplace.

We should now like to list our considered opinions of the advantages and disadvantages of the research facility environment, with the one-way mirror and viewing room.

Advantages

- The group is usually already formed when it arrives. People chat on the taxi ride to the facility and once underway the group gets going very quickly.
- The professional facility is a more formal businesslike environment in which the contract of exchanging information for taking notice of opinions plus some form of incentive is much more up front.
- Respondents are removed from local considerations, gossiping about friends and neighbours, opinions and prejudice about schools, local shops or whatever.
- Both the authors always tell respondents if clients or people are watching: the ability to observe consumers is of course, of immense potential value to clients but these disclosures can cause problems (see below).
- The professional back-up in terms of facilities (tea, coffee, paper, pens, flip charts and so on) and resources (separate telephones, etc.) provides an on-the-spot flexibility not available in suburban living rooms.
- Clients may observe the non-verbal signalling as well as the verbal record.
- Respondents often enjoy the outing and the genuine courteous respect and treatment they receive in the better facilities.

- Trainees and juniors as well as clients and agency personnel may observe and, hopefully, learn about group process, dynamics, content, structure.
- Depth or paired interviews may be observed.
- It is (usually) less tiring, and there is less travelling for moderators and clients alike.

Disadvantages

- Forming which takes place before the group proper (for example, when travelling to or meeting before the group) may introduce sub-group alliances or hostilities which are unknown to the moderator.
- Clients may and do misbehave behind the mirror. Raucous laughter and banging on the mirror have been experienced by both writers.
- Respondents, especially nowadays, may become suspicious and aggressive about being spied upon. Women are more usually concerned about a sort of voyeurism – 'Who is watching me and what is he looking at?'
- The use of facilities and 'bussed' respondents is expensive. It may nearly double the direct cost per group.
- The group dynamics (since there are two groups, one on each side of the mirror) are much more complex.
- The stress on the moderator is much higher.

10 The Interpretation of Qualitative Research

One of the least visible parts of a research project is the on-going process of interpretation. From the client's point of view, nothing seems to happen until the fieldwork is completed, after which the practitioner disappears for a time, emerging at the debrief with the findings, conclusions and recommendations. The fact that this process is hidden from non-practitioners is a cause of concern for some buyers and totally without interest to others. Concerned buyers are worried about thoroughness, lack of objectivity and the ability of the practitioner to reach below what people said to understand what people meant. Unconcerned buyers are simply interested in the practitioner appearing on the right day at the right time with the results – no matter how these are obtained.

One of the most basic buyer misunderstandings about qualitative research is that the results are reached by a scientific and objective process. This is simply not the case, as we have repeatedly claimed throughout this book. Qualitative research, particularly the interpretation of what consumers said or did in the interviewing situations is not a science. There is no single truth (or series of truths) that lies buried in the tape recordings which can be excavated by a practitioner. Interpretation depends on the individual – his unique combination of personality, experience and theoretical training, as well as demographic criteria such as age, sex and socio-economic group.

Interpretation also depends on the broader context of knowledge and data that already exists, which is owned by the client company and the advertising agency. The process of interpreting qualitative research is therefore made meaningful in the context of the information which already exists, such as

- continuous research data eg. TGI (Target Group Index), retail audits, sales data, advertising tracking studies)
- the quantitative profile of the market, provided by ad hoc usage and attitude studies, omnibus studies
- past experience with the brand and awareness of future strategies or developments
- the nature of the manufacturing/service company eg. 'cautious plodder' or 'risk taker'

- the basic research problem, background, objectives and action standards (overt & covert, see p. 20)
- the researcher's historical experience with the brand, the product category or the same type of problem

There is a traditional Japanese play which involves a number of different people observing the same event. Each then provides a completely plausible but somewhat different account and interpretation of what occurred. The same is true of the interpretative process in qualitative and *also* in quantitative research.

This subjectivity of the interpretative process and its dependency on the constellation of attributes of a single practitioner should not be a source of concern or anxiety. It is the strength of qualitative research. A seasoned practitioner is an active participant in the qualitative process and his experience adds to the insights and understanding gained through his interchange with consumers, rather than detracting from it.

Another common misperception about qualitative research is the idea that interpretation forms a distinct stage in the progress of a qualitative project, following a period of passive absorption of information (see Figure 10.1).

Briefing → Fieldwork → Analysis → Interpretation → Debrief

Figure 10.1

Interpretation is an evolving, active process that begins at the first contact with the client's problem and continues through each consecutive and chronological stage of the project (see Figure 10.2). Interpretation is continuous, rather like the pattern of threads weaving through a piece of cloth. It consists of the development of rolling hypotheses which are continually being challenged and developed throughout the process. It cannot be divorced from the earlier stages of a survey. Sensitive interpretation begins at the briefing and design of the survey and is obviously very dependent on how skillfully the qualitative interviewing is conducted. It also cannot be divorced from the final stages when the findings are communicated (often a two-way process) to the buyers and users of the study.

Interpretation is *much* more than a conscious process of thinking about the study. Whilst the fieldwork is in progress or after it has been completed a subconscious process of interpretation takes place. Thoughts creep into the mind whilst driving or eating; sudden flashes of insight occur whilst involved in completely different activities, sometimes a practitioner even wakes up with new ideas or hypotheses about a particular pattern of consumer response, without being aware that it was even on the mind's agenda.

These subconscious interpretative thoughts are gold-dust to the qualitative practitioner.

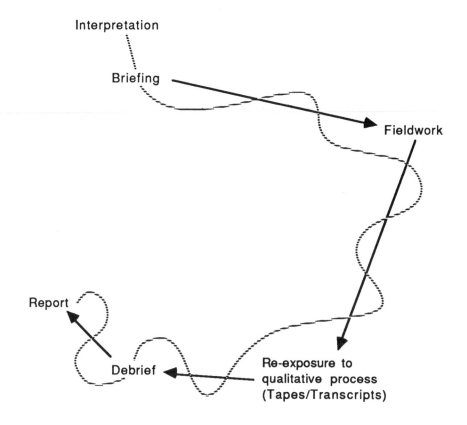

Figure 10.2

Although qualitative research *is* subjective and dynamic it is *not undisciplined*; conversely it involves a great deal of time and hard work. In addition to the continuous development and refinement of hypotheses which evolve as the project proceeds, the practitioner needs to re-immerse herself in the qualitative interviews (groups or depths) and organize or structure the content in a form relevant to the objectives of the study. This is often referred to as content analysis, which is a fair description provided the word 'content' is understood to mean the manifest content (what people said) as well as the latent content (what it all might mean — both the 'said' and the 'unsaid').

Why not rely on first impressions? After all if interpretation is a continuous process, and the practitioner is personally involved in the majority of the interviewing, why not simply write down an overview? The reason is simple — the problem of selective perception (hearing what one wants/expects to hear). This is compounded by the fact that the qualitative interviewer is taking part in a dynamic interaction with consumers during qualitative interviewing and is often more process-orientated than content-aware. Thus, there is a tendency to note and recall consumer expressions which support hypotheses expressed by the client or practitioner, or simply to notice points that support a personal point of view. This type of subjectivity is not acceptable in most market research studies unless it is particularly requested.

There is, unfortunately, no magic formula for dealing with a vast amount of unstructured information quickly. There is no short-cut. On the other hand it is not a mystical or guru-like activity beyond the reach of ordinary mortals. Interpretation involves two processes:

(a) Mechanical or functional, which involves the nitty gritty procedures of how one actually structures and organizes the data base.

(b) Interpretative, which focusses on answering the crucial questions 'What do the parts mean?' and 'How do the parts make up a meaningful whole?'

It is a well-worn cliché that 'people don't say what they mean and they don't mean what they say'. As we have pointed out in Chapter 1, the verbal record is insufficient, since it does not include the non-verbal cues to meaning, nor does it include verbal omissions. However it is the only method of allowing the practitioner to re-experience the qualitative interviews, hopefully bringing back to mind some of the covert signals that occurred.

THE MECHANICS

The only place to start is with the research objectives and issues on the one hand and the verbal record of the qualitative interviewing on the other. The verbal record can be tapes, transcripts or, increasingly, video(s) of the group discussions.

A great deal of discussion takes place amongst practitioners as to whether it's better to listen to the tapes or to read transcripts. It is our view that choice of either method or a combination of the two depends on the predisposition of the practitioner. Some people, who according to the theories of neurolinguistic programming, are *aurally*-dominant, feel more comfortable *listening* and thinking. Others, visually-dominant, cope better by *reading* and thinking. It depends on the individual, but there are strengths in each method. Listening to tapes allows the practitioner to re-experience the tone of response, the mood of the group, the process factors operating, the silences and the overall energy or lack thereof. It is far more difficult to do this from a typed transcript. The latter on the other hand, allows the practitioner to read at a fast pace, particularly when 30–40 individual depths have been conducted and to divide up the transcripts so that reactions to a particular advertisement/pack, or a discussion of a certain issue, can be read across the sample as a whole. Working from transcripts allows the practitioner to duck and dive between segments of the sample rather than necessarily dealing with each interview (group or depth) separately.

Whatever the method used, some kind of ordering or patterning of the content is required. This is not a purely mechanical process, since judgement is necessary to decide which bits or parts are worth structuring or organizing and which are not. Qualitative practitioners do not order every single item of the qualitative interview — certain parts of the content are ignored or highlighted. How this occurs will be discussed under Interpretation (see p. 138).

We shall describe two mechanical methods. No doubt there are others, but these two are likely to be the most commonly used.

Large-sheet-of-paper approach

The practitioner begins by ruling up a large sheet of paper into squares. Along the top of the sheet, in each column, are written the *key* variables by which the study was designed, such as male, female; upmarket, downmarket; North, South; users, lapsed users, and so on.

Would-be followers of this method are strongly advised to use only one of the variables, such as age *or* usership, to avoid having to write down the important points twice or more often. The other variables can be taken care of by using different-coloured pens.

Along the side of Figure 10.3 are written the most important issues of the research project. These are derived from the objectives and the way in which the interview was structured.

Whilst listening to the tapes or reading the transcripts, the practitioner transfers parts of the content into the relevant box. This transferral can take many forms, such as verbatim quotes, observations, interpretations or a précis of behaviour and attitudes. When all of the tapes/transcripts have been treated

	Current user	Lapsed user	Non-user
Awareness of brands in the marketplace			
Usage of Brand X			
Usage of Brand Y (Main competitors)			
Image of Brand X			
Image of Brand Y			

Figure 10.3

this way, the result will be a structuring or organization of the content of the qualitative interview.

Then, depending on the objectives, the structured data can be summarized and written up in a form that is both accessible to the buyer/user of the study and forms the skeleton of the final report.

The advantages of this approach are numerous:

- it brings reassuring order to chaos;
- it ensures that each transcript is treated in the same way;
- it allows two or more researchers to tackle the task simultaneously – a very important factor when analyzing 30–40 one-and-a-half hour depth interviews.

The disadvantage of this approach is that it can become mechanical. The practitioner constructs the frames prior to re-immersing himself in the data and then searches through each transcript to find the information to fit in a particular box. Insights or observations which do *not* fit into the framework are ignored, and these could be extremely valuable. The mechanics of the transferring procedure take the place of interpreting the relevance of consumer feelings and behaviour.

Annotating-the-transcripts approach

The practitioner begins by reading through the transcripts (and/or listening to the tapes) and annotating the margins. These annotations summarize relevant points *and* whenever appropriate include interpretative thoughts about them, for example:

Annotation	*Interpretation*
Majority claim product will suit teenagers/OAPs.	Symptom of alienation from product.
Spontaneous reaction to advertisement very negative.	*But* – communication is on target.

The annotations also highlight differences between the sample segments, consumer contradictions, majority and minority points of view, interesting verbatims for use in the report, differences between earlier responses and later ones (for example monadic versus comparative) or ways in which consumers 'warm-up to' or 'cool-off from' concepts, advertisements or products. The practitioner then reads down the margins at the end of the process and writes the summary for the debrief or constructs the report.

The main advantage of this approach is that each transcript is examined and understood *as a whole*, not as a series of discrete responses to particular question areas. It allows for contradictions to emerge and for the practitioner not only to analyze what respondents say but to interpret what they mean in an on-going manner, thus continuing to evolve hypotheses and understanding.

Other mechanical techniques

Although neither author uses the mechanical methods described here, we have both met practitioners who do.

Some practitioners have found computers very helpful in bringing order to chaos. A high-tech method such as this is used in many ways one of which is to classify and count the frequency of mention of a particular product attribute or brand name. It can also be used to provide an inventory of consumer language in relation to the product area or brand, the manipulations of the data leading to interesting conclusions or hypotheses.

It is our firm belief that no computer software has yet, nor ever will, replace the brain of a skilled qualitative practitioner, whose past experience and understanding of the 'said' and 'unsaid' aspects of the data, form the basis of the interpretation and recommendations.

Other practitioners, who perhaps have a strongly visual rather than verbal orientation have developed methods of mapping the information so that causal links are graphically demonstrated. This is a somewhat idiosyncratic (but no less valid in approach) way of organizing the findings but it does mean that the process may be less accessible to others such as co-researchers who may be working on the project simultaneously.

Whatever the mechanical method used, there is no short-cut. Total involvement is essential together with a system of structuring and organizing the content of the qualitative process. Practitioners all develop personal styles of doing this – would-be practitioners need to experiment.

INTERPRETATION

As we have stated, interpretation of qualitative content is more than a matter of restating what was said. The record also involves what was not said, silences, contradictions and inconsistencies, tone of voice, levels of energy or flatness of response and so on. The practitioner is required to interpret what respondents said (or did not say) and to discover what it all *means*. This is not always easy because respondents:

- are often inarticulate.
- may be ambivalent, defensive or self-contradictory.
- have not thought about why they believe what they do, or why they act in a particular way.
- may not want to admit to others or themselves how they feel or behave.
- bring beliefs about advertising and manufacturing to the qualitative interview which affects what they say they feel or do.
- feel pressurized, intimidated or simply uncomfortable in the interview situation and environment.

Notwithstanding all these difficulties, the longer one practises as a qualitative researcher, the less frightening or impossible the interpretation task seems. Common sense is the main guide. We all make sense of other peoples' conversations, behaviour and expressed or non-expressed feelings every day of our lives. For example, as human beings in socially interactive situations:

We *know* when someone is interested or uninterested, friendly or hostile, bored or curious, by their body language.

We interpret what is said by the context in which the remarks occur.

We note contradictions, inconsistencies and denials.

We listen for tone of voice, and notice whether remarks are made with enthusiasm or lack of emotional content.

We evaluate, in group situations, the effect other group members' views have on a particular person.

We listen carefully.

We make intelligent judgements about what's said or why an individual is silent in a given situation.

Exactly the same process occurs in qualitative research. It is not difficult. It is simply an application of what all of us do every day. Alan Hedges (1983) describes two levels of interpretation:

(a) Basic level — making sense of the content of the qualitative interviewing process, that is, what do people mean (as opposed to what they said).

(b) Higher level — what conclusions do we, as professionals, draw about what people meant.

For example suppose, as so often happens, respondents are shown a new advertising campaign for a brand, and they say they dislike it intensely.

At the basic level of interpretation, the practitioner has to decide if they really meant what they said and with what level of intensity. Were they influenced by the style of execution of the campaign? Did one hostile voice influence the majority? Was their hostility due to some group process component rather than directly due to the advertising?

At the higher level there is a further problem. Say one concludes that respondents were indeed hostile to the campaign. The next question to be asked is 'What does this hostility mean in relation to the objectives of the advertising?'. If the advertising clearly communicated the main message and appeared to have impact, does it matter that respondents did not like it?

At this second level a number of factors become important:

- The objectives of the study (covert rather than overt);
- The objectives of the advertising/pack design/new product;
- The level of experience the practitioner has in similar product fields or types of research;
- The role of the practitioner.

At the higher interpretative level, the covert objectives of the study become crucial. The practitioner needs to keep the overt and covert objectives in mind in contextualizing what respondents meant in the particular research study in question. Are the objectives described in words such as 'describe', 'demonstrate', or 'detail' or are they described in words such as 'evaluate', 'understand', 'explain', 'provide guidance'? The more the practitioner is required to 'judge' rather than simply 'describe', the more likely the subjectivity of the interpretation.

Subjectivity is *not* a dirty word, but an inherent part of the qualitative process. Different qualitative practitioners have different backgrounds — both academic and experiential, which provides a conversion mechanism through which 'what respondents said' is converted into 'what respondents meant' and furthermore 'what conclusions or action this indicates'. Practitioners usually work in a wide variety of product fields as well as specializing in certain types of research study such as NPD, early creative development research, pack designs or press advertising, to name but a few. A process of cross-fertilization takes place, so that what has been learned about what consumers meant in a particular product field or research problem can be enormously enriching when analyzing what they meant in a different product field. Thus depth of knowledge and experience underlies the 'subjectivity' of a qualitative practitioner. Experienced researchers intuitively know that when consumers say that they 'never watch ITV' or that 'they always read the ingredient list on the back of a pack', the respondent is making a statement about who she is in relation to the other group members (that is, 'I am a discerning viewer' or 'I am in touch with healthy eating') rather than necessarily accepting the statement at face value.

In addition to the study objectives, practitioners need to understand the objectives set for the advertising, the pack or the new product. Surprisingly often, clients believe that such information is of no use to the practitioner and it is not offered at the briefing. In our view it is crucial. How can one conclude the importance or otherwise of what respondents meant about an advertisement, pack or new product unless one has a benchmark for evaluation? Interpretation does not occur in a vacuum. It is only sensitive, action-orientated and relevant if it takes place against the backdrop of advertising and marketing objectives.

This brings us to the last point — the role of the qualitative researcher.

We have described alternative ways of reviewing and organizing the data and a notion concerning a couple of levels of interpretation and we have yet to face up to the most difficult and tenuous aspect of the whole process: the internal psychological process of examining and understanding the meaning of what took place during the interview. How do we do this? How does it work? We aim to offer a general theory of how the process works and then to suggest a couple of specific mental techniques[1] that we have taught with success in our own organizations for you to try out for yourself.

Returning to the more esoteric field of psychoanalysis for a moment, it is a widely accepted belief that the subconscious mind contains a pretty accurate record of everything that has ever happened to us and that elements of the mind 'work' on this record to shape its meaning. Uncomfortable parts or occurrences are repressed or distorted, just as in ·the 'bad' group where it is so difficult to remember anything about it — after all, nothing happened did it?

Reinterpretations or new shades of meaning are then grasped by the conscious, which attempts to implant them indelibly inside the awareness as the true record of what went on. And so, by the time we come round to sitting down and thinking about the fieldwork, some interpretations will already have been made. They may be appropriate, instructive and insightful but they may just as equally be distorted, false and inappropriate. We must find out which.

Just simply revisiting the ideas above for a moment allows us to see that we have a new addition to our armoury of interpretive weapons. In addition to the tape recordings, transcripts, content analysis, whatever, we now have the notion of a *complete, internal psychological version of what went on.* The best idea seems to be to compare the two and look for accord, discord and a sense of synergy or, conversely, disharmony between them. Of course, this is much like what actually happens when you play the tapes or read the transcripts. As you do so you revisit the group at an emotional level.[2] Depending on your own psyche, you may play your psychological re-run as pictures, voices, movements or mixtures of all three. This is the point at which you must relax. Once the psychological tape has begun to run, in whatever medium, *let it roll.* Don't get anxious and start worrying 'Did that really happen?': let it happen.

We'll check back over it for validity in a moment. Again we find ourselves at a point in the qualitative process where anxiety can spoil everything. By all means be a little anxious about getting the best interpretation for your client — that's what he's paying you for and it will spur you on — but don't be anxious about your competence or ability to make an interpretation; believe in it, and go for it.

Now that the tape is rolling you will re-experience elements of the group at a very profound level. You may see a series of flashbacks or hear snippets of conversation or see 'important' body language. Don't force it, let it run to its natural conclusion and then look back over it. What was going on? Were process factors or task defences at play? Is this straight talking we're hearing? What is the psychological climate like — the emotional atmosphere in the room? If you ever wonder whether you're experiencing a true version of what happened or not, become aware of your own body as you replay the tape. You'll find yourself re-experiencing the postures, facial expressions, heart-rate, eye movements and so on of that time back there when you were in the group.

Now that you have re-run the tape, what sense of meaning do you get when you look at the visual, or listen to the auditory, record? If you have a clear feeling about that then annotate it. If it's unclear this usually has one of two different meanings: if the feelings are indistinct and shallow then probably nothing much was going on worthy of interpretive intervention and you may rely on the verbal record. If they are indistinct *yet intense* then almost certainly something of sufficient importance to work through was going on. So very often we have unlocked the door of new insight which has shaped a whole study by revisiting these intense, fuzzy moments!

Fortunately for us, the subconscious tends to arrange these feelings or sequences in order of importance and that's the hidden work that gets done between the interviewing and the formal construction of the analysis. So as a rule you may start by actually replaying the first detailed sequences that come to mind and be fairly likely to strike gold. At the very worst you'll re-energize your experiences of the fieldwork.

Returning to our pyschological run-through, we were left with the problems of intense but indistinct feelings about what was going on. How may we shed light on that? We've found the technique of *changing perspective* a most useful and illuminating one for dealing with this problem. Look at Figure 10.4 for a moment.

Of the two vertical lines, AB or CD, which is in front for you? Whichever it is, look intently at the figure and change perspective until the *other* two lines appear to be at the front. You'll notice several things about this exercise. Firstly, that you've done nothing more than look at the data from a different point of view — yet *everything* has changed its orientation and meaning. One moment you're looking *up and under* something, next you're looking *down on* something. Secondly, notice how absolute or fixed the change can seem. How could you have seen it any other way? It seems so right like this. Imagine for a moment how fixed the way that you may have been looking at the data from the group interview might have been. Now let's change perspective on that.

Going back to the re-run snippet or sequence, it's time to replay it. Whether it was a 'film clip' or 'sound track', some people, speakers or others in the group, will have dominated it. Look around the group *in your mind's eye* — who else can you see or hear? Does anyone look fuzzy or sound indistinct? If they do in your mind's eye then turn up the sharp focus on this individual until they emerge *clearly* and watch their actions, listen to their utterances or words. What were they experiencing: what does their body language say? What has happened to the rest of the group? How has the balance of things changed? What do you now feel about what was going on? Looked at through this new central figure's eyes, what did they feel about it? What are you feeling as you replay the tape from this new perspective?

Sometimes a third or fourth person springs into view and you may repeat replay until you have exhausted all changes of perspective. Things will be clearer now that the relative significance of events has been explored. You've experienced several levels or types of experience, you're free to choose the most salient one or combination of two or more.

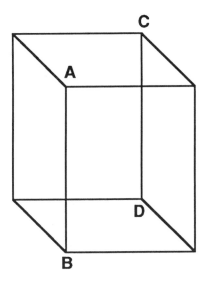

Figure 10.4

One of the marvellous things about this technique is that it only takes
a few seconds to do, although several minutes to explain or read about, and
some hours and hours of practice. But you don't need a group discussion
to practise, you can do it *anywhere*, choosing as a subject something from
your recent past, distant past or even in the present. Look at several people
in a meeting and deliberately transfer your level of rapport from one to another.
You'll find that the whole climate changes each time. Since it helps us towards
finding the most appropriate framework for our interpretation, we call this
technique *interpretive reframing*.

Another advantage lies in the fashion in which application of the technique
changes the form but not the content of the data. Going back to Figure
10.4 for a moment, let's imagine that an interpretive task is to determine
what's inside the box. Our changing perspective technique has now enabled
us to view the box from two angles rather than one. Merely reorganizing
our data has potentially doubled its power. Looking at two views separately
and then perhaps together may give us a huge increase in resolution and
hence information about the box. The top and the bottom may have different
patterns on them which when added together offer some clue to the contents
which neither alone could do.

To extend the analogy for a moment, we could pick up the box and rattle
it to see what sound it made — here in a real example we might be adding
the audible record to our picture of what was going on in the group. What
happens if we speed the conversation up, or concentrate on a different speaker?
We further increase our power of resolution on the raw data.

It is important to remember that the contents of the box have not been subjected to any manipulation whatsoever. In no way have we transformed, tampered with or injected any fanciful thinking into these. We have merely altered the way in which we study the data, thereby increasing our ability to make deductions about its inner contents or meaning. This, then, is one way of honestly recounting what occurs in the pursuit of meaning in qualitative interpretation.

Understanding confusion

In some way confusion is a special problem, since its source is so often obscure, yet so often does it represent a blind, behind which lies something of such importance that it is worthy of exploration. Looking back on a confused group (that is, where either you or the respondents were confused), go through the replay technique and when you come to the first instant of confused experience, stop. Who looks or feels confused? What has changed? Does some form of explanation (even if you didn't do it at the time) make any difference? Offer it to the group in your mind and see what happens. In other words, even at the psychological level, *try something new*, don't just repeat what happened over and over again. You already know that it's confusing, if you repeat it you'll get more and more confused. If you practise this, you'll become quicker to spot and deal with respondents' confusion in the actual group which is much better than trying to understand it afterwards. After all you can only surmise the reasons for it after the event; it's preferable to deal with it at the time.

This brings us to the point that most people have a completely inappropriate way of dealing with confusion in qualitative data. They regard confusion as a threatening, disorganized, vulnerable state. But it is not really like that at all. Being confused about something is not the same as 'not understanding' something. You don't understand many things, often because you don't know anything about them — brainwave patterns or nuclear physics, for example. You're not confused about them: you don't know about them. Confusion, looked at another way, always indicates that you are on the road to understanding something. You already have a body of data but haven't yet found the right way to organize it to create meaning or sense from it.

This sounds all too familiar a dilemma for the qualitative worker in pursuit of meaning from his findings. Now we're going to offer a technique for helping you to understand your confusion that we've used often. It doesn't always work and when it doesn't we try something different (like going down the pub) — but more often than not it does work on standard problems where the data has been collected reasonably well. Since, like the interpretive reframing, this technique involves no distortion of content (i.e. the record) *at all*, we merely change the arrangement of the raw components; it violates *none* of the rules surrounding the distortion or 'falsifying' of data or results. The best way we ever heard it described was as being like when you move a log on a dying fire and suddenly new flames spurt forth. You've added nothing to the fire and taken nothing away, but things are different.

To start with you must go inside your mind and re-run the sequence or series of events that confused you. Forgetting the content for a moment, what was being said or done, how does the situation appear, sound or feel to you? If a series of pictures, is it blurred or fuzzy? If a sound record, is it hard to hear or distorted in some way? If feelings or impressions, is it fleeting or imprecise? In whichever modes of experience you sense your experience of the confusion, hold it there. How does it look/sound/feel? Actively form a freeze frame or repeat loop of that moment. Don't worry about content, you'r just replaying the *form* of the confused experience.

Now try to think of a similar occasion, try another group of a similar age/sex grouping (it doesn't matter on what subject; only the form of the situation is important) during which your feeling of understanding the group was great. Re-run this experience in your mind. How do the two experiences differ? *Not in content but in form?* For example is one fuzzy and indistinct, the other sharp and clear? Is one a free-wheeling film sequence and the other a series of blurred stills? Is one vital and full of feeling and the other dull and lifeless? Whatever it is, it's the difference in the form of the two experiences that you must try to notice. When you've done this, *try to re-run the confused experience in the form in which you experienced the clear one.* If the clear one was a film then try to run the confused one that way. If the clear one was a distinct sound track then try to run the confused one that way. You're only trying to make the processes the same; we're not attempting a reconstruction of meaning. As you do this, if you succeed (and you should after practising a couple of times), you'll experience whatever feeling of clarity you first experienced in the good group situation becoming attached to the confused situation. It will appear more clearly, you'll be more relaxed and you can examine its significance more easily.

The idea underlying this is really very simple. It's simply that when we leave a group discussion we already have enough information in order to understand its meaning. More often than not we have too much, but it's very poorly organized and so feels like a little rather than a lot. We've been trained to cope with a feeling of confusion by getting more data in order to solve our problem, so in the next few groups we ask even more questions, get even more data and become even more confused. Does this sound familiar? It should. There are often far too many questions asked in group discussions. Qualitative researchers themselves are responsible for bringing all this about. Most people's picture of confusion will contain a huge collage or jumble of images, all frenetic and higgledy-piggledy. By contrast their picture of understanding will be clear, well-organized, *even spare in detail.* Almost always, in our experience, you generate too much data. Don't just keep asking more questions. If the answers just contain raw data they won't add anything, and you'll feel you have to keep on asking. Take time to start organizing the data you have as you go through the study, using both the practical and the psychological techniques we've described. If, once you've done this, you still need more data, then we guarantee you one thing – you'll know for certain what questions you need to ask and why.

INTERPRETATION IN ACTION: SOME EXAMPLES OF USING A THEORETICAL FRAMEWORK

Transactional analysis

Around 1980 we started the search for a more coherent interpretive system that would enable us to work with a number of different levels of experience from conscious rational processes through to more hidden fears and fantasies. It was also a requirement that the system should be capable of explaining conflict or at least of describing it in a realistic fashion. Consumers often have complex relationships with cars, diet food, banks or travel companies, being rational about them at one moment and emotional at the next. Both fact and fantasy seemed to be important in prompting people's behaviour.

We found just such an interpretative system in transactional analysis (TA). With its brilliant flexibility and its range from simple explanations to the most profound, it proved ideal. In that so much of consumer behaviour is based upon transactions, it seemed custom-made for our needs.

It is possible to use TA in groups and interviews, but this is often time-consuming and can be laborious. It's as an analytical and interpretive tool that it really comes into its own, and we will concentrate on those uses here.

Firstly we began to apply the structural analysis of the 'ego states' to the area of consumer decisions. The three ego states are the Parent, Adult and Child, and they are typically depicted as in Figure 10.5 overleaf.

Each one of the three has a special place in our psyche, and they may be used singly or in combination. We may flick quickly from one to the other and they may 'talk' to each other in our minds. Our Parent may encourage or rebuke our Child. Our Adult may give our Parent information as the basis for a judgement. Sometimes the states get mixed together and this produces a contamination. Parent/Adult contaminations result in prejudice. Adult/Child mixtures produce delusions. From person to person, the different strengths of their ego states will produce noticeable differences in personality. People can be overly parental, stuck in their Adult, or playful or sulky in their Child.

Well-balanced people tend to utilize all three ego states, switching easily from one to the other when appropriate.

Products and services have dominant ego states too. Banks are Parental

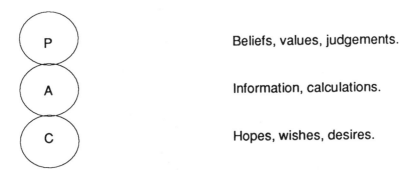

Figure 10.5

with Adult overtones; they have very little Child. This is why we often feel oppressed or impressed by them. Computers are Adult, as are calculators, and some of us find them boring, others are fascinated and play endlessly with them with child-like glee. Toys and games are usually in the Child, whether they're for children or not, although complex games like chess require the combination of all three ego states.

Advertisements aim to trigger our desires, and so often attempt to engage our Child ego states. They may do this by being playful, exciting, colourful or witty. Sometimes they like to appear Parental – particularly when offering us reassurance. Others appear as entirely Adult or information-based, but since our Adult ego state is not a source of our motivations, most Adult-type ads have Parent or Child components too – an authorative voice-over, bright colours or a witty thought.

In our general experience, the best advertisements engage all three ego states at once. This maximizes the interaction with the viewer and increases the chances of getting his or her interest. Quite often, when we are researching commercials and we discover a weakness, it can be pinned down to the absence of one ego state or the excess of another. Commercials may be too playful or too serious, too silly or too patronizing.

When analyzing a commercial's appeal, or lack of it, we would outline the transactions between the commercial and the consumer as Figure 10.6.

A figure such as this might represent a hypothetical commercial for a new toy at W.H. Smith. The solid lines represent the overt transactions – the manifest aspects of the commercial. The dotted line is a covert transaction – a hidden, latent message in the commercial, imbued or implied by tone of voice or details of execution. A very good example of latent communication are certain Proctor and Gamble washing-powder commercials which appear rational ('We took this shirt, cut it in half and washed one half in X, the other in Y') but in fact are experienced by consumers as bossy and patronizing.

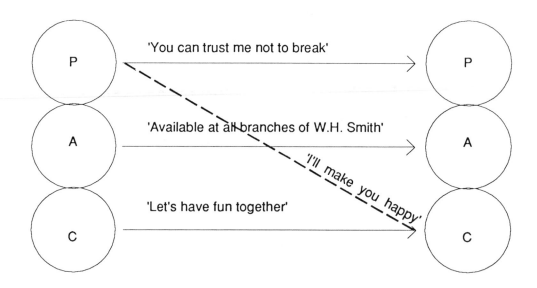

Figure 10.6

This is what is called in TA the 'pseudo-Adult' and refers to Parental instructions which pretend to be Adult information.

Another aspect of TA has helped us to understand the patterns in consumers' lives. This particular understanding is derived from the area of *script analysis*. Our scripts are the underlying rules and messages which influence and may govern our behaviour. They contain all of the permissions, injunctions, discounts and adaptions passed on to us by our parents. Some scripts are tragic, most lead to fortunate and unfortunate repetitions of patterns of behaviour of one kind or another, and two consumers' scripts which describe two different types of consumer follow as examples.

'They're all made by the same people anyway'

Manifesting as a rational, in-the-know observation on life, this is usually a pseudo-Adult position which superficially overlays a lot of Parent-Child injunctions. Typically Parent instructions which would facilitate the foundation of such a script are:

  'They're all out for what they can get'
  (Either men, manufacturers or whatever).
  'Don't believe in fairy stories'.
  'You get owt for nowt'.

Such a child would tend to doubt the existence of Father Christmas early in life and come to view the world from an Adapted Child which was full of suspicion. What seems like a rational standpoint actually borders on the paranoid: If you believe that the whole world is a con ('They're all made by . . .') then *nothing* may be trusted and you must be constantly on the look-out or be on guard. Adopting such a position leads to the suspicious, intransigent, typically working-class consumer who's always trying to beat the system or waiting for a bargain to fall off the back of a lorry.

The discomfort of this script leads to three common escape routes:

Bargain hunting

Spanning market stalls to carpet warehouses, cut-price holidays, betting on the pools or the horses, these are the attempts to get something for nothing and beat the system. Since this is a searching-out process, lines like 'Watch out for' or 'Be on the look-out for' are very motivating, as is 'Beat the Budget' or 'Buy one, get one free'. Essentially, anything that evokes the 'Aha, I've spotted a bargain!' or 'I've beaten the system' will appeal here.

Fantasy

If everyone's out to con you, then you might as well do something pleasant while you wait for the bills to arrive. Confectionery lines like Bounty pick this feeling up well (note the resemblance to 'bargain hunting' in the Bounty Hunters), as do holiday advertisements and all other advertisements which offer a pleasant fantasy as an imprecation to buy the product. At a superficial level, the John Smith's Bitter advertisement. may be witty, but it is also pretty obviously about getting one over on the scheming woman who is out to prevent you from enjoying yourself. Escape into fantasy also obviates the need for thinking about manufacturers ('Them') who make the products (for the likes of 'Us'). This is brilliantly demonstrated by the Japanese tape cassette advertisements which, by offering fantasies about the experience you'll have when you switch on, avoid the potentially boring or irrelevant implications of Japanese cassette tape functional claims.

Hoarding

One of the most positive adaptations of bargain hunting developed with the opening of the cash-and-carries and the retail warehouses. These places rapidly filled with 'They're all made by' type people, hoarding by bulk purchasing items that they would be bound to use anyway − or so their reasoning went. A couple of retailers have traded extremely profitably on this 'bargains galore/ change your whole life' kind of appeal − notably the carpet superstores, B & Q, Texas Homecare and MFI. The level of hysteria in these shops crackles through the air like electricity.

Nonetheless, for the 'They're all made by' type of person, this type of behaviour does represent a positive adaptation. Occasionally it gets out of control and becomes a spending spree, followed by a visit from the repossession agents.

Of course, supermarkets' own brands, the major new force in High Street retailing, are built upon precisely the assumption that their own brands are made by the big manufacturers anyway.

'Mum knows best . . .'

Almost *the* favourite consumer script, much beloved of advertisers and consumers alike. In its origins in the psyche, the script is much concerned with striving for perfection, issues of right and wrong and good and bad, as they affect the struggle to achieve the Perfect Life. At an even deeper level, much of this perfect behaviour is, of course, directed towards avoiding death or the fear of death – after all, the promise of *everlasting* life is open to all those of us who strive to be good. As you may guess, Perfect Mum is often a culmination of a fairly conventional Catholic, Jewish or Church of England upbringing.

She is, too the Perfect Woman of the commercials. There is never chaos in her house, her children are always clean, everything is supremely organized, there is plenty of food on the table, and everyone has clean (new) clothes. She is the role model that much of our early upbringing and virtually all of 1970s advertising urged us to emulate. Words like: best, perfect, efficient and absolutely proliferate in advertising that strives to reach her.

Unilever in particular have used her as the inspiration for much of their work on Oxo, Persil, Comfort, Flora and Birds Eye, where mum is the hub of the family, bestowing wisdom, love and bounties (of one sort or another depending upon the product field) at the centre of it all.

More recently she's changed. During the 1970s all of her perfect behaviour was directed towards the satisfaction of *others* ('Give unto others'). One effect of the women's liberation movement in terms of emancipation is in the home, and the portrayal of the stereotype of Perfect Mum is that she now has permission to *do things for herself*. In recent work, both from Oxo and Persil (the originators of Perfect Mum above all other brands), mum still knows best but she has permission to (and does) use that knowledge to her benefit rather than for the family's. She chides them for attempting to stereotype her or coerce her into satisfying their whims, and leaves them to get on with it while she does her own thing. Nevertheless, this new mum still behaves in a morally appropriate way – she is 'good' for them, she does not spoil them and ruin their character and competence to become independent beings – just as she has. The most brilliant summation of this is the recent Persil 'Out on the Streets' film.

Another example of this is the new Comfort work where the advertising attempts to encapsulate a sequence of perfect textural sensations: the feeling of the wind by the shore and soft fabric on your face, the sensation of flying with your clothes spread like wings behind you, or twirling like a dancer. Each is in itself an expression of intimate textural perfection offered not to the family, but to 'mum' herself.

'Mum Knows Best' is not about comparison of better or worse, it is about absolute confidence as expressed in 'Beanz Meanz Heinz' or 'Hovis : as good today as it's *always* been' or 'A diamond is *forever*'. In the world of moral perjoratives there are no shades of grey; there is only right and wrong.

It can, as any script may, go wrong and the most obvious negative evocation of 'Mum Knows Best' or Perfect Mum is – you've guessed it – Plastic Woman. If described insensitively, Perfect Mums become Plastic Women, manifestly living their lives according to a programme which they neither question nor understand. Examples of this include the film 'The Stepford Wives' or the portrayal of the mother in the Lenor advertising where she tours the house having little 'thoughts' as she picks up everyone's cast-off clothes, or the dumb women acquiescing to the male voice-over as it instructs them in appropriate behaviour from on high.

The mini-scripts

These are smaller, simpler versions of scripts which give rise to constantly recurring segments of behaviour or attitude. There are commonly agreed to be five main mini-scripts:

Be perfect

Much concerned with right and wrong and moral judgement, Be Perfect is often obsessed with efficiency and organization. Much of the advertising for household cleaning products has a strong Be Perfect element – whiter-than-white washing, floors you could eat your dinner off. The inclusion of the word 'perfect' itself is a sure indicator of the presence of this mini-script – a perfect cup of coffee, perfect pizza, perfectly square thin mints; all are examples here.

Be strong

Super-rational, controlled, dutiful and emotionally withdrawn. Manifesting as supreme reason, Be Strong may appear dogmatic if somewhat cold. Be Strong appears very sure of its facts – Domestos is a good example here, as was the role played by Arnold Schwarzenegger in *The Terminator*. A robotic or monotonous tone or appearance is a Be Strong characteristic. Be Strong things are made to last and can be dropped without breaking, like Volkswagens.

Try hard

Longing to be successful: it is very concerned with status and words like superior, better and best. Any advertisement which guarantees success or money back if not satisfied has a strong appeal to Try Hard people. They love a gamble and are desperately afraid of failure. Advertisements offering to cure your speech defects or make you a millionaire overnight are Try Hard. The best example of Try Hard advertising around right now is the television commercial for coffee which parodies a situation where a woman imitates the noises made by a percolator while making coffee for her guests. Although intended as a joke this lovely commercial exemplifies the 'Try Hard' antics.

Please

Determined to be NICE: he, or more typically, she, is desperate to conform, to be one of the decent folk that make up the silent majority. She wants to be fashionable but not to stand out in a crowd. She's a bit reluctant to ask for anything for herself and has great difficulty in showing her true feelings – or any real feelings at all. Combined with Be Perfect, she shops at Marks & Spencer. Have a nice day! is about the most pleasey commonplace remark.

Hurry up

About running away from things: many convenience products are Hurry Up – they're quick and easy, like Pot Noodles. The harrassed housewife is under the influence of Hurry Up, waiting to be soothed or relieved by the product or service. At McDonald's we've got time for you is an excellent example of an appeal to Hurry Up. In fact, McDonald's is so Hurry Up that its promise is 'no waiting' and in many outlets the seats slope downwards so that you don't sit on them for too long! The DHL advertising for its express delivery service is also a good example of the evocation of Hurry Up feelings.

Life scripts

Most recently we have also become interested in 'life scripts' and how these influence our life-positions and the things we buy and use.

In this next section we consider the Timotei advertising from the point of view of life scripts. Quite obviously the commercial is a romanticized fantasy – a kind of fairy story, so let's break down the elements of the script. We open on a young innocent, blissfully preparing her hair and communing with nature while she dresses. A parental voice whispers soothing, reassuring, wish-fulfilment-type messages to her as she carries out her grooming. Lo and behold, from the very spot into which she was a moment ago brushing her hair, a young man emerges on the screen and they go off into the sunset together. Apart from the magical implications (that brushing your hair will make men appear), there is a well-established life-script for this story. It's called Little Princess.

Little Princess is quite a common script in women, quite well-known as Jewish Princess, or identified by such phrases as: 'Who does she think she is?' 'Anyone would think she was royalty' 'She's giving herself airs and graces, isn't she?'

Usually it's created by daddy, who indicates to his precious little daughter that one day he'll come along (the man she loves), but that almost certainly he won't be good enough for her! Inevitably, most girls don't grow up to be princesses, yet never lose these coded instructions from their parents or the fantasies that arise from them. In later life, Little Princesses usually develop either a variant of a Waiting Script (the most tragic version of which is an Old Maid) or an If Only variant. 'If only I'd waited to get married' or 'I only took it up as a temporary thing . . .' Both of these are essentially tragic scripts imbued with a strong desire to escape back to the fantasy of being a Little Princess again. 'If only I'd never grown up'. Is it at this unconscious level that Timotei really exerts its pull, enabling those of us who wish it to return to the Little Princess of our childhood when we use the product and to feel safe in daddy's arms again as often as we wish?

INTERPRETATION IN ACTION

Example 1: The use of consumer vocabulary to reach an interpretation of the dissonance between a new product idea and the dynamics of a market

In view of the restrictions on cigarette advertising and the current vast expense of sports sponsorship, a tobacco manufacturer wanted to explore the possibility of increasing the opportunities for brand exposure and image-building through franchising the use of one of its major cigarette brand names on a range of men's toiletries.

Qualitative research in the form of group discussions amongst male users of toiletries (aftershave, soap, deodorant) was commissioned. Respondents were all smokers but the fact that this was a relevant criterion had been masked on recruitment. The first part of each discussion began by exploring attitudes to men's toiletries, using aftershave as the starting point. Respondents were given a large range of aftershaves to 'map', being requested to group them into categories in any way they wished so that each category consisted of brands similar to one another. Whilst doing this simple task, respondents were encouraged to talk to one another about the reasons for placing a brand in one category or another. During the ensuing chat the female moderator was struck by the extent and richness of vocabulary men used to classify the 20 brands.

After the research study had been completed, the transcripts were combed to produce as comprehensive a list as possible of the words used by male consumers in talking about aftershave. The vocabulary proved to be *no different* from that used by women when discussing perfume products. This led to the interpretation that in the 1980s men use aftershaves exactly like women use perfumes – to enhance, refresh and provide confidence, and for this reason subtlety, sophistication and individuality of smell are the key criteria which differentiate aspirational brands from the others.

The incompatibility of this perfume requirement with a new product branded with the name of a famous type of cigarette was, with its associations of stale tobacco smells and social negativity, deep and insurmountable. The recommendation was to avoid any product area where perfume was a key motivator.

Example 2: The use of typologies to develop a positioning for relaunching a brand of instant coffee

During the course of numerous qualitative advertising studies (strategy development, creative development, pre-testing) which were conducted in the early 1980s, we noticed a repetitive pattern of response. Someone in nearly every group discussion whatever the subject would say 'I think the ads are better than the programmes nowadays'. This statement would be met with agreement by some members of the group who cited examples of current TV advertisements (which incidentally had also received positive comment in the trade press) whilst others strongly disagreed. Because of the repetitive nature of these comments and the fact that they emerged when the group discussions were 'performing' rather than 'forming' (see Chapter 3), we began to take this seriously as evidence of a trend rather than simply posturing remarks. We isolated a number of types of consumers in terms of their attitudes to advertising, the two main types being Advertising Appreciators and Advertising Rejectors. The main problem with advertising rejectors in early creative development research is that the negative and hostile opinions they hold towards advertising interferes with the development task.

The philosophy 'why don't they stop advertising and take money off the product' is extremely destructive in trying to understand how a commercial might reward its viewers – not only in its content, but in its *form*.

One of our clients, an advertising agency, took the concept of differing levels of advertising sophistication amongst consumers to its ultimate. In examining the instant coffee market in the mid-1980s (UK), consumers expressed boredom with the advertisments, criticizing them severely for being patronizing or predictable. The agency (Still, Price Court, Twivy, D'Souza) on behalf of its client Brooke Bond Oxo decided to create a campaign for Red Mountain which was aimed at 'sophisticated appreciators' of advertising. Group discussions were recruited which in addition to coffee-drinking criteria, excluded all those who through the use of an attitude statement battery, were advertising rejectors. A highly unusual and impactful campaign was thus developed with the help of consumers who were sophisticated about advertising styles and content and who enjoyed good compaigns. Interestingly, the Red Mountain campaign has been applauded by consumers and the industry alike and has helped the brand to move from minor to major league.

NOTES

1. The techniques described later in this chapter borrow heavily from the practices of NLP as described by Richard Bandler and John Grinder. Nonetheless they provide a very accurate description of the processes which we have evolved and applied to our studies over the years. It was edifying to discover that NLP practitioners had furthered the understanding of these sorts of procedures. A full list of texts on NLP is given in the bibliography.
2. We're talking mainly about group interviews where the problems of shades of meaning are so much more complicated, but this 're-run' technique works equally well for depth interviews.

11 Recruitment

The subject of recruitment of respondents for qualitative group discussions or interviews has long been an issue in the UK market research world. Depending on whether one is a research buyer or practitioner, recruitment elicits a range of responses from intense concern about standards of recruitment to lack of interest in issues which have been discussed repeatedly over the past ten years, with no apparent resolution.

There are two main sources of standards of recruitment in the UK, one published by the Market Research Society (MRS) and the other by Association of Users of Research Agencies (AURA). Both are concerned with detailing minimum standards of good recruitment, summarized by Feldwick and Winstanley (1986) as follows:

1. The required number of respondents should turn up on time for the group.
2. The respondents should be on quota.
3. Respondents should ideally have never been to a group discussion and certainly not in the last year/six months and/or a limited number of times in the past.
4. Respondents should not know each other.
5. Respondents should be unknown to the recruiter.
6. Respondents should not know the subject of the discussion.
7. Respondents should be randomly recruited.

Feldwick and Winstanley discuss each of these points in turn, critically examining the real contribution of each point to good recruitment. They conclude, and we concur, that only points 1 and 2 are crucial on every single recruitment occasion, whilst point 3 is debatable, as will be discussed later in this chapter. Points 4–7 were considered by the authors to be an attempt to avoid cheating and bad practice such as that satirized by Abbott (1975) in 'Oh, didn't know you was in on this one Ethel. Haven't seen you since shampoos last Tuesday', but are not based on anything other than conventional wisdom. Above all, the authors conclude with the plea for openness and flexibility, if it is not feasible to recruit a group within impossible time restraints, recruiters should be encouraged to ignore any of points 3–7 *provided the quota requirements are rigidly and obsessively met*. To anyone interested in the policies and practice of recruitment which is highly relevant to contemporary qualitative research, we recommend the Feldwick and Winstanley article.

In this chapter we propose to address recruitment from a different perspective, that is *the recruitment experience* as it affects recruiters, respondents, moderators and buyers. Each of the four participate in the recruitment experience, each affect the experience of the others and each has different needs and expectations surrounding this event.

Table 11.1 summarizes some of the positive and negative attitudes and expectations that each of the four participants experience during recruitment *or* in the early stages of a group discussion. A glance across the columns shows that only a few aspects of the experience are similar across the four types of people, and that each comes to the experience with a unique set of attitudes. The more that we can all understand how the others feel, the more likely we are to make the recruitment experience positive rather than negative.

THE RECRUITER'S VIEWPOINT

In order to improve relationship between management and recruiters, one of the authors conducted a survey in 1984 amongst the company's field interviewers to find out motivations underlying choice of this work. The findings (unpublished) revealed that married women chose this type of job for a number of reasons. High on the list was the opportunity to meet people without the pressure of selling a product whilst equally important was the flexitime which ideally suits women at the childbearing/rearing lifestages with the demands of domestic responsibility. Interviewing was considered lucrative (in providing 'jam' rather than 'bread and butter'), challenging, rewarding and enjoyable. Most recruiters claimed to enjoy the job despite the difficulties. One of the striking characteristics of recruiters was the amount of professional pride shown by those who had been practising for some time.

On the downside, many recruiters disliked working in the evening: thus recruiting for male group discussions was considered less enjoyable. Group discussions, particularly, if convened more than once a week, were considered to intrude into the family's living space, so most attempted to control the acceptance of jobs. On one level, recruiters acknowledged the importance of clients attending groups but complained about their behaviour – using the recruiter's home as an office, the recruiter herself as a secretary and making demands for drinks or the use of the telephone when the recruiter was busy hostessing the arriving participants or worrying about whether or not they would all arrive. Not surprisingly, unreasonable quotas and short notice were mentioned as a major pressure. The unreasonable demands on recruiters was pointed out by Feldwick and Winstanley, who showed that 82% of the groups recruited by Boase Massimi Pollitt (BMP) (for 20 clients) involved recruiting

Table 11.1

Recruiter	Buyer	Moderator	Respondent
Positive			
A way to earn money	A way to learn about my consumer first hand	What is the research problem – will I solve it?	Curiosity – never been to market research before
Not overtly selling			
Fits in with domestic responsibilities	An educating experience	This is a good group – insights, help, guidance	Will it be as much fun as last time?
Stimulating/a challenge	Enjoyable hours out of the office	This is fun – I enjoy speaking to people	What will I say/ contribute?
A way to meet people, get out	Appreciation of qualitative methodology	Concerns about group and content	The incentive helps
Rewarding – to complete a job well	Admiration for moderator – how will she interpret all this?	Are these consumers correctly recruited?	Enjoy idea of usefulness – my opinion matters
Negative (Anxiety)			
Poor briefing about the sample and research objectives	Is this a con – are these people genuine?	Is this a con – are these people genuine?	Should I go – is it a con?
Intrusion of strangers into home	Have I been here before?	How anxious are the respondents?	I feel very conspicuous
Abused as facility not a person	This is better than the zoo!	How much withholding?	Should I say what I really believe?
Hard work	Work must go on – keep in touch with office	How much is client observer affecting me/issues?	Who is that guy watching?
Pressure of deadlines	Is the moderator doing a good job for me?	Will they all come?	Will it turn out to be a Tupperware party?
Will the respondent(s) come		Will it be a good group?	
Anxiety – about client	Is this a good or bad group?		

people who represented less than 5% of the population. Impossible quota controls have been discussed elsewhere (see Chapter 2).

Recruiters demonstrated both skill and imagination in successfully recruiting difficult groups. Many believed it necessary to find the most difficult respondents first so that one is not left with impossible 'needles in haystacks' later. Good recruiters were described as those who planned how and where to recruit, setting daily targets and moving into appropriate neighbourhoods. Door-to-door recruiting was *not* standard practice since recruiters preferred to evaluate age and social class before approaching a potential respondent. Thus supermarket queues, nursery schools, high schools, clinics and the local High Street tended to be favoured for cold recruitment.

Feldwick and Winstanley reported that recruiters relied enormously on the use of an existing network. Thus former respondents were recontacted after the statutory fallow period, or members of the respondent's family or friends were co-opted by telephone – the previous respondent serving to reassure the new recruit that the experience would be enjoyable. This form of 'snowballing' was very successful in raising the chances of attendance.

Recruiters, although recognizing the need for recruitment questionnaires, often tended to fill them in *after* establishing that the respondent fitted the quota – having asked the questions qualitatively rather than exactly as specified in the questionnaire. Although AURA and the MRS consider recruitment questionnaires crucial, it is the experience of many practitioners that comparatively few recruiters use them *at the first contact*. This is because most qualitative recruitment questionnaires are too long, too complex and poorly designed. A very simple list of criteria may well be an improvement on the current method.[1]

Given that recruiters are not likely to be recruiting according to the rules laid down by the companies for whom they work, nor according to the methods laid out by their training supervisors, it is not surprising that many recruiters are edgy at the beginning of a group, particularly if new to the moderator. This is because, in addition to the normal time pressures and anxieties about attendance, many recruiters are withholding because they feel unable to be honest and open with the moderator.

There is without doubt a process of collusion taking place which cannot be beneficial to any of the participants involved. Collusion does not mean dishonest recruitment – it simply means that *all the rules*, outside of quota requirements, are often broken.

Compared to other countries, UK recruiters are poorly paid and lack the status they deserve. In order to ensure high recruitment standards, it will be necessary for buyers of their services (research agencies and research buyers) to develop a more understanding relationship so that all of us are working towards the same goals.

THE BUYERS' VIEWPOINT

It would seem that recruitment is an important issue to buyers of research, for when asked *directly* 'which aspects of qualitative research caused most concern and might affect the validity of the results'[2] about half the sample of AURA members and advertising agencies — 71 in total — mentioned standards of recruitment. Nonetheless, it is our belief from practical day-to-day experience that the majority of buyers are totally unconcerned about recruitment. If the buyer trusts the qualitative researchers sufficiently to commission the study, it is assumed that the recruitment process will be entirely professional and competent. Standards of recruitment only become a concern when the relationship between buyer and researcher has, for whatever reason, become vulnerable. It is the first sign of breakdown.

Never in our combined experience of some 30 years of conducting qualitative research, has a client ever asked to see the recruitment questionnaires or asked about our standards of recruitment practice. None have been curious about back-checking quality control procedures or even asked the recruiter how easy or difficult her recruiting task was.

Buyers' experience of recruitment manifests at the group discussion itself — thus it is more relevant to talk about the qualitative experience than the recruitment experience.

On the positive side many buyers and end-users of qualitative research find the group discussion experience both highly enjoyable and very educational. It allows direct access to consumer attitudes and behaviour rather than as an abstraction which so often occurs in client or agency meeting rooms. Observers can thus have first-hand experience of the consumer-brand relationship and learn how a new idea, whether it be for product, packaging or advertising is received by consumers themselves. It offers a salutary lesson such that some wag once remarked 'that dumb consumer is your wife'. Attendance at group discussions soon reveals that consumers are far from stupid and it is a gross mistake or mistaken arrogance on the part of client or agency to view them as such.

Observers of qualitative research are also struck by the complexity of the moderator's task in bringing order to the vast amount of information gathered and interpreting it in an actionable manner for the marketing or advertising teams.

Conversely, client observers (whether manufacturer or agency) also experience qualitative research in a negative manner, primarily because of cynicism about the process itself, previous poor experience with the applications or misuse of qualitative research or prejudice due to a variety of personal or company-related factors. This negativity manifests itself in hostility towards the respondents or the recruiter, being denigratory about the former and casting doubts about the professionalism of the latter, treating the occasion like a day out at the zoo or a circus and demonstrating an inability to 'let go' of the office, the result of which is a sequence of telephone calls to or from a secretary. Such negativity is often displaced on to the moderator, because so many buyers of research have no criteria by which to evaluate whether or not the group discussion in progress is a good one or a bad one. This is because many clients do not understand the qualitative process and mistakenly use the wrong criteria for judgement. A chatty, lively group is not necessarily a good one, nor is a group that has troughs of quietness alternating with peaks of chattiness a poor one – the truth may be the reverse. Until buyers learn the basic principles of group dynamics and begin to observe the consonance or dissonance between the verbal and non-verbal content of a group discussion, qualitative methodologies will remain a mysterious process and its practitioners will remain gurus – a situation which exacerbates buyer anxiety and mistrust.

THE MODERATOR'S PERSPECTIVE

The moderator's experience of the recruitment process is, on the whole, minimal. Most are unaware of the difficulties the recruiter might have encountered in recruiting the group, often only realizing that the recruiter's task might have been far easier if a small detail of the sample had been well thought through in advance. Again, as for client buyers/users, the qualitative experience is more important than the recruitment experience.

Moderators in the UK have to travel extensively to qualitative group discussion locations. As the majority of interviewing takes place in the evening, moderators are having to work 5–6 hours after the end of a normal working day. This can be exhausting, with the result that the moderators often initially feel resentful, as the group begins to convene, at the intrusion of work into personal time.

The moderator also has a number of concerns, at the beginning of a group discussion, concerning the structure of the group – will sufficient people attend? Have they been 'properly' recruited, that is are the respondents 'on' or 'off' quota? How anxious are the respondents as they arrive? Will the observer report back positively or negatively on the moderator's expertise? Has the recruiter been honest? Are the respondents professionals? Does it matter if some have been to qualitative research before?

As the group discussion begins, the moderator's concerns shift to the dual role of understanding and orchestrating the natural process of the group dynamics as well as keeping the research objectives in focus and ensuring that the areas discussed (content) are relevant to the client's problem. Once the group itself is established and 'performing' (see Chapter 3), the moderator is oblivious to the lateness of the hour or the unsociability of the job but is enjoying the experience, deriving pleasure and satisfaction from the skills implicit in the role of moderator. The satisfaction of finding solutions to advertising/marketing problems is rewarding whilst the simple pleasure of experiencing a group of people enjoying the process of self-analysis and the sharing of views is extremely enjoyable.

THE RESPONDENT'S EXPERIENCE

In 1982, a research study was commissioned by the R&D committee of The Market Research Society[3] to understand the qualitative interviewing process as experienced by respondents. This study was the first which examined an interviewer-interviewee relationship as it exists in a non-clinical environment such as market research.

The findings revealed that the recruitment experience plays a significant role in the positive outcome of the qualitative process itself. The study clearly indicated that members of the public, on being approached by a market research recruiter, felt a mixture of interest and curiosity as well as suspicion and nervousness. To achieve a commitment to attend the group discussion or depth interview, the recruiter had to overcome distrust by being persuasive and reassuring and being seen as friendly, open and honest. Additionally, the incentive is crucial — 27% claimed that they would not have participated had it not been offered, whilst 53% believed that the incentive 'tipped the balance' between attendance and non-attendance.

Recruitment questionnaires can and do cause hostility, particularly the collection of demographic details such as age and socio-economic group. The classification of women by their husband's occupation — especially amongst working women — causes resentment. We believe that it is essential to determine both partners' income in today's society where 60% of women are working full or part-time.

As discussed earlier, it is conventional wisdom in the market research industry that good recruitment involves selecting respondents who have *never* participated in market research before. What the survey revealed was that the first experience was considered (by those who had been interviewed qualitatively more than once) to be more stressful, less enjoyable and a more self-conscious experience than subsequent occasion(s). It is the authors' view, based on this study and on practical experience, as well as on the observations of Feldwick and Winstanley, that previous knowledge, experience and hence familiarity with the qualitative process, produces a more relaxed, open and participative respondent.

One of the most important reasons for the high levels of tension at the beginning of a group discussion or depth interview (easily noticeable by defensive body language) is the fact that respondents do not know what to expect. In spite of having been told that the interview (whether group or individual) is a 'market research' one, as opposed to any other type of interview, the level of understanding of market research amongst the general public is very low. Thus respondents are nervous because the whole procedure is unknown.

Anxiety is high too, because people present are strangers; moreover the fear of speaking in public is one which many people experience.

Moderators and recruiters are often at fault in not explaining the qualitative experience clearly, both on recruitment and at the beginning of a group or individual interview session. Respondents require a great deal of reassurance and the more honest the moderator about the subject matter, the purpose of the survey, confidentiality, the end-use of the public's opinions, the tape recorder, the timing and the structure of the discussion or interview, the more relaxed will be the respondent.

The first ten minutes of the qualitative experience is important in that all the participants are sizing each other up. The group members or individual respondent display caution whilst they ascertain how to behave correctly and to seek clues as to how to act/react.

Respondents understand that by agreeing to attend and accepting payment something is expected in return. But what? This lack of definition of expected behaviour results in anxiety, cautiousness and defensiveness, which manifests itself in many ways all of which interfere with the successful outcome of the qualitative process.

Projective techniques used in the MRS study indicated that the anxiety manifested itself in one or more of the following ways:

- fear of not giving the right answer.
- fear of appearing stupid in front of stranger(s).
- 'fight' responses such as criticizing the skills of the interviewer or other members of the group.
- 'flight' responses such as feelings of boredom, loss of concentration, concerns about home-related activities.

The chapters on Group Processes and Group Dynamics (Chapters 3 and 4) describe other manifestations of anxiety.

On the positive side, respondents experience the qualitative interview as enjoyable, informative, a reinforcement of their 'own' beliefs, a way to earn money and an aid to the understanding of marketing or advertising.

Practitioners of qualitative research are aware that anxiety and tension do dissipate after a while, respondents demonstrating relaxation and comfort through both verbal and non-verbal behaviour.

The early stages of the respondent-interviewer relationship are interesting to explore. Respondents are acutely sensitive to the interviewer at the start of the qualitative process and have a clear and conservative view of what an interviewer should be like and how he should behave. Interviewers are expected to look neat and tidy, listen patiently, never be patronizing, appreciate respondent nervousness or inability to articulate and be able to relax people in a warm and friendly manner. Interviewers who differ markedly from the ideal have to work harder at gaining the co-operation and trust of respondents.

It is our view that the quicker the interviewer can project her real personality breaking through the stereotypical expectations and the more she can be open and reveal parts of her real feelings in the situation, the more quickly respondents will reciprocate on the same level, sharing heartfelt feelings rather than socially acceptable ones. The more anxious the individual or the group, the more withholding takes place to the detriment of the study.

Qualitative recruitment is ripe for change, and this is beginning to happen. Central interviewing facilities with one-way mirrors and/or video monitoring are mushrooming in London and the major urban centres. Soon, we predict, the UK will fall in line with the rest of the Western world. Group discussions will be convened in specialist locations situated in major urban/suburban areas, thus allowing buyers to observe the qualitative process without having to pretend to be someone other than the client!

Qualitative recruitment is also becoming more honest and realistic. For example panels of socio-economic group A respondents are being set up so that when required these difficult respondents are readily available 'on tap'. Other specialist panels are also being recruited such as business travellers, gold credit card holders, people who own stocks and shares, high-earning career women and so on − difficult respondents to find under pressure, but willing respondents if correctly approached and motivated with appropriate incentives.

In the UK today, recruitment practices are responding to new challenges. It is our firm belief that conventional wisdom should be questioned and innovation should be encouraged. Only two commandments are worth engraving in stone − 'Thou shalt ensure that all the required respondents arrive on time' and 'Thou shalt not recruit out of quota'. The remaining rules should be applied with discretion after consultation with buyer, agency and recruiter.

NOTES

1. See P. Feldwick and L. Winstanley (1986), *Qualitative Recruitment: Policy and Practice*, The Market Research Conference.
2. See note 1 above.
3. See W. Gordon and S. Robson (1982), *Respondents Through the Looking Glass*.

12 The Presentation of Qualitative Research

INTRODUCTION

One of the crucial differences between qualitative and quantitative research lies in the presentation of the results to the client. Quantitative research can be presented very effectively by any experienced researcher, even if the individual has not personally been responsible for the questionnaire design or has not interviewed one single respondent, or even read some of the questionnaires.

Qualitative research on the other hand can only be well presented by a researcher who was personally involved in the project, whether observing the qualitative interviewing process or personally moderating/interviewing.

Historically, quantitative research has the image of a scientific, objective process. Therefore the sample size, percentages and statistical references to, for example, probability, significance or error provide a backbone of authority to the presentation. Most clients will concede that a quantitative researcher is a specialist and therefore he is treated as a professional.

Qualitative research, on the other hand, has always been beleaguered by its obvious lack of statistical validity or reliability. Its antagonists have repeatedly criticized its subjectivity or moderator/interviewer bias and, in contrast to 'hard' quantitative data, it is often described as 'soft'. Qualitative research, it is widely believed, is an art-form.

To many buyers it seems that qualitative data is simply collected by chatting to people, either in groups or individually. This requires an ability to get on with people, and the possession of a personality that is warm, approachable and empathetic. These characteristics are not believed to be exclusive to qualitative researchers – in fact anyone with this type of personality will successfully (it may be believed) 'chat up' a few respondents, so specialist skills are not required.

For these reasons, qualitative research lacks the image of authority inherent in quantitative research. Presentation skills are therefore crucial, since no matter how excellently a particular qualitative project is conducted, if it is not presented in a persuasive, professional and authoritative manner, it might well be rejected by the client along the lines 'What does the man in the street know about design/advertising/marketing anyway' and so on.

THE DEBRIEF ARENA

It is easy for the researcher to become engrossed in the project and to arrive at the presentation not having given enough thought to the debrief arena. The feelings experienced before the presentation may include excitement at the problem-solving stage, interest and involvement in the complexity of the problem, anticipation of sharing information and insights with the client, yet if the politics of the debrief have not been carefully considered, all this effort may be totally in vain.

Remember the audience consists of individuals, each with a unique perspective depending on his role in the company, status, experience, age, sex and personality. Each therefore enters the debrief with a different 'set' which affects the selectivity of what he hears and absorbs and the way in which he relates to the researcher as a person as well as to the debrief content.

Creative teams do not feel warm towards researchers who insist upon going through five concepts which failed abysmally before getting to the two successes.

Busy marketing directors do not appreciate listening to two hours of largely irrelevant background information before getting to the main purpose of the research project.

Pragmatic sales directors, or in fact any reasonably intelligent but research-unsophisticated member of the audience, will become defensive (and subsequently hostile and rejecting) if made to feel a fool by the use of jargon, over-intellectualized explanations or research arrogance.

Researchers should be as sensitive to non-verbal cues in the debrief as they would be in a research situation. A senior manager (whether client or agency) will not respect a researcher who 'presents' to a junior member of the meeting because she happens to look the oldest/wisest/trendiest/sexiest. Make use of body language. Crossed arms and legs indicate non-acceptance or negativity; open sitting postures and inadvertent nodding suggest positivity; indirect eye contact, hand tapping, yawning, vacant staring, examining hands all suggest levels of uninterest, the observation of which should immediately help the presenter to diagnose potential problems before they occur (see Chapter 7).

Most practitioners, hopefully, would not think about conducting a group discussion without knowing the recruitment criteria: for example, users or non-users, BC1 or C2D; younger or older. The same applies to debriefs. It is essential to find out who the audience is going to be. Each member of the debrief audience will go to that meeting with a slightly different orientation – sensitivity to this fact is a prerequisite of persuasive communication of the findings. When numbers are not available to provide evidence, the persuasiveness and authority of the presentation is vital.

How is it possible to determine in advance which debriefs are likely to be particularly fraught and which are not? It is quite easy. Research is commissioned for two basic reasons (although the buyer may not be aware of his motivations).

(i)   Early learning, such as basic market studies, exploratory work, NPD, diagnostic studies and some tactical decision-making research.

(ii)   Evaluation, when the role of the research is to provide evidence (perhaps couched in words such as 'guidance', 'aid decision-making','insight' etc.) about the performance of a particular concept, advertisement, executional solution, alternative routes, and so on.

True learning research is always appreciated and, unless poorly conducted, is always greeted with enthusiastic thanks at the debrief. Evaluative research simply means BE WARY. Creative teams feel threatened easily, pack designers can be defensive, agency and client have to support their positions and the researcher can and does get branded as the culprit if the presentation is not well thought out and presented.

The structure of the presentation

There are some guidelines to remember here which largely apply to any type of research, but have special relevance to qualitative research.

(i)   Restate the objectives and *scope* of the research (quantitative researchers have the discipline of their tabulations to set the parameters of the study – the qualitative researcher does not).

(ii)   Provide a brief description of the methodology used, particularly relating to the sample. It is not possible to answer questions about people who were not interviewed.

(iii)   Inform the meeting of the agenda and when questions will be appropriate. Give them an overview on the structure that will be adopted and inform them that notes are provided.

(iv)   Begin with any necessary scene-setting but do not overlabour background information which is not relevant to the project unless you have been asked to do so.

(v)   Deal with the data in a way which is relevant to the type of project. Decide whether to start with the general and home in on the specifics, or to begin with the 'conclusions' and develop the ideas which led to these conclusions. This will be dependent upon the nature of the particular project and the needs of the audience.

   Exploratory research is usually best treated by starting with the general. Strategy development or executional evaluation is often best dealt with by starting with the ideas that have most potential. Like a lawyer it is necessary to consider how to present one's case; the order of the group discussion guide is *not* appropriate in many cases.

(vi)   Use visual language, particularly if the audience includes agency creatives or designers. Aids to expression such as metaphor, analogy or the type of data gained through the use of projective techniques (for example brand personification) help those less sophisticated in research jargon to understand, feel and even 'see' the subject being discussed.

(vii)   Be constructive. Whatever the project, particularly if its aims are evaluative, begin by drawing out the strengths and positives. The negatives or weaknesses have to be communicated but should be couched in terms of *direction* rather than absolutes. For example instead of saying 'This pack design was a no-no' a better approach would be to say 'The important point to learn from this pack is that a very contemporary tea pot and crockery are dissonant with the traditional values of the brand'.

(viii) Be polite. It is surprising how many qualitative researchers suffer from attacks of megalomania whilst debriefing to a captive audience. The individuals in the audience have feelings, particularly if their own work or thinking are being evaluated, so tone of voice is critical.

(ix)   Remember to separate the views of consumers from the interpretations of the moderator. Saying that 'consumers believed the advertising lacked impact' is quite different from saying 'judging from consumer reactions, it is my view that the advertising lacked impact'. The audience may have a different interpretation from that of the researcher.

(x)   Watch the time. Many qualitative researchers are performers at heart and once given the opportunity of a captive audience, enjoy being hero of the play. Remember how it feels to be lectured to or talked at for longer than 45 minutes – your mind wanders, you begin to hear even more selectively than you did at the beginning, the outside world intrudes.

We firmly believe that presentations or debriefs should be planned in advance so that only the main themes are presented, not all the thousands of details which confuse rather than clarify.

At the end of a verbal presentation remember that the audience will only remember about five main points – so make sure they are the ones you want them to retain.

As a rough guideline, 30–45 minutes talking without a break of some kind (for example, discussion, watching a video or commercials) is about the maximum. If, for whatever reason, the overall time is longer, plan it like a performance, using a colleague to break the monotony of one voice, a strategic coffee break, examples of projective techniques to re-energize the audience and so on. Do not be over-indulgent!

(xi)   Summarize the main themes. Some of the audience will not have managed to concentrate throughout so it is a good idea to finish by *succinctly* highlighting the main conclusions so that everyone leaves the meeting with those points in mind.

Presenting qualitative research does not make visual aids unnecessary. In some ways they are essential because they focus attention on the key points while the remainder of the picture is being painted and coloured.

It also helps to break the presentation by the use of various visual aids, so that it is not a monotonous 'blah blah'. Although the majority of people present may be familiar with the stimuli used (concept boards, packs, products, animatics and so on), it helps to show them so that the audience may relax and collect its thoughts before the next verbal onslaught. The use of projective techniques or quotes helps to bring the consumer and the subject to life.

Presentation manner

Qualitative research should be presented in a qualitative manner. The researcher is the link with consumers and has to be able to convey the *feelings* experienced in the contact with them, not just the facts that have been collected. Somehow, qualitative researchers have to bring consumers to life for an audience which is very unlikely to have the same lifestyle, attitudinal framework or behaviour. But a note of warning – balance is necessary. Overly anecdotal accounts reduce the findings and interpretations to the verbatims of Mrs Bloggs from Pinner. A fine line exists between the researcher as consumer spokesman and the researcher as professional diagnostician or marketing analyst.

Present with enthusiasm, but ensure that the presentation is paced so that the logical thread to the argument is retained. Jumping ahead and dealing with issues out of sequence will lead to a jumbled effect overall.

Qualitative researchers are required to be chameleons in that they need to be able to talk to all types of respondents yet also able to present professionally to senior management. If aiding in the process of major decision-making, clients will expect a researcher to be a professional presenter.

Presentation dress

It is a personally held view that the way one dresses for a presentation is crucial. Just as one would not arrive to interview C1C2 housewives in a Jean Muir outfit, so one needs to think about what to wear to a presentation.

Unless the researcher is extremely well known and highly regarded it is not worth risking credibility by wearing jeans and open-necked shirt or the latest style fishnet stockings and mini-skirt.

Again, bear in mind the audience. If it is an informal presentation to the planner and creative team, dress accordingly, but remember sometimes an informal chat turns into a fully blown presentation by the time it actually takes place.

Visual aids

There are numerous methods of presenting, in a visual manner, qualitative research to an audience. What follows is simply a guide to the options available. Examples are shown on pages 172 to 184.

Overheads

Types of overhead

Stabpoints	— phrases or single words which 'headline' or summarize key points. See Fig. 12.1, 12.2
Brandmaps	— diagrammatic representations of consumer perceptions of the brands in the market and their interrelationship. See Fig. 12.3, 12.4.
Diagrams	— illustrating the sequence of decision-making or a purchase process. See Fig. 12.5
Verbatim Quotes	— illustrating, with consumers' vocabulary, particular and relevant responses. See Fig. 12.6
Thought-Bubble Cartoons	— responses to a projective technique. See Fig 12.7, 12.8
Cartoon drawings/illustrations	— bring to life prevailing consumer attitudes, behaviour or segmentations. See Fig. 12.9, 12.10.

Figures 12.10 and 12.11 are visualizations of two different types of lager drinker drawn from explicit verbal 'portraits' generated in the group discussions. They were used to exemplify segmentations of consumer types in a presentation. The rather sulky looking gentleman in the matelot shirt is as consumers saw the typical Pils drinker (circa 1979), described as a student or lecturer type, a Marlboro smoker, excessively self-confident, sure of himself with women and a bit of a loner.

The chap standing at the bar is a Hofmeister drinker. He's Jack the Lad, full of jokes, desperately seeking attention and affection, tending towards 'medallion man' type of heavy jewellry — he's OK as long as his easy going style isn't challenged. 'Get the picture, squire?' describes his tone of voice. He and the Pils drinker would despise each other.

Figs. 12.12 and 12.13 bring to life two very different environments available to the motorist in search of spares/repairs for his ailing car. The Autotrend Superstore is superficially ordered, but the bored sales girl miserably flicking her duster over the pre-packed items and the general 'special offer' atmosphere demonstrated to consumers that no-one here really understands motor cars. This impression is confirmed by the fact that the man in the car spares booth is chatting up another sales girl, not helping customers. Children idly pull the products from the lower shelves.

The alternative, Harry's, is superficially disordered but his untidiness conceals the fact that Harry is a true expert. If he didn't have a part your car needed he'd make it out of something else. Harry's is a much more serious, professional environment and for all its messiness, infinitely more reassuring than the Auto-trend store.

These visualizations were used to bring home this essential difference to a retailer who was just about to re-design his automotive spares shops.

Usage indications   Larger audiences (8–12 or more), relatively informal broad, dense, information such as basic studies of market, strategy development, NPD and creative development.

Advantages

Cheap
Quick to produce
The room need not be darkened, so audience reactions can be observed.

Disadvantages   Hand-drawn overheads are often 'tacky'. With the best writing they still look amateurish and therefore the researcher runs the risk of undermining the authority of the presentation. Professional artwork overcomes this problem.

Handwritten flip charts

Types

Stabpoints
Maps   } as for overheads
Diagrams
Quotes

Usage

Smaller audience (very informal)
Any type of study, but particularly those focussed on a particular issue.

Advantages   As for Overheads.

Disadvantages   As for Overheads.

Segmentation

★   Commemorative

★   Collectable

★   British

★   Pretty but practical

★   Ornamental

Figure 12.1   Stab point chart showing different types of gifts

Decision Process

★ Process of choosing extremely complex

★ Occasion and recipient
 Occasions: major → minor
 formal → informal

★ Recipient:
 − closeness vs distance of relationship
 − degree of knowledge about recipient

Figure 12.2 Stab point chart − choosing gifts (summary of key points)

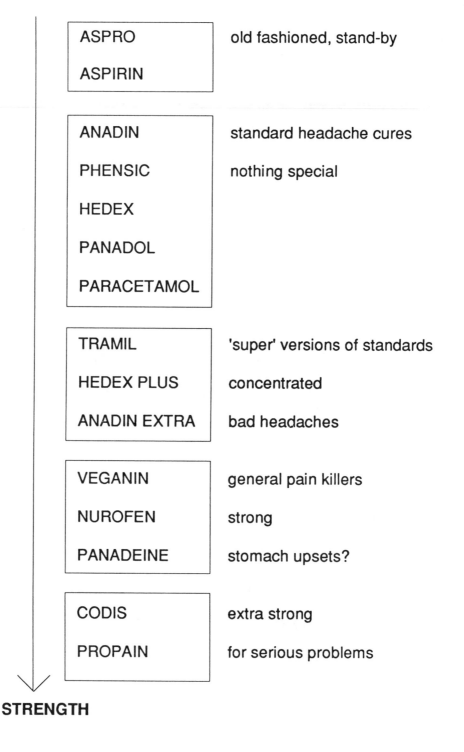

Figure 12.3   Brand mapping

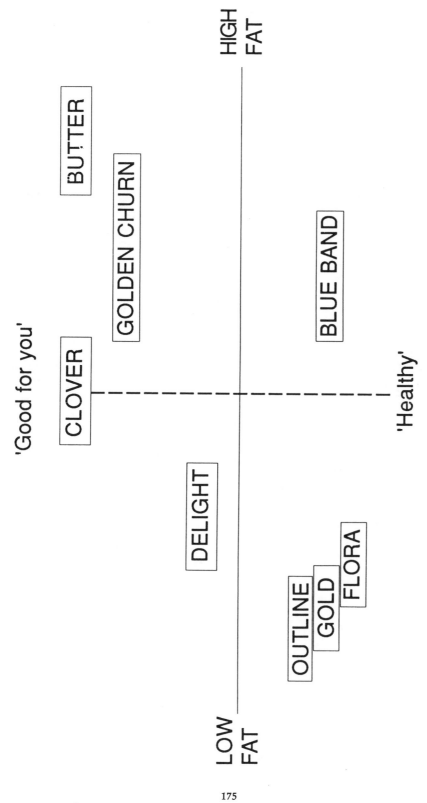

Figure 12.4   Brand mapping butters and margarines and low fat spreads

WILL I REALLY TAKE EATING HEALTHY FOOD SERIOUSLY

When and where are decisions made?

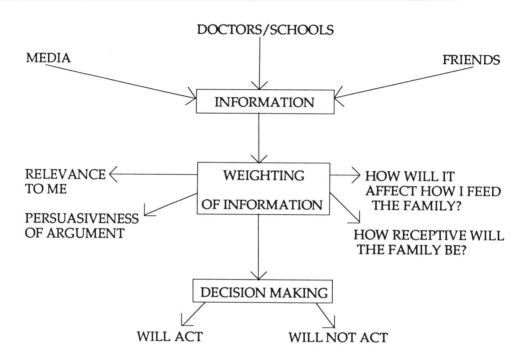

Figure 12.5   Diagram

God-daughter 21st present

'I think this item is important enough to stand on a shelf on its own for most of the time, but would be useful to hold fruits, nuts, desserts on special occasions. It would be nice to add the lamp at a later date. I think there is scope for other designs to be made up as lamp-stands'

Mother birthday present

'This was a very hard choice. If I were to choose for myself I would choose the Ladro, but for my mother the chokin plate. The chokin plate would suit their house. My parents have many valuable collections and I think they would appreciate this item. The plate would be very easily spotted as it's very stunning and beautiful'

God-daughter 21st birthday gift

'I chose this black labrador because I felt it would give my God-daughter the most pleasure for many years after her own dog would have died'(!).

Figure 12.6   Quotes: decisions on gifts

Figure 12.7   A thought bubble cartoon as completed by an informant

Figure 12.8

Figure 12.9   Cartoon illustration: travelling by tube

Figure 12.10   Consumers visualization of the trendy Pils drinker (c) 1979

Figure 12.11   Consumer's visualization of 'Jack the lad', the lager drinker

Figure 12.12 Consumer's visualization of the modern motor spares market

Figure 12.13   Consumer's visualization of the repair expert's shop

Projectives

These are the results of the use of projective techniques in the research project.

Types

Words and picture collages.
Thought bubble themes.
Sentence completion.
Brand personification.
Psychodrawings, clay modelling.

Usage   Any type of study, that is, whenever projective techniques have been used during fieldwork.

Advantages   The results of projective techniques, because they use visuals or visual imagery, are extremely powerful in communicating *emotional* levels of reaction or experience.

In our experience every single person in the audience finds this type of productivity of consumers in qualitative research fascinating and a sensitive discussion of 'what the drawings tell us', provides important insight and understanding. Although a cliché, it is so true that a picture is worth a thousand words.

Figure 12.14 represents the personification of a well-known brand of lavatory cleaner. Can you guess which it is? Confidentiality prohibits us from revealing more! The character in the drawing was described as a city businessman, authoritarian, cold, clinical, efficient yet uncaring.

Disadvantages   Projective techniques and the product thereof require careful explanation prior to their exposure. The audience needs to understand how and why they were used and what insights they bring to the problem. Unless this is done both seriously and professionally, the actual material becomes food for generalized mirth, thus undermining its usefulness.

35mm slides

Types   Slides can be produced to illustrate any point the researcher wishes to make. They can also be verbal, illustrative, diagrammatic or photographic.

Usage   Formal presentations to large numbers of people such as conferences, PR exercises, part of a client/agency presentation.

Advantages   Well produced and designed slides scream professionalism.

Figure 12.14 Can you guess which brand of loo cleaner this man represents!?

Disadvantages

Slides require time and effort.
With the exception of simple verbal slides, 35mm is very expensive.

Tapes (audio)

Types   Extracts of interviews or group discussions.

Usage   Any type of audience – small or big, informal or formal.

Advantages   Like verbatim quotes, extracts (audio) help to bring the consumer alive for the audience.
Tapes help to illustrate a tone of response, for example, enthusiastic, guarded or uninterested.

Disadvantages   If the sound quality is poor, the tape may do little to help the presenter and may indeed cause anxieties about the quality of the equipment used to record the group discussion. Re-recording particular excerpts is an option.

Video

It must be said that video is not often used by qualitative practitioners since most qualitative interviewing is not videoed.
Increasingly in the UK however, in line with Europe and the USA, more and more qualitative research is being conducted in research laboratories rather than in consumer homes. With this development, it is foreseeable that video snippets or edited sequences will be used to illustrate qualitative presentations more frequently.

The presentation summary of main findings

Even in note form, this should provide a cohesive summary of the debrief. It should not be necessary to have attended the meeting in order to make sense of it, although obviously some of the qualitative feel will have been lost to those who did not attend. However, the report, by the use of verbatim quotes, ought to be able to provide that feel.
The conclusions or recommendations should be carefully thought out and written in full. Clients and agencies discuss the debrief after the researcher has left and it is important that the concluding remarks are not open to various interpretations.

13 Research with Children

The development of qualitative research among children below teen-age has rather lagged behind the mainstream growth area of research with adults. There seem to have been three main reasons for this:

(1) That children do not buy all that many things. They have a low income and as such, in common with other low-income groups, don't represent potential profitable investment for mass-market manufacturers.

(2) Even in the many instances where children may affect the purchasing and consumption patterns of adults, the nature and extent of this effect is poorly understood, transitory or incidental in nature and difficult to measure. We may as well, therefore, the argument runs, rely upon the reports of adults.

(3) Children present special problems to researchers. Their level of comprehension, verbal and motor abilities vary widely from individual to individual and from age to age. How do we ask them questions and know what their answers mean?

When we've talked to clients about their feelings about research with children, one constant niggling deeper anxiety emerges, which relates to point (3) above – people feel that you need to be an 'expert' to understand children and they worry that researchers will not be able to disentangle real or meaningful responses from irrelevant and playful ones. Another powerful factor compounding clients' doubts here is the worry that in their reactions to adults (the researchers) children will, even more than adults, say what will please the adults in order not to risk their wrath or disapproval. This leads clients to worry about the excessively positive feedback from children's research. How can kids say they don't like something to someone in authority who's giving them rewards?

In the remainder of this chapter we will provide answers to as many of these questions as we can, and along the way we will outline some of the methodological problems and solutions we've encountered in research with children. First though, we'd like to state our conviction that a good, methodologically sound researcher can adapt his or her appreciation of qualitative processes just as well to studying children as to anything else where variable human behaviour is under observation. Providing that, as always, he takes the respondents' perspectives, abilities and stage of development or sophistication into account when designing the research technique and mode of questioning. Just as it makes no sense to ask someone who's only drunk sweet white wine their opinion on the importance of vintage years in red Burgundy, and then to regard their answer as 'wrong' because it's inaccurate, so it makes no sense to interrogate children on topics with which they are unfamiliar or, even worse, to assume that youngsters are capable of modes of thought which are beyond them.

Just to remind you, Piaget and others have striven to produce descriptions of the developmental stages of thinking, and while you must judge each child on his/her own manifest level of competence, when you are designing surveys it may be as well to bear these notions in mind.

DEVELOPMENTAL STAGES

2nd Stage: Pre-Operational Thought (POT: 2–7 years)

The first stage – *Sensori Motor* (0–2 years) is the pre-language stage, and is thus not of interest to market researchers.

The ages cited are not absolute guarantees of a particular individual's stage. Some develop more quickly than others, but they do give a rough guide to the level of development you may expect across an age range.

You may assume, for example, that up to seven years children will find it hard to operate in a group structure, although they may well be able to participate in activities together – drawing, choosing, preferring, looking at things.

There are three main things to take into account about the thoughts of children throughout these early years:

(1)   Their thinking is *intuitive*. For example, they may grasp that a key might unlock a door but they won't be able to explain locks and keys, and may not understand that the key won't operate *all* locks.
(2)   It's *animistic*. They imbue the physical world with the properties of human things. Water runs downhill because 'it wants to'. Clouds move because they want to get to the other side of the sky.
(3)   Their thinking is *egocentric*. This doesn't mean that they are selfish – selfishness presupposes knowledge of other's point of view and a disregard of it. The egocentric child doesn't know that there is another point of view.

Some later work reported by Margaret Donaldson suggests that children may be able to take another's point of view when something is directly relevant to their life. She described an experiment where a child is asked: 'If two policemen were standing at the corners of A and B, and a child wanted to hide from them, where would he/she stand?' (The experiment was done with a 3–D model: see Figure 13.1).

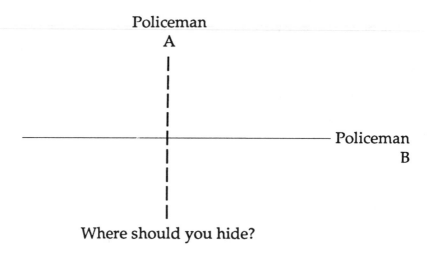

Figure 13.1

Many children, even as young as three years old, got the right answer, as shown in Figure 13.2.

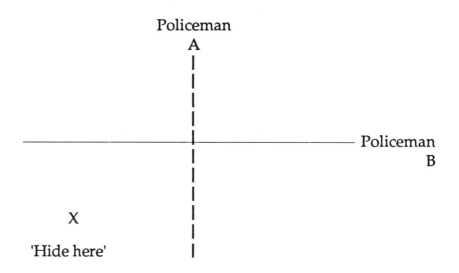

Figure 13.2

And so, depending on the type of task, you may get a thought that appears egocentric or doesn't, but if the task is made relevant to the child's life then he *may* be able to take the other's point of view. This provides our first guideline for researchers; choose research tasks that make human sense and are related to the children's own experience.

As a general rule, however, we try to avoid this type of question with children up to the age of seven. We would not ask 'Would mummy buy you this?' since this involves taking the other's point of view. You need to ask mummy herself this question. We ask 'Which do you like best? This direct form of question avoids both the use of the conditional ('would'-type) thinking, and looking at things from another's perspective.

With older children (6–7 years old) we've been quite successful with *asking* them 'why' they prefer something. With the younger ones it's often good practice to ask them to *draw* the thing they've chosen, then to describe the drawing to you. In this way you may get more information on the features of a product or experience which are of importance to a child.

Another aspect of egocentricism is that the child can't see things in terms of others' social feelings about objects, thoughts or social relationships. It's no use saying to children: 'How would you feel if I did this to you?' or 'How would you feel if you had an X?' (Contrary to fact conditionals like these are definitely out.)

Children also have problems on moral issues, again those questions that start: 'How would you feel if . . .' should be avoided. For example, for a child, breaking ten cups by accident may be worse than breaking one cup on purpose. It may be the opposite way round for an adult.

One way of *fudging* issues in this area of working with the 2–7s is to get into 'child-speak': 'Would Daniel like to play with teddy, then?' where it may appear that you are communicating with the children, that is you may talk to your children as if they understand you because you are using 'baby talk', but there's no guarantee that they do. It may be Double Dutch to them.

Egocentrism gradually lessens but never entirely disappears – all of us have difficulty in seeing the other's point of view from time to time! You'll have noticed this tendency particularly in research debriefs and other tense social situations!

3rd Stage: Concrete Operational Thought (7–11/13 years)

Now children are capable of doing the conceptual tasks which they typically can't do in the pre-operational stage: they have acquired the concepts of conversation, time, space, number and so on. It's important to remember, however, that children can only understand these concepts when working with concrete objects. They cannot work in the abstract, they are not yet capable of working with hypothetical thought. If for example you were asking children 'Which one of these have the most in it?' you would need to show the boxes, packs or whatever.

4th Stage: Formal Operations (11/13 years–adulthood)

It is at this stage that the 'child' is able to deal with abstract concepts and to form test hypotheses. The child is a little scientist and is capable of all forms of thought necessary for scientific reasoning. At this age the child should be capable of logical thought and can follow the reasoning of a syllogism as in:

> 'All children like cabbage.'
> 'John is a child.'
> 'Therefore John likes cabbage.'

In other words, they are able to accept that something is true just for the sake of argument even if they don't believe in it – for example that all children like cabbage!

It's important to note that some people never reach this stage and others only reach it in limited areas of their mental life. For example people might be able to use this form of hypothetical deductive thought to work out a DIY problem but would be very unlikely to use it in deciding where to go on holiday. When emotions enter into our thought processes we are all much more likely to revert to earlier forms of thought – something which all propagandists have always known!

There can be little doubt that the free spontaneous world of play which children inhabit when left to their own devices is different from the more structured question and answer, right and wrong world of their relationships with adults. For most children their normal everyday world is made up of adult-constrained time (particularly school) and free time, just as for adults where the things we say and do in the evenings may bear little or no relation to those we say and do at work!

Entering or observing the spontaneous world of play is not difficult; there are a number of ways of going about it. We may run play groups or observe them from behind a one-way viewing screen, for example. It's just that we don't necessarily want all of our responses to emanate from the child in his play persona. Even with toy products, more so with foodstuffs, clothing and durable items, the child's interaction with adults and how he sees this may contain important material.

For most studies what we ideally want is an arrangement where we may combine information generated from spontaneous moments with that from more structured questioning or tasks so that we may examine both and look for fit or discord in areas like the expression of feelings as opposed to opinions or 'facts'.

To take an analogy from the more familiar world of the adult group discussion, here we often feature sections of the group which are structured as rational discussion. However, there are usually one or more areas where our more spontaneous playful expressions are encouraged – participating in role plays, projective techniques or whatever. Laughter, jokes and word play are often used to encourage spontaneity in group discussions too – just as they may be with children.

On balance then, our methodology with children tries to strike the appropriate combination of techniques to allow us to look at the child's view of things from a series of different perspectives. As we've outlined elsewhere, this changing of perspectives facilitates the widest possible examination of the respondent's picture of reality. All of us, except for the very uptight, have more than one way of describing or reacting to most things.

It now remains to suggest a series of practical methodologies for children of various age groups combining an awareness of Piagetian developmental capabilities with these other considerations in pursuit of fulfilling the research brief.

ENTERING THE RESEARCH SITUATION

Imagine for a moment the standard interview or group discussion where people gather to talk about subjects like food or drink, consumer durables, work or leisure. This research situation appears rather an unusual set-up to the child. In the first place, children do not usually have conversations about 'topics' with adults they do not know, and many have relatively few of these even with those they know well. Right from the outset several aspects of the situation may seem bizarre to the child:

(i)   The unfamiliarity of the other children if there are any, or the absence of them if there aren't.
(ii)   The unfamiliarity of the adult.
(iii) The strange surroundings.
(iv)   The unpractised, perhaps poorly understood activity that seems to be expected of the child.

Given this view of the situation it seems rather remarkable that researchers get anything out of children at all! Of course, in many cases, the simple fact of the presence of an 'adult' will induce compliance to a degree, but every researcher has experienced the dramatic difference between his/her fantasy of a room full of children playing and talking creatively, and the stony silence where the only sound in between one-line questions and one-word answers is the sound of the clock ticking. What's wrong? Why won't they talk? They may even have been screaming with energy and conversation as they entered the research facility or house, then suddenly plunge into silence when they meet the researcher.

In other places in this book we've already come to appreciate that some form of anxiety about the situation is usually the cause of such dramatic shutting down. Let's think for a moment about the possible sources of such anxiety among a group of seven-, eight- or nine-year-olds as they are introduced to their interviewer:

(i)   Their closest existing model for this situation – going into a room with a strange adult who might ask them questions – is the first day of term with a new teacher. Where to sit, what will he be like, will he pick on me, will he tell me off – all these thoughts and more buzz through their minds.

(ii)   If they don't know them, who are these other children? Do they know more about things than I do? Will they like me? Are they the 'teacher's' own children?

(iii)   There are (probably) no familiar things here. Where are my toys, children's things and the like? Does this mean that children don't often come here? Why not?

(iv)   What are we going to do now? Shall I join in? I wasn't listening when he said that. What if I can't do it?

You can begin to appreciate the extent of the problem. Children do not encounter unstructured interaction with adults very frequently, they are waiting to have it explained to them why they are here and what they're going to do. During the next ten minutes or so our aims must be six-fold:

(i)   To help the children get to know each other.
(ii)   To let each child bring something of himself into the room.
(iii)   To provide a stable and secure environment that's not physically or psychologically daunting.
(iv)   To explain what's going to happen during the session and what is expected of them.
(v)   To indicate that they'll have a chance to practise things if they want to, to get them right. They're not expected to do everything perfectly.
(vi)   To appreciate their context by asking them a little about what *they* expect to happen or would like to happen.

Before coming on to consider some of the more esoteric aspects of theory and practice, we have to be able to create rapport with our child informants, simply in order to establish a dialogue and some form of agreement about the task ahead. Here is a list of 'Dos' and 'Don'ts' which are designed to help you in this situation:

DO:

(i)   Have mum (or dad) present with the under-sevens. Use their Christian names from time to time.

(ii)   Use eye contact occasionally and appropriately.

(iii)   Have orange juice, biscuits, etc. available.

(iv)   Use vocabulary and sentence length geared to children's age.

(v)   Have a firm idea of structure of session and tell children what this will be.

(vi)   Work at their physical level, especially with younger children.

(vii)   Make sure they understand what they have to do, giving help or practice if necessary.

(viii)   Start off the session with familiar activities like drawing, eating, drinking, group games, etc.

(ix)   Respond to fidgeting, racketing and other signs of tiredness by starting to draw the proceedings to a close. You won't get useful material from exhausted children.

DON'T:

(i)   Make value judgements about what they say or do *individually*, unless you can give each member of the group similar praise or encouragement. *Do*, on the other hand, use occasional encouragement to the group as a whole.

(ii)   Be surprised if they produce unexpected answers – these can be useful too. In a sense, no answers are wrong.

(iii)   Expect young children to concentrate for more than ten minutes on any one activity.

(iv)   Try to work with a large group of children, i.e. over seven or eight members.

(v)   Forget that the form in which questions are asked may affect the replies you get.

METHODS AND MEANS

Methods

Taking the question of structure and size of the interview first, we operate the general rules outlined in Table 13.1.

Play groups for toy research, leisure wear or consumption (how things get eaten) can be run with any of these age groups.

Means

Following Table 13.1 we include a list of techniques that we have found particularly useful in our work with children:

Table 13.1

Age	Sex	Number	Duration
Under 7s	Boys or girls.	Individual interviews or pairs with mothers present. Accompanied shopping.	30–40 mins
7–9	Boys & girls mixed or, more usually, separate.	Friendship pairs or small friendship groups (4–5). Accompanied shopping.	45 mins–1 hour
10–12	Boys & girls separate.	Friendship pairs or trios or small groups (4–6). Accompanied shopping.	1 + hour
Family interviews		In which all members of the family are interviewed together, separately or in pairs. These help overcome the posturing and overclaiming that can emerge in pair group interviews with children. For example, a little girl trying to appear grown up may claim never to play with Care Bears. In the presence of an elder (or younger) sibling such a remark, if untrue, would quickly be rebutted with something along the lines of 'Oh yeah! Then how come you took one to bed with you every night last week?'	1½–2 hours

Familiarization games

It's always handy to have a few ideas to help children get to know each other in those instances where for experimental or demographic reasons, children who don't know each other are gathered together. Our three favourites in this vein are:

Hangman   Divide the children into pairs *before they are introduced* and tell them not to tell each other their names. They then play 'Hangman' using their own Christian name as the clue. The other child must guess the letters and then the name. The children take it in turns in each pair to put their name up as the clue. Then, when all have finished, each child introduces the name he guessed – that of his partner – to the other members of the group. This is suitable from seven upwards and takes about ten minutes.

Chinese whispers   This is always an amusing game and encourages the children to listen to each other. The moderator whispers something (which he has also written down) to one child who passes it on to the next, who whispers it to the next and so on back to the moderator. The moderator then compares the whisper he received to the original written down on paper.

Drawing home and family   Really an aspect of projective drawing, this enables children to introduce elements of their real-life background into the research situation. They feel comfortable drawing familiar objects, and very often the researcher may learn relevant details about each individual from his execution and description of his/her drawing.

Sorting/mapping games

Children love sorting things out into groups and patterns. It's much better with children to let this become a fairly active procedure with everyone getting involved at first, in order to familiarize them with the things being sorted and then to introduce structure in the form of suggested categories. Very often, particularly among the under nines, kids will sort products on quite pragmatic attributes like colour, size, shape, rather than on conceptual bases like 'For Adults – For Kids' or 'Good For You – Bad For You'. It's quite acceptable for the researcher to introduce a number of simple dimensions which she wants the children to work with, but it's well worth observing their spontaneous sorting first – all sorts of interesting perspectives on the child's world may arise out of this.

We sometimes, with six- and seven-year-olds, play a simplified version of sorting, called 'Labelling'. In this game, each child has a handful of five or six cards, each of which has a simple drawing and word on it. These words are relevant to the product area under investigation, so for a new toy we might have:

cuddly	to look after
for boys	for fighting
fun	breaks easily
my favourite	strong
not for me	too hard
for girls	messy
exciting	fiddly
boring	(and so on).

Each of the cards is first explained to the participants and then they have a practice run with the cards and familiar toy, putting those that go with it in one pile beside the toy and those that don't in another pile away from the toy. At the end of the sorting you may give the children a blank card and ask them to draw or write something of their own which would go with the toy.

In this game we take one product at a time, up to three or four products.

With the 10–12s you may use quite sophisticated association matrices as long as you explain the meaning of each attribute as you go. An example of such a matrix is included in Figure 13.3. This is quite a useful and advanced method for studying children's perceptions of the relationship between the five products involved:

Lemonade
Coke
Quatro
Dr Pepper
Tizer

You must, of course, explain to the children that they can put a tick in any box where they think a word applies to the product named above it. Help and encourage them and make sure they have correctly understood the task.

Role playing and enactment

Children love acting and miming, and providing the atmosphere is supportive and secure, they will usually respond warmly to an invitation to role play. One of our favourites, particularly useful for studying children's perceptions of their mothers' behaviour and attitude, we call 'The Shopping Game'. It is suitable for seven years upwards and it runs something like this:

The Shopping Game

Interviewer: Who'd like to pretend to be her mum for a bit? (Pick a respondent)

	Lemonade	Coke	Quatro	Dr Pepper	Tizer
Refreshing	☐	☐	☐	☐	☐
Fizzy	☐	☐	☐	☐	☐
Sweet	☐	☐	☐	☐	☐
Sticky	☐	☐	☐	☐	☐
Interesting	☐	☐	☐	☐	☐
Strong taste	☐	☐	☐	☐	☐
A treat	☐	☐	☐	☐	☐
Everyday	☐	☐	☐	☐	☐
Expensive	☐	☐	☐	☐	☐
New	☐	☐	☐	☐	☐
Exciting	☐	☐	☐	☐	☐
Different	☐	☐	☐	☐	☐
Sharp	☐	☐	☐	☐	☐
Nasty	☐	☐	☐	☐	☐
Boring	☐	☐	☐	☐	☐
For young children	☐	☐	☐	☐	☐
For older children	☐	☐	☐	☐	☐

Figure 13.3   A brand association matrix for older children

Interviewer:	Now, *Julie,* I'd like you to tell me your mum's name.
Child:	Mrs McConnell.
Interviewer:	Okay then, Mrs McConnell, you are Mrs McConnell, aren't you!? I'd like you to imagine you're in a supermarket buying some fizzy drinks for the family. Here you are, Mrs McConnell, these are the fizzy drinks in front of you. Pick the ones you want for the family and then bring them to me at the checkout, Mrs McConnell. Off you go!

As the child picks and chooses you watch her actions, what she picks up and puts down. When she brings them to you at the checkout you may ask 'Why did you buy that one?' for each drink.

The important thing here is the frequent calling of the child by her mother's name in order to aid her getting into role, and to remember to ask a simple, fairly direct, but open-ended question about each of her purchases.

Next, another child may have a go and the results may be compared and contrasted.

Acting out the advertisements   We often play games like this as a variant of 'Give Us A Clue' (a TV game based on charades) in which one, two or three children (depending upon the number of characters in the ad) act out elements of a TV advertisement and the other children, who are excluded from the room while the screening of the commercial and the practice are going on, have to guess what the advertisement is from the enactment. It's important to let the children themselves decide which elements to portray and it can often be useful in a competitive advertising situation to allow them to choose which advertisement to act — you may then ask them later why they chose it.

You must be prepared to allow practice time (10 minutes or so) and to offer support if the children get stuck. You may offer to take a minor part or to hum a piece of music — providing it is not pivotal to the scene. You could be one of the marching children in a Captain Birds eye advertisement, for example, but it's important for you *not* to play the Captain himself, just because you're the adult. It's their view of the Captain that we need to discover.

Once they are ready you may call the others back in and ask them to watch. Remind them that it's an advertisement they're watching. After the enactment it's very interesting to ask the audience what they think of the characters, for example 'What did you think of Captain Birds Eye?' Children are quite likely to be frank about other children in role or not; they are much less likely to be frank about an old grandparental adult. You may also use the experience to note which parts of the advertisement offer seminal communication as opposed to parts which may be ignored or deleted from the enactment.

Acting real life   In a recent study of cereals we invited children to act out 'Breakfast at Home'. They were encouraged to arrange the room as much like their home as possible — other group members were invited to play the key roles of other participants in the real scene — brothers, sisters, parents and so on. The protagonist mimes and vocalizes his own behaviour and tells the other participants what to say and then they say it. He gives his response and the scene moves on. The important thing is to stand near the protagonist at all times and make sure that he directs the essentials of the action. It's his breakfast-time scene that we're studying — what are the influences operating on him during this scene? How do the brands figure? How does his choice come about?

PROJECTIVE TECHNIQUES

The variants of these techniques in common use with children in our practices are:

(a)   Projective drawing.
(b)   Sending postcards.
(c)   Word association
(d)   Completion tests (word-bubble completion).
(e)   Picture/collage construction (with older children, 10 +).
(f)   Story writing or completion.

Projective drawing

Projective drawing is by far the most versatile, especially with the young, and we shall concentrate on that. However, more recently we have found it advisable to leave the child to choose whether she draws, writes or draws *and* writes.

Some *advantages* of projective drawing or writing are:

- It's a medium with which children are comfortable.
- It represents a move away from school/question and answer session.
- It helps overcome difficulties in articulating certain ideas.
- It overcomes shyness.
- Children are more uncomfortable with silences in question/answer sessions. Anxiety blocks responses.
- It engages the child (rather than pseudo-adult in the child) — particularly important with toys, etc.
- It helps break down posturing — there is a reluctance to admit to an interest in things they see as too *young*.
- You may gain a better measure of children's understanding of something; if they can't talk about it, let them project in drawing or writing. If they

still have problems, it may be that the child doesn't have an internal concept of the subject matter at all and this may be an important finding.

Practical guidelines for projective drawing

- Use felt pens, not crayons (with both the children and clarity at debriefs in mind)
- Have plenty of materials available.
- Have a table to work at.
- Be flexible – allow for drawing *or* writing.
- Don't tell children that there is no correct answer (this is a concept adults understand; children have just learnt at school that there is always a correct answer).
- Join in. (You move into a less judgemental position.)
- Give them plenty of time.
- Let them practise (firm up ideas/relax).
- Note any copying going on (difficult to eliminate – can create upset), notice who is having which idea.
- *Always ask the child to interpret her drawing.* Ask for clarification if you're not clear.
- Don't make assumptions. It's easy to think that they haven't *understood* what you asked them to do because they didn't produce what you expected. Tell them you've forgotten what you asked them to do and ask them to remind you. Were they working on the right lines or not?

Establishing rapport/getting to know the child at a deeper level

All projection contains something of the self, both at the manifest (clearly revealed) and the latent (deep, hidden) levels. We can see this principle at work in projective drawings right from an early age.

One of the best ways of getting to know the child and bringing the child's real-life experience into the room, is to ask him/her to draw (or write about) their family/home. These drawings often contain important latent feelings about the family, as well as practical details such as size of family, siblings, and so on.

The type of things we often see are:

(i)   Children drawing themselves close to one parent, yet far away from another (or with the other parent absent).
(ii)   Child on one side of the house or outside the house, while the parents are on the other side or inside.
(iii)   Child being separated from mother by a younger sibling. Sibling rivalry is often indicated by placing other siblings far away from mother, or leaving them out altogether.
(iv)   Child leaving herself out of the drawing altogether.

As we mentioned earlier, it is important to let the child interpret these drawings. These examples are often (though *not* always) representative of:

(i)   One-parent families, or families where the father works away. One parent is particularly dominant, child is keen to have time with the parent they have placed themselves close to.

(ii) Child feels lonely or excluded by parents, child feels that the house is more important than they are.

(iii) Position has been usurped by arrival of younger child/baby. Mother now gives more attention to it. Sibling rivalry.

(iv) Low self-value, or does not see self as intrinsic to family group.

Sending postcards

Sending postcards is particularly useful for investigating activities like attitudes to or fantasies about going on holiday, going to an amusement park, a day at the museum, a visit to McDonalds. You invite children to send a postcard to someone (whoever they choose) drawing and/or describing an event or activity.

Word association

This is usually played as a group game, with a small prize being offered to the 'last out'. Each child has to make an association with the word that went before as words pass from person to person. The moderator usually starts with a trigger word like 'chocolate' and each child who can't think of a word drops out until only one is left in. The words generated may be compiled and sorted by the children or used as a trigger stimulus to other groups.

Word/thought bubbles

The same technique we described with adults (see p. 106) is easily applied to children.

Picture/collage/story construction

With older children, especially those of ten years and upwards, you may use tear sheets from magazines and invite children to construct a collage of pictures to represent a theme or aspect of their lives, for example:

- A fashionable scene.
- A food page for teenagers.'
- A letter page in a teenage magazine.
- A review of a new BMX or motor bike.
- A great day out.
- Things you always wanted to say to your parents.
- Your motto.
- An advertisement for yourself.

The main uses of projectives in children's research

- To enable further understanding of the subject from the child's perspective.
- To facilitate and access both the child's latent and manifest knowledge and beliefs.
- To engage the true child aspect of the personality (moving away from pseudo-adult questions and answers), which is particularly relevant for products which are to appeal to the uninhibited child (for example toys).
- To see which aspects of advertising or a concept is of most interest to the child by allowing him/her to draw whatever part they want to. (Here practice is important, as the child may initially choose the element which they feel they can manage most effectively.)
- Inventing new products (children are usually far more creative when asked to invent or consider new product ideas when they are allowed to projectively visualize them rather than verbalize about them).
- Communicating perception of brand personality, brand image and attitudes towards products. These are particularly difficult areas to investigate verbally with children.
- An interesting example of uncovering beliefs in such areas was an exercise which we carried out concerning Ribena. When we *talked* to children in groups, it was difficult to differentiate Ribena other than on taste and treat status. However, through projective drawings we established a clear difference in that whereas orange squash is known to have a natural and organic origin — the orange — Ribena is seen to come from an inorganic origin, i.e. the factory. This turned out to be a result of the fact that children had very low awareness and knowledge of blackcurrants as a fruit and of their important associations with Ribena. (See Figures 13.4 and 13.5)

THE VALIDITY ISSUE OR, CAN WE TRUST THE RESULTS?

The question of the reliability of the answers and perspectives generated by children's research is a source of confusion among researchers and research

Figure 13.4   Children's perceptions of the origins of Ribena (the Ribena Factory)

Figure 13.5   Children's perceptions of the origins of orange squash (an orange tree)

users alike. Can we trust anything they say? They change so much. Boys are not the same as girls, are they? Isn't that a leading question?

Once again, we find the confusion stems from a relatively simple source: our adult tendency to take children's answers and reframe them in our own context, using our own map of reality to set the boundaries. If, for example, a child says 'Green is a brilliant colour', taken literally this might imply that our client should make his package bright green. Our job as researchers is to avoid this literal translation – unless it is appropriate – by probing to find the meaning of the utterance to the child. We must, of course, find out what the signifier 'brilliant' means. If the child simply means bright then he/she will say so. If, on the other hand, he means great or favourite then we have a different piece of information, with separate implications.

Green may well be a favourite colour of a number of children but may have cultural inappropriateness in other ways. For example, it is not very favourable as a colour on crisps or potato snacks – here, green means bad, as it does on meat products.

Looking at things through the child's eyes is the key to understanding. Let us demonstrate this point again with a true story from a research project.

Daniel is six. He has been asked by his mother, at the request of the researcher, 'What are the advertisements for?' He replies 'For selling things.' So far, so good. Daniel obviously knows what's going on. But does he?

When asked a little later in the interview 'Who gets the money for the things that are sold in the advertisements?' Daniel thinks for a moment and then says 'The shopkeeper'. The response is a crestfallen client – oh blast! a wasted interview, this child is too young to understand! He doesn't realize that the brand is responsible for the advertising. He doesn't even know what a product is! No more advertising research with the under-sevens.

Thinking more clearly for a moment, back to our developmental stages, we can realize that it *is* inappropriate for Daniel at six years to have an abstract concept like a brand or company, but that notwithstanding, *Daniel's answer makes complete sense within his own context.* In Daniel's life, the commercials are shown on TV and subsequently he or his mum and dad hand money over to the shopkeeper in order to acquire the product. What this implies is that the shop and the shopkeeper are much more closely related to the product in Daniel's life than in yours or mine, and that they might represent potent triggers for Daniel (the nice shopkeeper giving him the product and helping him open it). But, of course, this is *exactly* the same for adults in the area of retailing chains and own labels where Sainsbury's itself is the trigger for all the related brand and product values. In the case of the multiple stores, the shops (and shopkeepers) themselves have taken over from the products. What about store advertising for children?

As you can see, by treating Daniel's answer seriously, as he meant it, not as we initially construed it, we have gained a new perspective; that for a six-year-old, enhancing the experience of the product may involve heightening his perception of the transaction with the storekeeper or the store itself. We would guess that the first store advertising directed specifically at the under 10s is not far away.

It seems to us that the key considerations when thinking about the validity issue are:

(a)   Not to expect children's answer to be the same as adults' − if they were, there would be little point in talking to them.

(b)   To be prepared to understand the significance of the answers from the child's point of view − and then to go on and judge whether this has implications for the strategic, marketing or creative objectives of a communication.

14 Research Stimulus Material

INTRODUCTION

More conflicting and contradictory opinions and beliefs have been stated or written under the heading 'Stimulus Material' than in any other area of contemporary qualitative research. Buyers of research in client companies, buyers and practitioners in advertising agencies, NPD specialists, pack design experts, and researchers all have pet theories about how to present 'ideas' to consumers. There is very little agreement amongst all those professionals and certainly no body of knowledge as yet exists in a collected form, which would allow buyers and practitioners to make informed decisions. The current state of the art is that anyone and everyone has an opinion and one person's views are as valid as the next (see Rose and Heath, 1984).

It is high time that the current myths and beliefs about 'stimulus material' are collected and seriously examined. This chapter attempts to do so.

One of the major reasons for the muddle over stimulus material is that creative development research for advertising, pack design and NPD is relatively new. It is a youthful area of research and therefore one where pragmatic rules are being developed all the time. In the UK, prior to the mid-1970s almost no creative development research was conducted. Qualitative research was used to explore a market, develop hypotheses, understand consumer language prior to quantification and verification. Qualitative research was almost invariably called Stage I, and because it lacked statistical reliability or validity, was rarely used as a method in its own right.

In the last ten years the role of qualitative research has changed entirely, to the situation at present where it is an end in itself and is considered valid without the need for further quantification. This has come about for a number of reasons, of which one of the most important has been the advent of account planning. A planner's role is differently defined according to the advertising agency in question, but on the whole there is agreement that a planner is the *link* between the consumer and the creators of the advertising, ensuring that not only is the advertising memorable and impactful but that it is relevant to the target consumer (in both strategic and executional terms). There is only one way in which a planner can fulfil this difficult task and that is to use qualitative research early on in the creative development programme to help define the (most consumer-relevant) strategy and subsequently to guide the creative process towards the (most consumer-relevant but also executionally exciting) expression of that strategy.

Although planners as such do not exist in pack design companies, and are not necessarily involved in NPD programmes, the same orientation is beginning to become more widespread. Pack design based on creativity alone may be very successful in isolated instances, but on the whole it is more likely to succeed when built on consumer feedback at an *early* stage of development. The same applies to NPD programmes. No one would deny the crucial role of qualitative research in particular, in helping develop an NPD proposition.

WHAT IS STIMULUS MATERIAL?

In order to obtain early feedback from the consumer on a new product, new pack design(s) or new advertising for a brand, something needs to be shown to consumers which sums up the thinking of the creators thus far. This something is 'stimulus material'. Our definition therefore is as follows:

Stimulus material is anything visual and/or aural used to:

a)   communicate a product, pack or advertising IDEA to consumers
or to
b)   trigger consumer responses to a particular area of enquiry

We term the first type DIRECT STIMULUS MATERIAL since its relationship to marketing and advertising is perfectly explicit. The second we term INDIRECT STIMULUS MATERIAL because its form bears no resemblance to a product, pack or advertisement.

Stimulus material takes many forms nowadays. It can be a 3–D pack or a drawing of a pack; a tape explaining a TV commercial or an animatic; a frame by frame representation of the storyline of a TV commercial or a single board outlining the idea, and so on. Each of these has advantages and disadvantages which will be discussed further on in this chapter. At this point we shall simply list the main types in use in the mid-1980s, giving a short explanation of each.

Concept boards
Animatics
Storyboards
Flip-over boards
Narrative tapes, with/without key frame visuals
Photomatics
Mock-up packs
Admatics
Mock press releases, editorial, direct mail shots

Concept boards

These are single boards on which the product, pack or advertising idea is expressed verbally and/or visualized. Usually a set of concept boards are used rather than one in isolation.

Animatics

Key frames for a commercial are drawn and then filmed on video with an accompanying sound track. The effect is of a somewhat jerky animated TV film, using drawn characters to represent live action.

Storyboards

Key frames for a commercial are drawn consecutively, like a comic strip. The script is sometimes written underneath and/or is played on a tape recorder with special effects (for example, a jingle, the sound of water, running footsteps).

Flip-over boards

Key frames for a commercial are drawn as above, but to avoid the respondents reading ahead, are exposed one by one, by the interviewer in time to a taped sound track.

Narrative tapes

This consists of an audio tape on which a voice artist narrates the dialogue and explains the action of the commercial. It is not simply the sound track, in as much as the action is explained, the characters described and the dialogue narrated by a voice. This tape may or may not be accompanied by key visuals.

Photomatics

A form of animatic using photographs instead of drawn key frames, thus showing the characters and scenes realistically rather than drawn representations.

Mock-up packs

The new design (box, label or physical shape) is mocked up in 3–D, to make the product look as 'real' as possible.

Admatics

These are a development of animatics, changing crudely animated storyboards into something more nearly approaching the level of a finished commercial by using computer-generated and manipulated images.

Mock press material

A new product (usually) is written about in editorial style and presented to consumers as part of a magazine, or newspaper (that is, a mock 'interview', 'write up' or 'press release').

Before one examines the advantages and disadvantages of each of these types of stimulus material in relation to the different stages of the creative development process as well as to the different media, it is essential to examine some basic principles.

● What do respondents 'see' when we show stimulus material?
● The issues of 'rough' and 'real' in relation to stimulus material.
● 'Decoding' stimulus material — how do consumers create meaning?

WHAT DO RESPONDENTS REALLY 'SEE'?

As professionals operating in a marketing and advertising environment, we are used to discussing products and advertising as abstract ideas, well before their execution as a reality. We have developed our own language for communicating with one another such as 'concept', 'rough idea', 'creative idea','positioning concept', 'positioning statement', 'adcept', 'total proposition' and so on. When material is developed for research it has usually been 'briefed' to the visualizer using this sort of terminology and it is here that a 'Chinese Whisper' game begins to operate.

Take for example the brief to develop a number of positioning concepts for a product. Those involved may well isolate five to six different possibilities which require visualization: that is, a drawing or photograph together with a concise statement of each positioning. The creative assigned to this task, given his background, training and own unique style of expression, produces five to six boards which look like 'posters' or 'press ads' but which everyone involved, including the researchers who have to use the material, talk about as 'concepts' or 'the concept boards'.

Now what happens when you take these 'concepts' into qualitative research? Rose and Heath (1984) stated that *'Consumers evaluate all research stimuli as advertisements: most find it difficult to deal with concepts or ideas and need to evaluate these within a known framework'*. Consumers attend qualitative research sessions having been given an explanation about why market research is necessary and what their contribution will be. They therefore know in advance, if not in fine detail, that the unwritten contract between themselves and the interviewer is to do with an exchange of information which will eventually be used for marketing or advertising purposes. It is hardly surprising, then, that the 'concepts' when exposed are perceived as advertisements – in press or poster form.

If the research is being conducted at an early stage of the creative development process, when the concept boards represent various positionings or strategies, then the reactions of consumers to the boards as 'advertisements' is very misleading, if not destructive. The more often consumers are told that the board is *not* an advertisement (poster) but is an idea of what could be suggested about a product, the less likely they are to change their perspective. If you tell someone who is happily climbing up a very tall ladder not to look down to see how high he is, he is almost 100% likely to start feeling anxious and might well look down! So too with a concept board. If you tell a consumer, it is *not* an advertisement (but it looks exactly like one), he will not think of it in any other way unless you tell him what it *is*. Since the word 'concept board' is alien to him, some other context must be provided *or the stimulus must not bear any superficial resemblance to an advertisement*.

This problem occurs with other forms of direct stimulus material too. Narrative tapes are evaluated in the context of radio advertisements or plays and therefore respondents apply criteria of evaluation which are totally unhelpful to the development of the TV advertisement, such as: is the 'playlet' entertaining or boring; is the voice-over engaging, someone I know or a turn-off and so on. Animatics are evaluated as cartoon advertisements in spite of the instructions to the contrary, whilst storyboards are often evaluated in a 'cartoon strip' context. Against these perceptual contexts, consumers repeatedly use criteria such as impact, characterization, entertainment value, and finer executional details to evaluate the 'concepts' rather than responding to the idea, that is, the deep structure rather than the superficial expression.

The fact that consumers evaluate all direct advertising research stimuli as advertisements (excluding mock-up packs or 'press release' type materials), is just as much of a problem at the later stages of creative development, as at the earlier stages. Unless a great deal of care is given to the executional details, the material will be evaluated as a *poor quality* press poster, radio or cartoon-advertisement. In these cases both respondents and advertising creators have the same frame of reference (i.e. an advertisement) but respondents will not make allowances for anything that is unfinished. They see it as 'the real thing' and will harshly criticize its weaknesses.

THE ISSUES OF 'ROUGH' AND 'REAL'

We cannot emphasize too strongly the fact that consumers do not see 'rough ideas' when shown direct research stimulus material that approximates an advertising format; they see a finished execution, that is, a finished idea. An idea, as soon as it is expressed verbally or visually or both, becomes a complete entity, and responsibility must be taken for its existence.

Again, by telling consumers that the material is 'only a rough advertisement' or 'designed to give you a rough idea' does not succeed. Consumers see a reality, and because of the previous instruction are not sure how to respond. Often the response is very inhibited. For example:

> 'I know you said it's rough, but it doesn't do anything to me'

or

> 'I heard you said it's unfinished but I don't like the picture of the man and women looking at each other like that.'

Whether the form is rough or finished, the execution itself affects responses to it. Because of this fact, two schools of thought about this issue of rough and 'real' have come into being.

Many NPD specialists and pack designers now believe it is vitally important that the product (whether new or simply redesigned) comes across to consumers as *real*. Taking NPD as an example, consumers first hear about a product via a friend, see an advertisement, read about it in the editorial of a magazine or newspaper or simply see it on the shelves. The theory is, then, that in research the consumer should be exposed to the product in a form that's familiar to her, such as a radio commercial, a mock-up pack shown in a competitive context, an article in a magazine, a press release, a point-of-sale promotional item and so on.

Specialists in NPD have experienced, with much pain, the loss of good new ideas through ill thought-out research stimuli, and thus in recent years more innovative research stimuli have been developed. Some of these have been discussed on pp. 216–27.

In contrast, those working in pack design have paid little attention to the whole question of how best to expose new packaging concepts to consumers. All too often consumers are shown half-a-dozen front-of-pack designs mounted on white cardboard, or a drawing of a new pack shape showing a transverse section of the opening mechanism. With this type of material the consumer is encouraged to play the role of pack design critic, focussing on executional details and differences rather than reacting to the pack as a product or brand. In the latter case, mechanical drawings are completely confusing. A new type of opening for a sauce can only be understood as a reality, not as a drawing.

Thus, increasingly, manufacturers, researchers and designers are coming to the view that, expensive as it is to make 3–D mock-ups which approximate the reality of the product in weight or colour, it is worth it. Research is an expensive process, therefore its contribution needs to be maximized by 'feeding in' the stimuli which will help decision-making. If the stimuli are too artificial, the research guidance will be artificial too.

The question of artificiality or reality is very complex in relation to the development of advertising.

With the exception of a photomatic, admatic or a well-produced animatic, the issue of realism is almost impossible to deal with in early creative development research. Narrative tapes, storyboards, concept boards and so on are very far removed from real advertising and in fact each format bears no resemblance to the end product, that is, a TV commercial.

For this reason, many advertising professionals prefer to use these research stimuli *very early on* in the creative development process, to *explore* strategy options or to explore a number of different executional *routes* for a given strategy, but not to pre-test the advertisement itself.

Taking the TV types of stimuli as examples first (that is, all narrative tapes and storyboards/flip-over boards), such material cannot be used to evaluate communication of the commercial, assess branding or measure impact. It can simply be helpful to explore whether or not the underlying strategy is meaningful to consumers and whether or not the executional 'clothing' seems interesting, different and relevant to that particular brand in terms of the product category in general, and also in terms of contemporary advertising trends more widely. Provided the executional evaluations from consumers are ignored, such stimulus material can be extremely useful at the beginning of campaign development.

As a result of continual frustration with the range of direct stimulus material used in early creative development research, advertising and research professionals have been searching for new solutions. These research stimuli are even further removed from the advertising end product but add to the armoury already available.

HOW DO CONSUMERS CREATE MEANING?

We have shown in the two preceding sections that stimulus material does not occur in a vacuum. Consumers contextualize the stimulus in order to establish parameters for evaluation. Often this context is not one we, as product, pack or advertising developers wish them to use, but we cannot do anything about it because we have not created the appropriate context.

Alongside this problem of context is the fact that consumers decode a stimulus in a way that may be very different from that intended by its creators. The idea of decoding has come from semiology/semiotics, the study of signs and symbols, the principles of which are extremely valuable when applied to communication.

Using this theoretical background, we can understand how human beings within a particular culture or social group create meaning. *Meaning is created by signs or symbols operating within a system or code.* For example the sign 'red', shown in a 'traffic' code or system, signifies danger. But red only has meaning as a signifier because green signifies safety. Signs do not operate as independent units of meaning but only have meaning in opposition to one another. Thus red meat, in the code of food hygiene, signifies safety because green meat (or a non-red colour) signifies danger.

Returning to stimulus material, the creator encodes meaning by his unique choice of visual, verbal or aural signs and symbols. But it is not necessarily a corollary that the consumer will decode the integrated stimulus in the same way, because the creator may not have understood the codes in a particular system. For example, a Benson and Hedges cigarette advertisement showed a snake's track on the desert sand, the sloughed skin forming the shape of the cigarette pack. Consumers did not decode this advertisement (that is, these symbols) in a positive way. Instead the snake as a symbol of danger, the sloughed skin as a symbol of something discarded, all combined in such a way to be decoded as an anti-cigarette advertisement. Similarly, one of the famous Strand advertisement illustrates another decoding problem. The creator chose to show the Strand smoker alone at night, at peace with himself and self-contained because of his Strand cigarette; the consumer decoded the smoker as a loner, Strand thus symbolizing alienation.

Thus, stimulus material can easily be decoded in a completely different way to the way intended, resulting in the 'deep idea' being lost because the signs (and combination thereof) were chosen in an arbitrary manner.

In order to cope with the arbitrariness of much of the stimulus material used in creative development research, new thinking and new material is being developed, some of which can be used alongside the conventional material already described, and some of which makes the existing types of material unnecessary.

THE NEW STIMULUS MATERIAL

The new stimulus material is indirect. In its form and the way in which it is used in research it bears no resemblance to the direct research stimuli discussed in the first part of this chapter. Indirect stimulus material has been developed from an understanding of semiotics and post-structuralism, both of which have found more ready acceptance amongst French communications theorists and research practitioners than amongst their English colleagues.

However at the time of writing more and more qualitative practitioners and end-users in the UK are beginning to become receptive to these theories and to find ways of applying them to practical advertising and marketing problems (Dyer, G. 1984).

All of us, when faced with an incomplete or ambiguous stimulus, make efforts to complete or clarify it. We draw on our beliefs and attitudes, our past experiences and also the cultural norms and codes of our social group or society.

The indirect stimulus material is open-ended. It allows consumers to project their own meaning on to the material, thus enabling the researcher to understand the complex interrelationship of signs and symbols which carry meaning in a particular product field or for a particular brand.

The different types of new stimulus material which have been developed are:

Thought tapes
Creative or marketing 'talkie' tapes
Visual collages
Video collages
Vocabulary boards
Packaging shapes and mechanics

These can be used in many different types of research study, whether fundamental research studies of attitudes and beliefs in a market generally, a product category or a specific brand; or developmental projects of any kind (NPD, packaging, brand advertising). They cannot be used to determine or evaluate *how well* a particular advertisement meets the strategy objectives, since they are *not advertisements*.

Thought tapes

A mock consumer depth interview or group discussion which highlights known or hypothetical needs, attitudes or beliefs about a particular category or brand. The persons playing consumers are not given a script but are briefed carefully beforehand on the position each one should take in relation to the subject under discussion. The tape sounds extremely natural, giving respondents permission to be hesitant, jocular, serious or thoughtful. Often the 'actors' are briefed to articulate very different points of view, respondents being encouraged to place their own opinions on the spectrum defined. Thought tapes are invaluable alternatives to concept boards for strategy development but can also be used to understand the emotional tone of response in relation to a particular advertising, packaging or product idea. This type of indirect stimulus can also be used to break the ice when the subject matter is intimate eg contraception, AIDS, body odour.

Vocabulary lists

Most people when asked to articulate feelings about a subject which is normally taken for granted, such as advertising, supermarket shopping, image of day-to-day products, find it extremely difficult. Most have a fairly limited vocabulary which even experienced interviewers find impossible to penetrate eg:

Interviewer: 'What do you think of this?'
Respondent: 'I suppose it's quite nice'
Interviewer: 'What do you mean by nice? Can you tell me a little more?'
Respondent: 'Well it looks ok, quite attractive'
Interviewer: 'Attractive, in what sort of way?'
Respondent: 'It just appeals to me . . . I can't really say why'

A vocabulary list shown to a respondent at this point, which has been especially designed for the project will help her to find a range of words to express a view that may be *felt* rather than thought. A vocabulary list consists of adjectives, verbs or phrases. See Figures 14.1, 14.2, 14.3 and 14.4.

Visual collages

These are collage boards made up of scrap art cut from magazines or newspapers. They are carefully designed at the beginning of a research project and provide consumers with open-ended image options from which, for example they can create and express aspects of a brand's personality or can be used to explain the user-image of a product or advertisement. See Figures 14.5–14.8. Visual collage boards can be designed to explore abstract concepts such as romance, freshness, modernity, wisdom, balance and many more. They can also be used to understand the most meaningful symbols for a particular brand. For example, for a shampoo brand, visual collages exploring colour, consistency, cleansing, conditioning, perfume, ingredients, hair colour, women, and so on would be used to understand which combinations of elements most effectively and uniquely define a brand. Finally, they can be used to explore mood, through the use of colour boards or collages representing mood states such as excitement, depression, curiosity, amusement.

Video collages

Humorously called 'Stealomatics' by one Agency, these are becoming popular as a way of showing consumers the proposed *form* of the advertisement – its filmic style (quick cuts, cinematic devices), its mood, tone of voice, type of music, appearance of the characters, visual juxtapositions and so on. Video collages are used to supplement *direct* stimulus material which usually carries

If it made me feel . . .	*by easing . . .*	*in my . . .*
calm	aches	head
well	pains	stomach
healthy	discomfort	bowel
sprightly	tightness	eyes
sparkling	tenderness	neck
clearheaded	soreness	ears
comfortable	fullness	nose
strong	nausea	back
together	heaviness	limbs

Figure 14.1 Exploring the vocabulary for a new analgesic

the responsibility for conveying the structure of the idea such as the sequence of actions, the script, the time, place and characters.

Packaging shapes and mechanics

This type of research stimulus, which is a graphic illustration, allows the

If it has . . .

a car phone	cushions
a sticker	covered steering wheel
a dangling ornament	leather upholstery
a nodding dog	plastic upholstery
a St Christopher medal	fur upholstery
'Just married'	fabric upholstery
stripes on outside	skirts round outside

If it has . . . (as a standard option)

manual gears	back screen washers
automatic gears	an electronic voice
overdrive	digital dashboard
5-speed gear box	radial tyres
power steering	continental lights
heated rear window	radio
3-speed wipers	cassette player
air conditioning	dashboard warning lights
electric windows	sunroof

Figure 14.2 Exploring the images cues of car drivers

a house	property	small business
a car	stocks	venture capital
home improvement	shares	horse racing
luxury goods	unit trusts	casinos
antiques	bonds	dog racing
pictures	foreign currency	education – for me
clothes	pension funds	education – for my children
jewellery	insurance	education – for my grandchildren
furs	building societies	
expensive clothes	gilt funds	

Figure 14.3 Exploring investments

SAUCE	CREAMY RELISH
PICKLES	ACCOMPANIMENT
RELISH	SPICY PICKLE
CONDIMENT	MIXTURE
CHUTNEY	SALAD CREAM
MAYONNAISE	JUICE
GARNISH	DIP
DRESSING	SPREAD
KETCHUP	FILLER

Figure 14.4 Market segment vocabulary for a new product

Figure 14.5 Abstract collage representing competence, potency, control and dominance

223

Figure 14.6 Visual collage (exploring water symbols)

224

Figure 14.7 Brand personality collage (by excluding physical norms of beauty [hair, face] consumers create a brand personality in terms of fashion imagery)

Figure 14.8 Packaging shapes (exploring the imagery of shapes)

researcher to understand how the rational and emotional aspects of product imagery are communicated by packaging and mechanical design elements. The shapes (Figure 14.8) are explored in relation to the product category, (in this case whisky), and the brand, giving consumers a visual shape vocabulary to express their views. This type of board is particularly suitable to new product development research.

'Talkie tapes'

These are mock interviews (also unscripted) with an authority figure such as a Creative Director, Marketing Director, Policeman, Teacher, Doctor, Nurse or anyone relevant who might be perceived to wield authority or expertise in relation to the subject being discussed. The 'authorities' can be used in different ways; to explain the idea behind a new advertisement or product, to explain the problem which consumers are being invited to help resolve, or to explore a strategic route of endorsement (eg a hairdresser or restaurant owner discussing the brand). In each case, executional details do not interfere since the interview format, with its inbuilt hesitancy and realism, involves consumers. Additionally since the Talkie Tape in no way resembles a commercial or radio playlet, it is accepted without question for what it seems to be.

The most important point to make about this type of open-ended projective stimulus material is that *the interpretation of what it all means lies with consumers.* It is they who select a number of visuals or words and explain to the moderator *why* they have done so and *how* the images or words relate to the area being discussed. We want to emphasise that stimulus material of this type simply triggers response in the same way as the projective techniques described in Chapter 8. Consumers themselves create and explain the meanings they make. We researchers evaluate whether or not these explanations are relevant.

THE CHOICE OF STIMULUS MATERIAL

How do we choose which form of stimulus to use to convey the ideas we have in mind? There are two factors to bear in mind:

(i)   stage in the creative development process;
(ii) intended medium (press, poster, TV, radio).

We have covered the three stages of the creative development process in Chapter 1, when examining the role of qualitative research in advertising development. To recap, the three stages are:

Strategy Definition: What should we be saying and to whom?

Creative Development: How should we be saying this?

Pre-testing: How well are we doing this against the objectives we set ourselves?

Stages in the creative development process

Stimuli for strategy definition

In order to define an advertising strategy it is necessary to understand as much as possible about the relationship of the consumer to the product category in general and to the brand in particular. Currently, the majority of professionals would recommend *concept boards* which can be executed in different ways. Product or positioning descriptions are purely verbal and describe either what the product *is* (for example, 'a new chewy chocolate bar with a healthy filling made of honey, muesli and malt') or a possible strategic route ('a different savoury snack for the new health-conscious family'). This very same information can be executed differently. A product name and pack design can be drawn graphically and the benefit expressed in advertising copy accompanied by a visual representing, for example, a health-conscious family:

'JOGGER – the new health bar for the fit family'
(illustration of family in tracksuits jogging in the countryside)

Adcepts are a fairly new type of concept board and came into being in response to the problems faced by image-led products. Certain brands nowadays, for example in the countline and toiletry markets, have *no* unique properties but are differentiated from their competitors by the style of advertising or brand personality. These ideas cannot be expressed as bald statements since they only come to life through the clothing of advertising. Professionals have attempted to create advertising concepts, that is, integrated verbal and visual pieces of communication, that incorporate advertising *values*. Unfortunately, because of the problems of decoding described earlier, the authors' experience with these have been far from satisfactory.

However executed, concept boards are quick and easy to prepare, cheap and good for sorting out a wide range of ideas at an early stage. As with all stimulus material, there are good concept boards and bad ones. Good concept boards are those which are *considered* and *well thought through* in relation to the role of research at that particular stage and its overall objectives. Concept boards are, in essence, hypotheses about possible positionings for a product or strategies for the eventual communication to the target market. They need then to encompass *the extremes*, which help diagnostically to pinpoint what limiting parameters exist for the brand.

The main problem with concept boards is that they only use a few signs or symbols in one particular combination. The combination each time is arbitrary.

One either hits paydirt or one does not. Thus in executional terms, it is crucial to make the stimulus open rather than closed, presenting a range of possibilities or executional triggers for response rather than one. The example on page 224 shows how this can be achieved.

Additionally, visual collages, vocabulary lists, 'thought tapes' and 'talkie tapes' can provide a method of exhausting all the possibilities without exhausting the respondents. The consumer isolates meaningful symbols and relates these to each other in a particular code or system thus allowing the researcher to give direction and guidance based on careful analysis rather than intuitive hunches.

Stimuli for creative development

It is at the stage of creative development that professionals are most at odds with one another. Rose and Heath (1984) showed that the same script, when given to a sample of professionals, attracted widely different direct research stimulus recommendations namely narrative tapes, animatics and storyboards, all of which tend to be used most frequently in the current climate. All have strengths and weaknesses.

Narrative tapes have the advantage of being quick, easy and cheap to produce, and are therefore a very helpful option when a number of advertising ideas require evaluation. A significant indication of whether or not a narrative tape is appropriate or not is to decide whether the advertising idea relies on nuances of tone, mood, imagery, relationships, expressions and so on to convey the main and supporting messages. Such subtleties are impossible to communicate with any other type of visual research stimulus, and attempts to do so often result in consumer-literal responses which interfere with an assessment of the main idea.

Good narrative tapes are short (less than two minutes in length), free of jargon related to film production (such as 'cut to man's face' or 'freezeframe') and establish the emotional background of the commercial (whether the action is serious or a send-up; what kind of character(s); the type of setting – modern traditional upmarket; the period and so on). A well-produced narrative tape sets the scene, establishes the characters and conveys the mood rather than concentrating on the logicial sequence of actions. The use of open-ended material such as visual or video collages can help in providing creative guidance for future development (see David Stewart-Hunter, 1984).

A criticism of the narrative tape is that each consumer imagines a different scenario and/or different characters and these may bear no resemblance at all to the advertising idea as conceived by the creator. It has also been demonstrated that consumers apply judgements relevant to *radio*, rather than TV, because there are no visual aids to establish parameters and ground the imagination. Thus accompanying key visual frames are often used to give more control over what consumers are imagining.

Research has shown that consumers find narrative tapes the least easy stimulus to evaluate. There is no relationship between stimulus (aural) and end-product (visual), the length is confusing and consumers find it difficult to retain the large amount of information. Thus, narrative tapes tend to magnify defects in the narrative script or execution since the sound track assumes a relatively greater importance. The narrator's voice too can interfere with communication if perceived to be droning, irritating or even if recognizable, that is, famous. Consumers do not know where to look, and if accompanying visuals are used, focus on these so intently that some of the aural content can be lost.

Storyboards, like narrative tapes and concept boards, are relatively quick and cheap to produce. The advantage of the storyboard is that consumers are able to relate the form (cartoon strip/sequence of actions) to the end product (a commercial) and view each frame as a blueprint for each scene: for example, a commercial in three acts with two scenes in each act. There is also no confusion, in that without doubt, the stimulus is a commercial 'in the making'.

However, the problems of execution discussed previously are a problem here too. Storyboards are limited when it comes to conveying imagery, mood or atmosphere and suffer from being static if the final script relies on fast-moving film techniques or scenarios dependent on movement and action.

Storyboards are best suited to simple advertising ideas, that is, those where the characters are well known stereotypes and therefore immediately recognizable from drawings such as Dracula, cowboys, Royalty, aristocrats, rock stars or where the sequence of actions is straightforward and almost tells a story.

In order to overcome some of these inherent problems, storyboards are often accompanied by a well-produced sound track, particularly important if music, dialogue or special effects are key to the advertising idea or if the scene needs to be established prior to the first frame.

Well planned storyboards with an accompanying sound track, executed with care and foresight, can be extremely successful. Again, visual or video collages can be used to help consumers articulate the most relevant executional values for the development of the advertisement.

Animatics are widely used in contemporary creative development research and have their fans as well as their critics. Enthusiasts believe that an animatic gives the best indication of how a final film will work since structurally and in timing terms it is very similar. It is thus a realistic format for consumers and, from the viewpoint of the agency, can be made to incorporate some production values. It is more open, so it is believed, to objective interpretation of reactions, although we would contest this view (see Chapter 10).

As with all research stimuli, animatics can be good or bad depending on the orientation of those involved. As a general principle, however, great care should be taken in the choice of visualizer. Captain Pugwash[1] characters are difficult to imagine as real human beings and tend to heighten the likelihood of consumers evaluating the animatic against cartoon film criteria rather than those necessary for a live action film.

The main criticism levelled at the animatic is that it is inappropriate for many ideas, particularly those that are dramatic, stylized, reliant on mood or tone, dependent on human expressions for communication or are intended to be cast with a famous person. In fact the animatic is not that well suited to advertising ideas that are emotionally-based pieces of communication, unless all concerned are willing to use a large amount of judgement in evaluating its likely effect as a finished film.

Stimuli for pre-testing

Pre-testing, that is, that phase of creative development which is concerned with how well the advertisement meets the advertising objectives, is extremely contentious since the role of research is 'thumbs up or thumbs down' rather than developmental. As the name implies, the advertisement is being *tested* and therefore stringent criteria of evaluation are applied.

As mentioned in the previous section, the only way to pre-test a TV commercial (if this is deemed necessary) is either to make it or to make an animatic or admatic. However, as we have explained, the unsuitability of the animatic form for certain types of commercials almost guarantees that, unless judgement is liberally applied, the commercial will be seen to fail, thus fuelling the belief so often expressed by creatives that 'research kills all good ideas'.

Admatics are a new development of animatics using computer-assisted images and animation to create a more realistic facsimile of a finished advertisement. They may be created from scratch using visuals which are actually drawn on the computer by an artist, or developed from photographic or filmed material by digitizing the photographs, storing them in the computer and building up animated sequences from them.

In the case of film, we digitize approximately one frame in four and thus produce a very realistic recreation of the actual filmed material. Any elements of this sequence, such as clothes, faces or backgrounds, may then be altered, reshaped or recoloured to fit in with the advertising agency's creative intentions.

Admatics have several strong advantages over animatics:

- They avoid the 'Captain Pugwash' effect,
- They can realistically create difficult subjects like skies and landscapes, movement, explosions, animation, mixtures of animation and live action, subtle facial expressions, detailed packaging,
- Because every aspect of the Admatic is stored in the computer's memory, they may be altered in any essential detail as the research progresses. Every researcher knows the problems of an idea failing because of a detail of execution which, no matter how hard the moderator tries to explain it away, keeps tripping consumers up.

An example her was an animatic for lager in which the central protagonist for the brand was wearing a tartan shirt. When exposed to groups in

Scotland – a key market for the brand – all of the young drinkers rejected the idea outright since in Scotland the only people who wear tartan shirts are posers and tourists.

Using the Admatic format any detail of the commercial may be changed (hair colour, facial expressions, dress, backgrounds) usually within 24 hours or so of the first research session.

Advertising medium

We have discussed the medium of TV in some detail, emphasizing the importance of stage of development of the advertising and the nature of the idea itself in determining the form of the stimulus.

With regard to press, poster and radio advertising the issue of *context* has more influence on the form of the stimulus material than stage of advertising development.

One of the crucial questions to explore before deciding on the form of the stimulus material is *reality of context*. For example, if an advertisement is designed to be a 48-sheet poster, should it be researched as an A4-sized advertisement or vice versa; should a press advertisement be blown-up on to a 3' by 2' stimulus board for exposure to consumers? Since it is our belief that context is crucial, a radio commercial needs to be evaluated in a radio environment, a large poster in an outdoor environment, and press advertisements in an editorial environment. The closer the advertising idea is to a finished execution, the more importance should be given to context.

A radio commercial can be inserted into a 3–4 minute (or longer) excerpt from a commercial radio station in which the break includes other radio commercials besides the one being researched. Consumers are recruited on the basis that they listen to commercial radio, but are not told about the subject of the interview. The tape is played and the respondent questioned in terms of recall of programme content as well as advertisements. This methodology allows the researcher to evaluate, more realistically, the impact of the commercial, its intrusiveness compared to other commercials in the break, and the key points communicated. After further exposure to the commercial, the details of the advertising idea can be explored.

With regard to the outdoor media (posters and tube advertisements) there are two possibilities, depending on the level of finish of the advertising ideas.

If the advertisement is still unfinished (that is, drawn rather than photographed, written rather than typeset) respondents can be exposed to a number of photographs of the environment, for example, bus shelters showing Adshel sites, busy streets showing posters, underground stations showing advertisements. These are used to help respondents to imagine the environment in which the advertisement will appear, and are used to trigger the appropriate emotional mood, for example, irritation or boredom in the underground. The chosen advertisements are then exposed on *large* stimulus boards, since the medium is large rather than small.

If the advertisement is finished (or near-finished) it can be photographed on 35mm slide. Competitive advertisements are also photographed, together with outdoor scenes (buses, traffic, poster sites) or the tube environment. Respondents are shown the slides very quickly, the slides being projected to a size that bears some resemblance to reality, that is, large!

With regard to press advertising, two different methods are available. The first is to print the advertisement on the equivalent type of paper and to insert it loosely in the magazine or newspaper. Although the context of viewing the advertisement is realistic, this method cannot be used to measure impact since respondents will know which advertisement is being researched. The second method is to conduct a folder test. The advertisement is placed in a folder amongst other advertisements that occur in a particular newspaper or magazine or amongst a selection of competitive advertisements, for example, all shampoo advertisements. Editorial extracts can also be placed in the folder to give a more realistic environment. In both cases, the respondent is encouraged to page through 'as if paging through a magazine or newspaper in the doctor's waiting room'.

We have learned a number of important lessons about designing stimulus material as a result of being involved in hundreds of projects where the research stimuli interfered with rather than helped the development of the creative idea.

1   There is no off-the-peg answer. Each time material is required, time and energy need to be expended in making sure that the best solution is found.

2   If you are not yet at the stage of researching an advertisement (i.e. headline and copy or script) then design stimuli that bear no resemblance to the form of an advertisement or commercial.

3   Think in terms of a stimulus kit. No one piece of stimulus material may be able to convey the full idea to consumers, so use one type to convey the structure of the advertisement (e.g. the sequence of actions or scenes, the time period, the characters) *and* other types to convey the form of the advertisement (the mood, photographic style, characterization, humour).

4   Consider the implications of context and attempt to help consumers to enter into the particular advertising environment in which your advertisement or campaign will appear.

5   If you are using rough stimuli (whether packs, concepts or advertisements) *always* expect consumers to respond to the execution rather than the core idea, and when it comes to interpreting the results of such research, question whether or not the core idea was *ever* fully explored, or whether the arbitrary choice of executional details interfered with consumers' access to the idea.

6 Think carefully about the issue of rough and real particularly in relation to pack design development. Pack designs which are produced to explore directions can be less finished than a pack design that is submitted as a solution to a pack design brief.

In summary, there are a key number of points to be kept in mind in the design of stimulus material for advertising research. There are only a few questions, which, if asked every time, should lead to the design and production of stimulus material that nurtures rather than destroys creative ideas:

Where are we in the cycle of developing advertising – early strategy development, creative development (early or late?) or pre-testing?

What is the essence of the idea we need to communicate to consumers – is it dependent on imagery or is it a rational proposition?

Do we have an advertisement (or TV commercial) to explore? If not, then how can we produce a stimulus that looks nothing like an advertisement or TV commercial?

How real can we afford the stimulus to be given that the preparation of elaborate stimulus material is very costly?

NOTE

1. Captain Pugwash is a very simplified cartoon character on children's TV.

We would like to express our indebtedness to Ginny Valentine for her innovative work in developing new stimulus material.

15 Qualitative and Quantitative Hybrid Methodologies

The thirty-year war between qualitative and quantitative researchers still flares up in the form of the occasional skirmish with minor injuries on either side, but, on the whole, truce has been declared and happily we are beginning to see signs of co-operation and respect between followers of the two religions. Religions they are, since defenders of either side can still be fanatical and irrational in their denouncements of the other and completely blind to the weaknesses of their own faith.

It is the recognition of strengths and weaknesses of qualitative and quantitative research approaches that has brought about the new peace and indeed has triggered the development of hybrid methodologies which have been designed to maximize the strengths whilst overcoming the weaknesses of both approaches.

The main differences between quantitative and qualitative methodologies have been highlighted in Chapter 1. Most practising researchers and end-users would argue that a quantitative approach has two advantages over a qualitative one — numerical measurement and supposed researcher objectivity.

Quantitative methodologies certainly provide measurement — numerical comparisons between items within a survey (for example, attribute comparisons across brands) or between surveys conducted at different points in time. These measurements which are based on 'reasonable' numbers of people (usually not less than 50 and as many as several thousand) can be subjected to different kinds of statistical tests providing the twin benefits of validity and reliability. The understanding of the consumer-brand relationship is made on the basis of *patterns of numerical proportions* rather than insights provided by one or several individuals. We shall show later in this chapter that contrary to the myths in our business small qualitative samples of respondents can also provide useful, ordered and reproducable data.

In terms of process rather than methodology, the major difference between the two seems to centre on the role of the researcher. In qualitative work, the introspections of the researcher are regarded as a valuable, often essential, component of the data base. This is why the methodology in qualitative research has focussed on the extended individual interview or group discussion, to give the interviewer time to get to know the individual and how she sees things. It is in understanding how individual people create meaning from the world about them and how brands or services play a role in the culture to which an individual belongs, in both the micro and macro sense of the term, that the strengths of qualitative research lie.

The main danger of this type of approach is seen to be that the interviewer projects his own unique view of the world or his own fantasies of what the dialogue with the consumer meant after the interviewing event. This is why the controls of recording, content analysis and observation by other members of a research project are vital in qualitative work. In quantitative work, the interviewer who administers the questionnaire has no part to play in the compilation and interpretation of the results whatsoever. This is often viewed as a strength but in our view is a great weakness. The research executive who designs the study and is responsible for the structure, syntax and content of the questionnaire, as well as the interviewer who asks the questions and rewards or punishes with body language cues, both influence the results.

Neither quantitative nor qualitative methodology is without bias. By acknowledging and understanding the different types of bias, one can decide which approach is most appropriate for the problem in hand *or*, as is increasingly the case, combine aspects of both methodologies in an evolutionary approach.

It is obvious that in the increasingly competitive commercial world of the 1980s, where brand differences are more likely to be image- than product-led, it is important to understand both how a group of individuals who have been defined as the target market for a certain brand or service create meaning from the stimulus provided by the advertiser/manufacturer (for example, product, advertising, promotion, PR) and to measure how many individuals are creating meaning *in the same way*. This is what mass marketing is about — reaching a large number of consumers in such a way that they react positively to the stimulus in the desired manner (that is, buy the product, re-evaluate the brand, notice the promotion and so on).

In this chapter we will describe three ways in which qualitative and quantitative techniques have been grafted on to one another to provide a new and powerful tool for understanding complex marketing and advertising problems in modern commercial activity.

Each has evolved from a different perspective and thus the points at which the grafting has taken place vary:

- The grafting of qualitative interviews on to a quantitative fieldwork procedure.
- The grafting of qualitative forms of data collection on to a quantitatively administered questionnaire.
- The grafting of a statistical analysis procedure on to a small-scale qualitative study.

QUALITATIVE INTERVIEWING IN A QUANTITATIVE PROCESS

This is fairly common in the UK nowadays and came about in order to compensate for the loss of sensitivity to consumer feelings and emotions and increased distance from consumer language which results from a purely quantitative study.

By involving trained qualitative interviewers in quantitative data collection, a rich and colourful texture is added to the outline design of the quantitative survey. Qualitative interviewers may conduct a small number of depth interviews at the same time or in the same place as the questionnaires are being administered; the insights thus gained from a less structured and open-ended depth interview provide greater understanding of the meaning of the numerical data obtained.

Alternatively, qualitative interviewers may re-interview a proportion of respondents after the questionnaire has been administered, using the answers already given to explore further the nature of responses. This is particularly useful in understanding the meaning of consumer vocabulary. For example, a respondent may answer, in response to a question about a brand, that it is 'cheap'. The qualitative interviewer will need to establish whether 'cheap' means 'cheap and nasty' or 'good value for money' in order to understand the nature of this type of response. Many other consumer responses require sensitive clarification in relation to the overall business objectives so that the data is actionable. Is, for example, a high frequency of mention of 'modernity' for a brand a positive or a negative result? Modernity can indicate advanced technological design, convenience of use or aspirational user imagery, or it can mean a product that is soon obsolete, and which appeals to the young, which may not be relevant or motivating to the target market.

The usefulness of qualitative, alongside quantitative, interviewing extends into the structure of the coding frame. It is the qualitative interviewer who is most able, given the overall research, marketing or advertising objectives, to design a code frame that will yield the most sensitively grouped and/or classified set of responses. Thus a qualitative interviewer will separate those responses, in an advertising pre-test, that are related to the execution from those which result from the strategy itself. The fact that the two are often muddled is responsible for advertising agencies' paranoic distaste for quantitative pre-testing surveys.

QUALITATIVE FORMS OF DATA COLLECTION IN QUESTIONNAIRE DESIGN

Relatively few companies in the UK have explored this aspect of grafting together qualitative and quantitative methodologies. This is primarily due to the fact that most practising quantitative researchers have not been exposed to and trained in the qualitative techniques that can be applied in a face-to-face interview and, even more important, are unskilled in how these techniques are both administered and interpreted. It is only the few companies or individuals who practise both disciplines who are able to develop successfully this type of hybrid variety.

A number of types of qualitative data collection have been applied to quantitative studies:

- Sentence completion and word association verbal projective procedures.
- Other verbal projective procedures such as thought bubble completion, tell-a-story and brand personification.
- Visual projective procedures such as collage boards designed to work as visual rather than verbal.

Both the authors have often and successfully used 'thought bubble' cartoons in quantitative research. The examples shown (see Figures 15.1 and 15.2) are completed by the respondent (rather than asked as questions by the interviewer) and allow an individual to express thoughts and feelings, particularly 'gut-level' responses, through the vehicle of a fictitious third person. Response is spontaneous because inhibitions about articulating a feeling verbally or anxiety about satisfying an interviewer's expectations are removed providing, of course, the interviewer has been trained in administering this type of projective technique and abides by the basic rules (see Chapter 8). The range of different responses, interlinking thoughts and the volume of each, can be shown numerically.

The use of the Thematic Apperception Test (TAT), administered under self-completion conditions to a large sample has been used to segment consumers on a psychological basis (Schlackman 1986). Respondents are shown a drawing, photograph or scene from a commercial and asked to tell a story with a beginning, a middle and an end. They are encouraged to describe events leading up to the scenario shown and the consequences likely to result from it. These 'stories' are analyzed by trained qualitative researchers who isolate the main themes that emerge and classify the stories into typologies leading to the segmentation of the sample by the story contructs. Using this technique W. Schlackman (1986) described different types of male businessman air traveller and was able to measure the proportion of each ('Hawks' 'Rabbits' etc.) cross-tabulating each typology with attitudinal and behavioural information derived from other questions in the study.

Brand personification questions are easy to administer quantitatively and provide a richness of response for understanding brand personality. The responses to the question:

'If a magician were to wave a magic wand and turn this product [Wedgwood] into a person, what kind of person do you imagine would appear?'

show the power of this type of question in bringing the brand to life:

'Someone dressed in old-fashioned clothes, wearing a white wig and carrying a cane.'

Figure 15.1   Thought bubble as presented to informants for completion

Here, again, is a person seeing
this range of products on sale in
a shop. Now if you imagine for a
moment that these products could
speak to the person, to tell him
about themselves, what do you think
they might say? Please write in the
bubble from your impression of the
range.

Figure 15.2   Projecting from the product rather than the person

'Someone old, wealthy and very discerning.'

'Blue . . . I see blue figures on a white landscape.'

These responses can be used to illustrate other numerical findings within the questionnaire, or can be coded and counted.

An analysis of any language shows the importance of similes, metaphors, and other analogical constructs in making communication more vivid and meaningful. However, not all of us find it easy to invent verbal analogies, but with a little visual help are able to do so. This has led to the development of research stimuli used in the administration of a questionnaire which may be understood as visual (rather than verbal) adjectival checklists.

Thus instead of asking the question 'Judging from this commercial, at whom do you think the product is aimed?' or some other form of verbal user-image question, respondents are shown a picture board of people (see Figure 15.3) and asked 'Which of these types of people if any, do you think the commercial is aimed at? Why do you say that?' A purely verbal user image question leads to stereotypical responses relating to age, sex and socio-economic type, for example: 'mothers with children, housewives, women'. A visual stimulus yields responses that are more revealing and are more likely to lead to a greater understanding of how the commercial is working, for example: 'people who care about health, the young-at-heart'. It may be the choice of character which best illustrates the difference between two commercials and/or it may be the reasons why that character was chosen. Visual collage boards are tailor-made for each project, and are specifically designed to meet the research objectives, the brand, and the style of creative idea.

Visual collage boards can also be used to encourage respondents to think more laterally, for example: 'If this product were a car, what kind of car would it be? Why do you say that?'; or instead of a car one might use a board showing different types of drinks from cider and beer to exotic liqueurs or expensive brandies. Besides 'things' such as drinks, cars, houses, shops and so on, more abstract visual adjectives can be used to mine the underground store of emotional feelings. Colour boards have been used by the authors to help respondents articulate moods such as optimism, happiness, depression, vitality and so on. In all cases, it is the respondent's own reasons and explanations for the visual choice which is the most useful aspect of these analogies rather than any possibility of the researcher making sensible interpretations derived from the frequencies alone. It is little diagnostic use knowing that 64% thought Brand X was like beer, unless one knows whether beer was chosen because of its everyday acceptability, its cheapness, its masculine associations or its class origins.

Q.   Which of these types of people do you think this commercial was aimed at? Why do you say that?

Character chosen:	Commercial 1 %	Commercial 2 %
B	52	48
C	36	24
F	35	37

Reasons for choosing H:		
She looks fit, keep-fit type, sporty.	9	34
She'd care about her body/looks after herself.	5	19
An active person.	24	4
The right age.	7	13
Modern, looks trendy.	10	15
Glamorous, dresses well, looks good, stylish.	43	3

Figure 15.3   User imagery collage

STATISTICAL ANALYSIS PROCEDURES IN QUALITATIVE RESEARCH

Both authors have developed different hybrids in this area, which vary in the method of data collection and yet produce a similar computer product 'map' using statistical correspondence analysis. The Kelly Repertory Grid technique was all the rage in the 1960s but subsequently fell into disfavour. It is a technique of differentiation. Respondents in the traditional Kelly Grid procedure were given three brands (each on a separate card) and were asked to divide them into a pair and a single brand giving a reason why the brands paired were similar and the third different from the other two. This procedure was repeated with different combinations of brands until all the possible differentiating criteria were exhausted. The analysis involved both listing and counting all the criteria of difference and determining how many unique attributes were attached to the brand. This technique reached its zenith in the culture of the USP (unique selling proposition), a time when it was believed that if a brand had a set of unique attributes, this was sufficient to ensure its success in the marketplace.

The problem was that respondents tended to express *rational* rather than *emotional* differences between brands and even after exhaustive interviewing were still able to continue the game, but the differentiating criteria were simply irrelevant to brand purchase motivations.

Currently, the procedure described above has been adapted so that it is less sterile, and visual stimuli (such as those described previously) are used to evoke emotional image differences as well as rational product differences. The logos of the brands in a particular product sector are exposed to a respondent in threes with the instruction to divide them into a pair and a single brand, giving reasons for the similarity and difference. The reasons are explored as is normal in a qualitative individual depth interview. *All the brands are then sorted* on the pair of constructs isolated. The procedure is repeated until no more useful differences emerge.

Once 10–15 such interviews have been conducted, the list of product attributes and image differences are then analysed *qualitatively* and pruned and grouped judgementally, only the key differences being selected.

The resulting data matrix of isolated attributes and main associations with brands is subjected to correspondence analysis to produce a map of the products against the dimensions elicited.

A second mapping method has been called '*micro-modelling*' and it represents an alternative way of summarizing the attitudes of small samples. As a further benefit, the representation of this summary is treated graphically offering, as qualitative practitioners and clients alike often prefer, a visual representation of the data.

Before commenting on the technique, it is best to describe the methodology. Practitioners are aware that respondents gathering to enter a group discussion are in quite an energized, if not nervous, state. A degree of anticipation pervades the room, hallway or wherever.

These highly energized few moments can be used to start work, asking people how they feel, what they think is going to happen, if they can imagine talking about washing-up for an hour and a half, and so on. The amount of valuable 'leaking out' that occurs during these marginal times – when people are migrating between their everyday lives and the task-orientated group discussion experience – is quite surprising and often provides important cues for exploration in the group later on. But in practice moderators are often too busy fiddling about with videos, props, recorders or discussion guides to get involved in this preliminary group-forming process.

Once the notion of the significance of these marginal moments is recognized, small tasks can be designed for the respondents to become involved in before the interactive experience of the group begins. A form of simple projective procedure, such as word underlining or sentence completion, allows the researcher to list and count the brand associations. The findings from these procedures can be incorporated in the overall qualitative analysis, and/or they can be subjected to a quantitative analysis.

'Brand associations' is a tried and trusted quantitative method of data collection. Rather than constraining the respondents within the formal structure of questions and answer, it 'offers' a series of attributes, suggestions or opinions to which the respondents react *or not*, as they like. The attributes or statements may be collected from previous or pilot research, from the client and his view of what his customers think, or they may simply reflect a series of alternatives, describing things that the manufacturer/advertiser would *like* people to think about the product, service, commercial or whatever. Within limits, too, the number of times the small sample associates one particular attribute with any other thing, gives a steer on the prevalence of this feeling. This mapping task is presented to consumers using a brand association questionnaire, an example of which is included at the end of this chapter.

On samples of fifty upwards (eight groups or more), the analysis can be run and split by a 'before and after the group' method of administration so that the effect of the group discussion, including the test material, new commercial or whatever, on the topography of the sample's view of the marketplace can be examined. It seems appropriate to describe the nature and mathematics of the model now.

A mapping analysis is a graphical way of representing the views of people and, although mathematically based, it is a *non-numerical* representation in that it replaces numbers by space and distance. By so doing it lends itself to being incorporated into the other non-numerical data bases of qualitative research.

Correspondence analysis is a form of multi-variate analysis. The mathematics takes a large array of numbers and preserves as much as it can about the relationships between them. It then summarizes the data in a graphical form and offers a spatial representation of an array of numbers. In other words, it allows us to present what tables say in a graphical way. People don't think in numerical terms and it assists us to transform the numerical data back into more user-friendly pictures of brands and markets. Correspondence analysis is not awe-inspiringly complicated, it is simply a way of analysing data. For the technically minded there are a series of references describing the mathematics in the Bibliography.

Both the brands and the chosen attributes are similarly plotted and imposed on the map. The interpretation of the association between brands and attributes is accomplished with reference to the centre of the map. The further from the centre a brand or attribute lies then the more distinctive or discriminated they are. In Figure 15.4 for example, Sainsbury's is the most clearly discriminated brand. We then look for the disposition of the attributes relative to Sainsbury's and find that 'harsh', 'cheaper' and 'value for money' are the most salient discriminating attributes, roughly in that order of importance. Omo, likewise, is fairly clearly differentiated by being 'out of date'.

'Ariel' and 'biological', too, have the same disposition with respect to the centre and here we can infer that they discriminate each other quite closely. In this way we can pick out particular relationships but we can also pick out more general ones and by introspection arrive at a naming of the dimensions and quadrants of the map. In the example below the principal horizontal dimen-

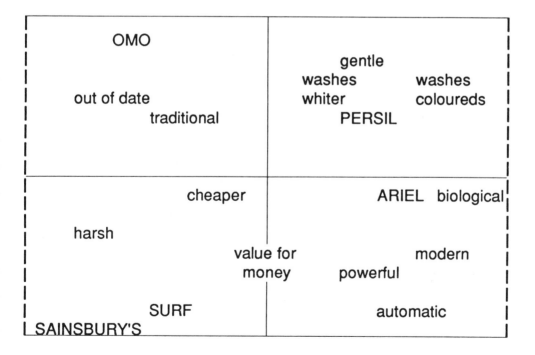

Figure 15.4   A brand map showing brands of washing powder and their attributes

sion is described in terms of 'out of date' versus 'biological'/'modern'. The vertical dimension seems concerned with 'power', 'value for money' and automatic' as opposed to washing and gentleness.

As you can see, the map includes a number of brands (five in this case) and a number of attributes. As described, these attributes may be predetermined by the research team and client, or generated by consumers from earlier pilot research.

For the technically minded

The mathematics employs matrix algebra and the extraction of eigen values from a linearly transformed matrix. Eigen values can be used to measure statistical variance. The first eigen value extracted accounts for the largest amount of variance, the second, the second largest amount of variance, and so on. Since the data has been taken through an orthogonal transformation, there is no covariance term, and therefore the total amount of variance explained is the sum of the eigen values.

For the less technical

Explaining variance essentially means how much information is lost or kept by representing the data in maps. Often, correspondence analysis explains between 80 per cent and 90 per cent of the data in the first two dimensions and therefore it rarely becomes necessary to present the data in more than two dimensions.

The correspondence analysis programme used has certain characteristics and properties not commonly found; outliers are fixed at three standard errors from the origin so that the data is not swamped by strong brands. In addition, supplementary variables or subjects, for example concepts, can easily be overlaid or market share can be shown as a variable, thereby indicating where market volume lies on the map.

The use of the map as a predictive tool is obviously of interest. What happens for example when variables are enlarged or diminished? Does the model react in a rational fashion or does it break up and behave in some other unfathomable way? Figure 15.5 illustrates a very rational response to this type of experimental tinkering. The first map represents the attitudes of people towards banks and building societies. This data was collected just prior to a series of group discussions on financial matters. Eight groups among dual account holders (holders of both bank and building society accounts) were conducted.

As can be seen, all of the building societies were seen in relation to banks, virtually identically. If one of them, say the Woolwich, decided to change

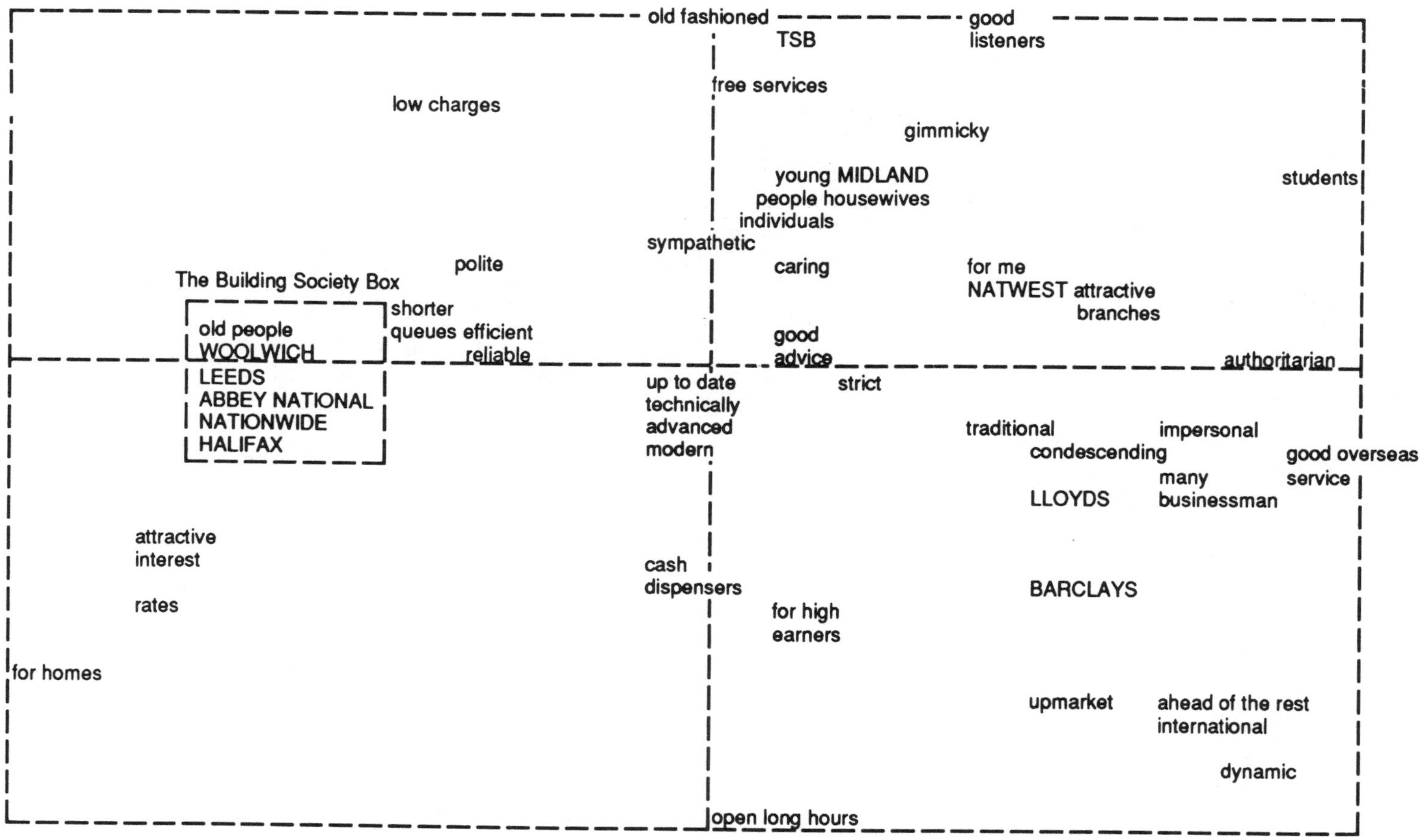

old fashioned

good listeners

students

TSB

free services

gimmicky

young MIDLAND
people housewives
individuals

sympathetic

caring

for me
NATWEST attractive
branches

authoritarian

impersonal good overseas
service

condescending many
businessman

traditional

LLOYDS

BARCLAYS

upmarket ahead of the rest
international

dynamic

good
advice

strict

up to date
technically
advanced
modern

cash
dispensers

for high
earners

open long hours

low charges

polite

shorter
queues efficient
reliable

The Building Society Box

old people
WOOLWICH
LEEDS
ABBEY NATIONAL
NATIONWIDE
HALIFAX

attractive
interest

rates

for homes

Figure 15.5 Map showing attributes of banks and building societies

247

its profile and break out of the building society box, what would happen? How could its image be shifted so that it:

> Maintained the traditional strengths of building societies, that is: good for your savings, and so on.
> Differentiated itself from other building societies.
> Took on some of the positive image characteristics of banks.

A Woolwich which possessed a lot of cash dispensers and offered business services, such as help with commercial property transactions or short-term facilities, was hypothesized and the Woolwich's score on these alternatives was correspondingly increased. The Woolwich was not given any higher scores on 'business' or 'cash dispensers' attributes than those obtained by banks. Then the map was run again.

The result is shown in Figure 15.6

As can be seen, the position of 'Woolwich Business' moves the society away from the others closer to the banks, particularly Lloyds and Barclays. It also increases the image of the society on the 'for high earners', 'modern' and 'dynamic' attributes.

Therefore if the Woolwich pursued this activity, it would increase its chances of being seen very differently from the other building societies.

Every qualitative researcher has been faced with the 'What would have happened if we'd done X or Y instead..?' type of question at the debrief. The alternatives are either to duck the question or say more or less the first thing that comes to mind. This type of mapping software allows much less superficial answers to 'what if?' questions. The maps can also be used to explore the additional variable of the effect of new activities by the competition on an existing or developing strategy. Recently the maps have been used to explore the image shift brought about by new creative routes – all of it done in group discussions.

As a caveat, it seems important to add that in order to make full use of the creative possibilities of mapping in both the qualitative and quantitative arenas, it is important for the researcher who is carrying out the analysis and interpretation to have access to his own software. It is at the terminal that the interactive process begins; the interaction between the data and the researcher stimulates new ideas, creates new chains of logic, patterns of association and so on.

How does this technique differ from straightforward qualitative market mapping, carried out by the whole group during the discussion process? It has several important advantages, ie.

1   As we described above, the programme selects those attributes of the data with the greatest discriminating power to be its basic axes. These main axes may or may not have end-points which are true opposites as in 'hard – soft' for example. Sometimes the ends of the dimensions are

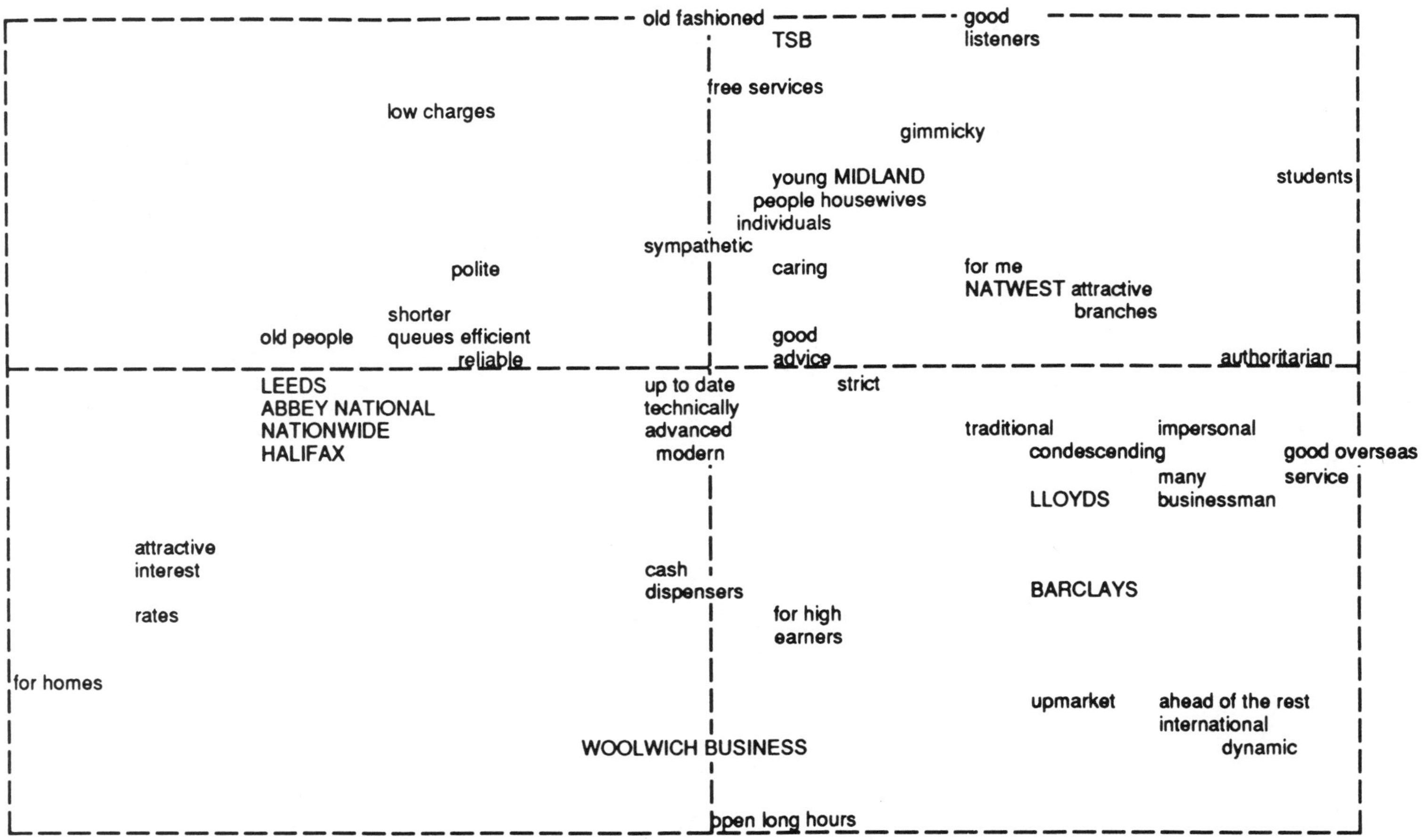

Figure 15.6 Map showing the new position of the Woolwich with business customers and more cash dispensers

not true opposites but are juxtaposed to each other. For example, we could find a brand that is long lasting juxtaposed with one that is inexpensive, as might occur in the following sort of exchange:

'A good electric razor lasts a lifetime.'
'Yes, but Bic disposables are so easy and inexpensive.'

'Inexpensive' and 'long-lasting' are not opposites, but in this example they *are* juxtaposed. The programme allows representation of these juxtaposed attributes in forming its axes: it does not create 'false' opposites where they do not apply.

2   In a group environment there is a degree of moderator and group influence in the production of group consensus-type market maps. The power of this brand association technique is that it enables each informant to contribute at the level at which he or she feels comfortable. The 'open' structure of the questionnaire gives respondents permission to avoid whole areas or brands that they do not feel qualified to comment upon.

3   An unexpected, but significant, advantage is that respondents do not know that they are creating a map. They feel comfortable just forming a series of plausible associations at their own pace. There is no anxiety of falsification based on attempts to 'get the answer right'. The associative-cognitive skills required may operate at a very easy, unpressurized level.

4   In a conventional group discussion it is very difficult not to lead participants in these mapping exercises. If some form of encouragement or enthusiasm is not offered, the mapping quickly takes on a desultory feeling. If too many 'strokes' are given the maps become slightly hysterical, producing ever more unlikely associations.

5   In connection with the last point, it is our belief that the qualitative market mapping in groups often works extremely well as an enabling technique – expanding and deepening people's awareness of their feelings about products or advertisements, (see Chapter 8). But the resulting maps are often peddled as something they're not – an objective representation of everybody's views. In our opinion they are as strongly influenced by group pressures as by individual introspection and expression. The experience is somewhat akin to a committee going out to buy a bottle of shampoo for an imminent visitor they have never met. The final choice may as easily be bizarre as appropriate.

The methods described here permit a much greater degree of confidence in the robustness of qualitative results. Furthermore, they achieve an easily comprehensible display of the overall views of the sample without disrupting the interview process or group rapport in any way whatsoever. They also allow individuals to contribute at the level they're comfortable with. Finally they represent, we hope, interesting examples of a fruitful marriage of quanti-qualitative techniques which are available to the *quali*tative practitioner.

Brand mapping questionnaire: washing powders

'Overleaf is a list of words that you might use to describe washing powders.

Across the top are the names of some brands of washing powder. Would you please, for each brand, put a tick beneath it in the appropriate column alongside any word which you think applies to it? (Give example). You may put as many or as few ticks on each line and for each brand as you wish.'

	Surf	Tide	Daz	Omo	Persil
Washes Whiter	☐	☐	☐	☐	☐
Traditional	☐	☐	☐	☐	☐
Out of date	☐	☐	☐	☐	☐
Powerful	☐	☐	☐	☐	☐
Washes coloureds	☐	☐	☐	☐	☐
Gentle	☐	☐	☐	☐	☐
Harsh	☐	☐	☐	☐	☐
Biological	☐	☐	☐	☐	☐
Modern	☐	☐	☐	☐	☐
Automatics	☐	☐	☐	☐	☐
Value for money	☐	☐	☐	☐	☐
Cheaper	☐	☐	☐	☐	☐

NB; As many as 30-40 attributes may be included. Single word attributes are the least open to misinterpretation.

Figure 15.7

Bibliography

Abbott, D. (1975), Group Discussions, Admap Creative Research Issue, October.

Bandler, R. and Grinder, J (1975), *The Structure of Magic*, Science and Behaviour Books.

Bandler, R. and Grinder, J. (1979), *Frogs into Princes*, Real People Press.

Bandler, R. and Grinder, J. (1982), *Reframing*, Real People Press.

Benzecri, J–P. (1979) 'Practical Aspects of Correspondence Analysis', *ADDAD Bulletin*, no. 6.

Benzecri, J–P et al. (1973), *L'Analyse des Données, Vol. 2: Correspondances*, Paris: Dunod.

Bion, W. R. (1961), *Experiences in Groups and Other Papers*, Tavistock Publications.

Blackstone, M. and Holmes, M. (1983), 'The Use of Transactional Analysis in the Development of a New Brand Personality', ESOMAR Seminar on New Product Development.

Braithwait, A and Lunn, T. (1985), 'Projective Techniques in Social and Market Research' in R. Walker (ed.), *Applied Qualitative Research*, Aldershot: Gower, 1985.

Deville, J–C and Malinvaud, E. (1983), Data Analysis in Official Socio-Economic Statistics', *Journal of The Royal Statistical Society*, Series A, Vol. 146, pt 4, 335–52.

Dilts, R. B. (1983), *Applications of Neuro Linguistic Programming*, Meta Publications.

Dyer, G. (1984), 'Semiology/Structuralism Notes for Market Research Society Course', The Market Research Society.

Estes, S. G. (1937), *The Judgement of Personality on the Brief Basis of Behaviour*, Cambridge, Mass: The Harvard Library.

Feldwick, P. and Winstanley, L. (1986), Qualitative Recruitment: Policy and Practice, The Market Research Conference, March.

Fisher, R. A. (1936), 'The Use of Multiple Measurements in Taxonomic Problems', Annals of Eugenics, no. 7, 179–88.

Frost, W. A. K. and Braine, R. L. (1967), 'The Application of the Repertory Grid Techniques to Problems in Market Research', Commentary 9, 3.

Gordon, W. and Robson, S. (1982), *Respondents Through the Looking Glass: Towards a better understanding of the qualitative interviewing process*, Market Research Society Annual Conference Proceedings

Greenacre, M. J. (1983), *Correspondence Analysis*, London: Academic Press.

Grinder, J. and Bandler, R. (1976), *The Structure of Magic II*, Science and Behaviour Books.

Hedges, A. (1983), 'The Analysis of Qualitative Data', presented to the Association of Qualitative Research Practitioners, One Day Event.

Hill, M. O. (1974), 'Correspondence Analysis: A neglected multivariate technique', *Applied Statistics*, no. 23, 340–54.

Jones, S. (1985), 'The Analysis of Depth Interviews' in R. Walker (ed.), *Applied Qualitative Research*, Aldershot: Gower, 1985.

Kleinman, P. (1985), *Market Research: Head counting becomes big business*, Comedia Publishing Group.

Langmaid, R. and Ross, B., 'Games Respondents Play', *Journal of the Market Research Society*, vol. 26, no. 3.

Lebart, L., Morineau, A. and Tabard, N. (1977), *Techniques de la Description Statistique*, Paris: Dunod.

Lewis, B. A. and Pucelik, R. F. (1982), *Magic Demystified*, Metamorphous Press.

Market Research Society, R&D Sub-Committee on Qualitative Research (1979), *Qualitative Research: A summary of the concepts involved*.

Rose, J. and Heath, S. (1984), *Stimulus Material: A dual viewpoint*, Market Research Society Conference.

Ryan, C. and Gordon, W. (1980), 'The Interface between Creative, Account and Research Groups in Advertising Agencies', article presented at the Market Research Society Conference.

Schlackman, W. (1984), *A Discussion of the Use of Sensitivity Panels in Market Research*, Market Research Society Annual Conference Proceedings.

Schlackman, W. (1986), *The Application of Projective Tests to Psychographic Analysis of Markets*, Market Research Society Conference, March, 27–41.

Shreeve, E., 'Getting the Best out of Qualitative Research', for OBM account and creative personnel.

Stewart, J. W. (1981) 'The Application and Misapplication of Factor Analysis in Marketing Research', Journal of Marketing Research, vol. 18, February, 51–62.

Stewart-Hunter, D. (1984) 'Narrative tapes, some notes for users' presented to Account Planning Group Education Course, October.

Worcester, R. and Downham, J. (eds) (1986), *Consumer Market Research Handbook*, 3rd revised edition, ESOMAR.

Yablonsky, L. (1981), *Psychodrama*, Gardner Press.

Index

Abbott, D. 156
accessing cues 82–8
accompanied shopping 19
Acorn (A Classification of Residential
    Neighbourhoods) 24
acquaintance 40
Acting out the advertisement game 200
acting real life 200–1
adcepts 228
admatics 212, 215
adolescents 12, 17, 74
advertising agencies 7, 8, 98
advertising rejectors 154
advertising tracking ix
aftershaves 153–4
age bias 27
aggression 99
analogy generation 14
anchoring 60
animatics 211, 213, 215, 230–1
anxiety 163, 194
association procedures 95–8
  word association 70, 95–6, 203, 238
Association of Qualitative Research
    Practitioners (AQRP) x, 73
Association of Users of Research
    Agencies (AURA) 156, 159, 160
attitude studies ix
attitudinal areas 6
attitudinal perspective 17
auditory people 83
aurally-dominant people 135

baby talk 191
Bandler, R. 82, 88, 155
banks 246–8
bargaining hunting 149
bias 234

Blackstone, M. 72
Boase Massimi Pollitt 157
boasting 48
body language 2, 41, 77, 86
    advantages 130–1
    in debriefs 166
    disadvantages 131
    external (social) 78–9
    in group dynamics 44
    internal (personal) 78–9
    in interviews 58, 62, 66, 69
    mirroring 55
Braine, R. L. 5
brainstorming 14–15
Braithwaite, A. 69
brand association matrices 198, 199
brand associations 244, 251
brand differentiation 5, 234
brand imagery 96, 98
brand mapping 101, 102, 170, 171, 174,
    175
    questionnaires 250–1
brand personalities 5, 185, 218, 225, 228,
    238
    as a projective technique 97, 98, 106,
    109, 111
briefing 20–3
    covert brief 20–3
    overt brief 20–3
bubble cartoons see thought bubble
    cartoons
building societies 246–9
buyers of qualitative research 158, 160–1

Captain Pugwash 236
caption writing 114
carpet superstores 149
cars 5, 17, 18, 78, 170, 183, 241

cartoons 170, 180, 213
cat food 117
children 12, 17, 75, 188–208
    developmental stages 189–93, 207
    methods and means 195–201
    projective techniques 201–4
    research situation 193–5
    validity of results 204–8
Chinese whispers game 197, 212
choice ordering procedures 111–12
cigarette advertising 153, 216
coding frame 237
collages 97, 98, 185, 202–3
    visual 218–27, 229, 230, 238, 241
colour 207
colour boards 241
commercial radio 232
commercials 147–8, 152, 154, 230–2
communication 8–9, 16, 21, 74
communication checks 74
competitive advertisements 233
competitiveness 48
competitive products 5, 9
completion procedures 98–101
computers 138
concept boards 211, 213, 215, 228–9
conflict interviews 17
confusion 144–6
construction procedures 101–6
    projective questioning 103–5
    stereotypes 105
consumer laboratories 31
consumer needs 6
consumer perceptions 4
consumer segmentations 4–5, 24
consumer vocabulary 5, 237
content analysis 134, 236
continuous monitoring ix
correspondence analysis 246
costs 25, 31, 74
covert brief 20–3
creative development research 7–9, 209–
    10, 228, 230
    executional guidance 7,8
    pre-testing 8–9, 240
    stages 228–32
    strategy definition 7–8, 228
creativity tests 115

cross-over 81

data bases 2
data-collection techniques ix, 237–44
debrief arena 166–9
decision-making 6, 169
decoding 215, 228
defence mechanisms 45–6, 50
demographic criteria 4, 5, 162
dependence 47, 49
dependent groups 46–7
depth interviewing 51, 64–76, 122, 237,
    243
    advantages 71–2
    completion of interview 70
    definition 15, 64
    disadvantages 16
    facilitative atmosphere 69
    flexibility 65
    objectives 73–4
    paired 30, 75, 196
    parameters 67–8
    problems 61–3
    projective techniques 70
    questioning approach 65–6
    rapport 68–9
    skill of interviewer 70–3
    strengths 15
    time taken 66
diagnostic studies 9
diagrams 170, 171, 176
Donaldson, Margaret 189
Dyer, G. 217

editing 57
egocentrism 189, 191
ego states 146–8
emphasis 87
enabling techniques 2, 89
enactment 109–11, 198, 200
encounter groups 14
Estes, S. G. 87
executional guidance 7, 8
expansiveness 87
experiential learning 33–4
exploratory studies 3–6, 13
expressive procedures 106–11
    psychodrawing 109

extended discussions 13
eye contact 69, 82, 87, 166, 195
eye movements 82, 84

facilitative atmosphere 69
facilitator 15
factor analysis 24
familiarization games 197
family interviews 196
fantasy 149
Feldwick, P. 157, 159, 162, 164
femininity 125
fight response 47–8, 61
financial matters 11
flight response 48, 62
flip charts 171
flip-over boards 211
flirting 49
focus groups 20
folder test 233
food products 4
forming 39–40, 131, 154
free association 13, 14
Freudian theory 72
Frost, W. A. K. 5

geographic distribution 27–8
gestalt dialogue 14
gestalt groups 90
'Give Us A Clue' 109
Gordon, W. 21, 25, 67, 164
Grinder, J. 82, 88, 155
group behaviour 36–42
    components of groups 37–8
    structural factors 37
group discussions ix, 10–15, 20, 193
    advantages 11
    attitudes towards 35
    brainstorming 14–15
    content 37–8
    disadvantages 11
    extended discussions 13
    hidden agenda 38
    location 164
    mini-groups 12
    problems 61–3
    reconvened 13–14
    recruitment 157

sensitivity panels 14
synectics 14–15
group dynamics 34, 43–50, 52, 131
    dependent groups 46–7
    dominant respondent 47–8, 61
    fight response 47–8, 61
    flight response 48, 62
    group experience 45–50
    material brought to the group 44–5
    paired groups 49–50, 62
    recruitment 45
group experience 45–50
group interviews 29
    extended groups 30
    mini-groups 30
    reconvened groups 30
    standard groups 30
group perspectives 50
group process,
    forming 39–40, 131, 154
    mourning 41–2
    norming 41, 56–7
    performing 41, 154
    stages 39–42
    storming 40, 41, 56, 57, 61, 62
group processes 33–6, 38–42
group psychology 50

hall test 16–17
hands 86, 166
Hangman game 197
head movements 84
health consciousness 4, 228
Heath, S. 209, 213, 229
Hedges, Alan 139
hoarding 149
Hofmeister drinker 170
Holmes, M. 72
home ownership 26–8
hypothesis-generation 6

incentives 32
individual interviews 15–19, 29–30
    accompanied shopping 19
    mini-depth interviews 16–17, 74
    observation 18–19
    paired interviews 17, 75
    semi-structured interviews 17

triangular interviews 17–18, 75
instant coffee 154–5
integrated group interviews 29–30
internal dialogue 81
interpretation of qualitative research 132–
   55
      annotating-the-transcripts approach
         137
      bargain hunting 149
      fantasy 149
      hoarding 149
      interpretation in action 153–5
      large-sheet-of-paper approach 136–7
      levels 139–41
      life scripts 152–3
      mechanics 135–8
      mini-scripts 151–2
      'Mum knows best' 150–1
      subjectivity 133, 135, 140
      theoretical framework 146–53
      'They're all made by the same people
         anyway' 148–50
      transactional analysis 146–8
      understanding confusion 144–6
interpretive reframing 143, 144
interviewers 237
      awareness 69
      dress 68, 163
      motivation 157
      sharing 68–9
      skills 70–3, 163–4
      types 71
interviewing ix, 51–63
      advanced skills 57–61
      anchoring 60
      basic contract 53–4
      creating rapport 54–5
      depth interview 15–19
      getting started 54–6
      listening levels 57–9
      listening for patterns 59–60
      location 31, 75–6
      mirroring 55–6
      silences 55–7, 62
      training 51–2
interview structure 2
intimate subject matter 11, 217

jeans 4
Jung, C. G. 95

Kelly Repertory Grid 5, 243
kinesthetically dominated people 83
Klein, Melanie 93

lager 170, 182
lateral thinking 14, 15
learning experience 33, 44
Lee 4
life scripts 152–3
life stages 27
life-style segmentation 4
listening levels 57–9
      intentional 58
      manifest 57
      subconscious 58–9
Little Princess 153
Lunn, T. 70

Machover Draw-a-Person Test 106
management consultancy xi
mapping 138, 243, 248, 250
mapping analysis 244
mapping games 197–8
market research, definition ix, 73
Market Research Society x, 156, 159, 162
markets, new 4
market sectors 4
masculinity 122–4
Mass Observation 18
matrix algebra 246
meaning 216
methodologies ix–xi
      choice of 10–19
      group discussion 10–15
      group interview 29
      hybrid 3, 17, 235–51
      sampling 29–31
      small sample 1, 233, 243
      statistical analysis procedures 243–51
micro-modelling 243
mini-depth interviews 16–17, 74
mini-group discussions 12, 30
minimal cues 78
mini-scripts 151–2
      Be Perfect 151, 152

Be Strong 151
Hurry Up 152
Please 152
Try Hard 152
mirroring 55–6, 80, 81
mock press material 212, 214
mock-up packs 212, 214
moderators
    attitude to recruitment 158, 161–2
    group discussions 36–42, 44–7, 49, 92
    in interviews 52, 58–60
    leadership 46
    observation of non-verbal
        communication 83
    in one-way mirror research 127–31
modernity 237
motivation studies 1
mourning 41–2
muesli 5

narrative tapes 211, 213, 215, 229, 230
negativity 160–1
Neuro Linguistic Programming 5, 81–8,
    155
new product development 3, 6–7, 13, 74,
    101
    stimulus material 209–10, 214, 217
non-smokers 55
non-vebal communication 2, 11, 60, 61,
    77–88, 95, 116, 117
    in analysis of meaning and
        interpretation 81–8
    anger 79
    body language 78–9
    boredom 79
    desire to speak 79
    discomfort 80
    hostility 79
    pacing 80–1
    procedural considerations 79–81
    shyness 80
    withdrawal 79
norming 41, 56
numerical measurement 235

objectivity 235
observation 6, 18–19
    active 18

participant 18
passive 18
simple 18
one-way mirror research 32, 37, 75, 76,
    127–31, 164
    moderators 127–31
    observers 129
    respondents 127–9
orange squash 204, 206
overt brief 20–3
own brands 150, 207

pacing 80–1
pack design 209–15, 228
paired groups 49–50
paired interviews 17, 75
pairing 49, 62, 87
Perfect Mum 150–1
performing 41, 154
perfumes 154
personal products 109
personification 70
personnel training xi
perspective changing 142–3
photomatics 211, 215
Piaget, J. 189, 193
picture boards 241
Pils drinker 170, 181
planning 209
Plastic Woman 151
playing in 109
positioning 101, 212–14, 228
posture 86–7, 166
posturing 63, 201
presentation of qualitative research 165–
    87
    debrief arena 166–9
    dress 169
    manner 169
    projective techniques 185–7
    structure 167–9
    visual aids 168–87
press advertising 232
problem areas for qualitative research 3–
    10
    broad market exploratory studies 3–6
    creative development research 7–9
    diagnostic studies 9

new product development 3, 6–7
tactical qualitative studies 9–10
product descriptions 228
projective drawing 116, 197, 201–3
projective questioning 103–5
projective techniques 2, 6, 13, 20, 74, 89–126, 201–4
  analysis and interpretation 118–25
  association procedures 95–8
  children 201–4
  choice ordering procedures 111–12
  completion procedures 98–101
  construction procedures 101–6
  definition 93–5
  depth interviewing 70
  and enabling techniques 89
  expressive procedures 106–11
  features 95
  guidelines for use 112–25
  history 89–90
  methods of administration 116–17
  presentation of qualitative research 185–7
  projective drawing 201–3
  scoring 96
  sending postcards 203
  tests 117–18
  word association 203
psychoanalysis 141
psychodrama 106
psychodrawing 13, 20, 70, 109–10, 185
psycho-dynamic market research groups 34, 35
psychographics 4
psychology 72
psychotherapy 34

qualitative research,
  definition 1–2, 64
  growth of x–xi
  and quantitative research ix, 1, 2–3, 165, 235
Qualitative Research Study Group 72
Quality Circles xi
quantitative research, and qualitative research ix, 1, 2–3, 165
question and answer group session 34–5
questionnaires 2, 17, 237–42, 250

recruitment 158, 160, 162

radio commercials 232
rapport 54–5, 68–9, 202–3
reclusiveness 87
reconvened discussions 13–14, 30
reconvened groups 30
recruiters 157–9
recruitment 45, 156–64
  buyer's viewpoint 160–1
  moderator's perspective 161–2
  questionnaires 158, 160, 162
  recruiter's viewpoint 157–9
  respondent's experience 162–4
  standards 156, 159, 160
recruitment experience 157, 162
repertory grid interviews 5, 243
reportage 57
representative groups 43
research debrief 21
researchers 23, 166, 169, 235
research objectives 20–3
respondents,
  dominant 47–8, 61, 128
  experienced 25
  inexperienced 25
  one-way mirror groups 127–9
  recruitment 158, 162–4
retail audits ix
ritualistic responses 59
Robson, S. 25, 67, 164
role playing 13, 20, 70, 109–11, 193, 198
Rorschach ink blot test 95, 96
Rose, J. 209, 213, 229
Rosenweig Picture-Frustration Test 99
Ryan, C. 21

sample design 23–32
  age bias 27
  geographic distribution 27–8
  preparatory stages 23
  representation 27
  sample methodology 29–31
  sample size 25–8
  spread 27
  target sample 24–5
sample size 25–8
scheduling 32

Schlackman, William xii, 14, 238
script analysis 148
selective perception 129
self-completion questionnaires 99
semiotics 72, 216
semi-structured interviews 17
sending postcards 203
sensitivity panels 14, 20
sentence completion 70, 99, 185, 238
shampoo 218
shopping game 198–200
signs 216, 217
silences 55–7, 62, 135, 193–4
skills acquisition 33
slides 185, 187
small sample methodologies 1, 235, 243
smokers 55, 154, 170
social class 27, 32
social marketing xi
social norms 11
sorting games 197–8
sports gear 4
sports sponsorship 153
stabpoints 170–3
standard groups 30
statistical analysis procedures 24, 243–51
status signalling 48
stereotypes 105–6
Stewart-Hunter, David 229
stimulus boards 232
stimulus material 56, 209–34
    admatics 212, 215
    animatics 211, 213, 215, 230–1
    choice 227–34
    concept boards 211, 213, 215, 218, 228
    definition 210
    direct 210
    flip-over boards 211
    indirect 210, 217
    mock press material 212, 214
    mock-up packs 212, 214
    narrative tapes 211, 213, 215, 229, 230
    new material 216–27
    photomatics 211, 215
    'rough' and 'real' 214–15
    storyboards 211, 213, 215, 230
storming 40, 41, 56, 57, 61, 62
storyboards 211, 213, 215, 230

strategy definition 7–8, 228
stream of awareness 14
subconscious mind 140, 142
subjectivity 133, 135, 140, 165
synectics 14–15

tactical qualitative studies 9–10
talkie tapes 103, 227, 229
tape recorders 42, 67, 135–7, 141–2
tapes (audio) 187
Target Group Index (TGI) ix, 132
target market 25, 236
target sample 12, 24–5
    overdefined 24
Task Forces xi
task-oriented groups 43–4
teaching 33
teenagers 23
telephone postures 81, 83
Thematic Apperception Test 101, 238
thought bubble cartoons 70, 106–8, 114,
    117–21, 203, 238, 239
    presentation 170, 178, 185
thought tapes 103, 217, 229
three dimensional techniques 114, 215
throw-away remarks 60
toiletries 153, 228
toys 92
trading disclosures 55
transactional analysis 5, 20, 72, 73, 146–8
transcripts 135–7
triangular interviews 17–18, 75
TV commercials 230–1

Unilever 150
unique selling proposition 5, 243
usage diaries 6
usage studies ix
user personality 111

verbal records 135–8
verbatim quotes 170, 171, 177
video 187
video monitoring 164
viewing rooms 31, 75, 130
visual aids,
    brand mapping 101, 102, 170, 171,
        174, 175

cartoons 170, 180
diagrams 170, 171, 176
stabpoints 170–3
thought bubble cartoons 170, 178
verbatim quotes 170, 171, 177
visually-dominant people 135
vocabulary 154
vocabulary lists 218, 229

Waiting Script 153
washing powder 245, 250–51
Winstanley, L. 157, 159, 162, 164
withholding 164
women's liberation movement 150
word association 70, 95–6, 203, 238
word lists 117
word underlining 112, 244